...And So We Pray

Guidance for Moms With College-Aged Young Adults

BY

MARIBETH HARPER

ISBN: 0-692-1-6206-2

ISBN-13: 978-0-692-16206-4

TABLE OF CONTENTS

When We Doubt

ABOUT...AND SO WE PRAY

...*And So We Pray* accompanies mothers like us, as we send our children off to college. The book is filled with encouragement, sound Catholic teaching, and real-life stories shared by women of faith who have experienced transitioning their teens from high school to college.

As mothers, we want to activate the most powerful weapon imaginable to help our children succeed in their college-aged years. That weapon is prayer. ...*And So We Pray* will help you pray in a deep and meaningful way through this time of transition by providing you with thought-provoking, faith-based, real-life applications to contemporary issues that you and your young adult may face during the exciting, and sometimes challenging, college years and beyond.

ACKNOWLEDGMENTS

As this book came together I felt surrounded by highly competent, generous women who wanted to help! Praise God. First and foremost, many thanks to the mothers and young adults who shared with me their hearts and their stories for the edification and blessing of others. Thanks also to the dedicated women of Praying College Moms, especially to the founder, Laurel Howanitz, and Liz Hild, Anita Alexander, and Frances Chamberlin for their support, encouragement, and example.

A very special thanks to praying college mom Julie Mantooth who poured her writing talent into several interviews and essays amidst a very busy family life. And I feel particularly blessed to include a chapter on the ill effects of pornography, written in part by Luanne Griffin, a graduate of Divine Mercy University, an excellent Catholic graduate school of psychology and counseling.

I am also grateful for Fr. John Pietropaoli, LC, and Fr. Justin Huber of the Archdiocese of Washington, D.C., who read the book for doctrinal soundness and offered their wise advice. I thank Melissa Overmyer, who generously created an excellent training video for small-group leaders that can be accessed on prayingcollegemoms.org.

For all the fine-tuning, I thank my friend Margie Davin who brought her own deep spirituality to the editing process and improved every chapter. And thanks to college coed, Inés Vera, who also read and contributed her perspective to the book. Finally, I thank my daughter, Sarah Nolan—my first reader of every chapter—and my husband, Denis, of thirty-four years, for their patience and loving oversight.

HOW TO USE THIS BOOK

...And So We Pray is written for individuals or for women meeting in small groups who want to explore issues that young adults face in the college-aged years and read, discuss, and pray about how faith in Jesus Christ can console and strengthen them. With 33 chapters and a different theme to read and reflect upon every week of the academic year, these pages were written to accompany women as they make the transition from mothers of children to mothers of young adults.

Each chapter includes the following elements:
- The body of the chapter, which focuses on a dilemma and proposes a principle of faith as a possible solution.

- The closing prayer.

- Questions for reflection which can be used individually or in small-group settings.

- Prayer intentions: A place for writing down prayers of petition.

- Answered prayers: A place for recognizing and celebrating answered prayers, which help to build faith and trust in God.

- Prayer practice: One suggestion made for each chapter to deepen prayer life.

- Scripture verse: Ideally, the reader will have or will develop a daily habit of prayer and reflection. These verses were selected to inspire ongoing prayer along the chapter's theme, with plenty of space for journaling.

Journaling is an important practice, whether reading the book alone or in the context of a small group. Journaling stills the mind, empties it of busy thoughts, and promotes deeper contemplation of the Scripture being read. The free-flowing nature of journaling encourages the mind to surrender to the Holy Spirit and can allow God to speak to us more clearly as we write. Over time, we produce a private record of our thoughts and God's actions in our lives which, when revisited, can deepen our trust in God, who we see has been working tangibly in our lives. The action of journaling is like praying twice, just as singing is thought by some to be "praying twice."

Praying College Moms (PCM) small groups read a chapter or more at each monthly meeting and spend time discussing the questions that follow each chapter. Prayer intentions are shared at the beginning or end of each meeting, at the discretion of the team leader. The prayer practice and Scripture verses are read between meetings. For more information, see Appendix 2, How to Use This Book in PCM Small Groups. To learn more about the organization Praying College Moms, see Appendix 1.

If reading the book outside of a small group, it is recommended that each chapter be read slowly, pausing for several days after each one to reflect on the questions, journal, and attempt the prayer practice.

All quoted Scripture is from the New American Bible, Revised Edition (NABRE) unless otherwise noted. Stories shared with the author are true, but names have been changed.

The pronoun *him/her* has been chosen arbitrarily for individual chapters, unless otherwise indicated.

PRAYING COLLEGE MOM'S PRAYER

Dear God, Our Father, You have graciously set me over my children as their guardian, their protector, and their first exposure to the faith. With the love of a mother's heart, I have poured myself out teaching, guiding and preparing them for a future of service to You. I am grateful for Your good gifts, especially for the grace You have given me to do my best at parenting.

But now, dear Lord, my child is entering the college-aged years. A new phase of adulthood beckons. Our relationship will change. United with Praying College Moms everywhere, I ask at this time of transition for Your superabundant blessings on my child and this whole generation of young adults:

- Please make Yourself known to them so that they always believe they are loved, sustained by, and find their purpose in You, dear Lord.
- Help them to master their studies, make good friends, and perhaps discern a career or vocation, according to Your perfect Will.
- Keep them safe and temperate in all things.
- Remind them often that their family loves them and prays for them.

With confidence in Your loving Providence, I ask all of these graces through Christ Our Lord, and through the intercession of our Blessed Mother Mary.

FOREWORD

It has become something of an end-of-summer ritual for our species—mom and dad bringing their child to college. It is an elaborate ceremony, the shopping and packing, loading and unloading, dorm room negotiations, awkward meetings, greetings, handshakes and hugs. It all ends with an uncomfortable farewell dance. Mom and dad linger, sensing that they are supposed to depart… but not knowing how. The children know they ought to treasure time with their parents…but they also hear college's freedom and fun calling them. The whole scene foreshadows the difficult dynamic that will characterize the coming years: Letting go of the children you love.

Parents have become clingy. Colleges and universities now have to contend with the "helicopter parents" who insist on assisting their children throughout those years that are supposed to bring growth and independence.Our technology exacerbates this clinginess with all the means (phone, email, texting…and whatever's next) for parents to keep track and to…hover, hover, hover. It is not good for the children, needless to say. But neither is it good for the parents.

In the context of the Catholic faith, this struggle takes on another dimension. It is no secret that most campuses are culturally, intellectually, and morally on a different track from the Catholic Church, and that most children lose their faith during those crucial years. The worry for many a Catholic mom is whether her child will keep the faith she has taken so much trouble to instill. Many ask: *How do I keep this from happening to my child? How much should I say…or not say? How much is too much…or too little?*

From my years working as a parish priest, I know the struggle and burden this is for parents—especially moms. They have heard (perhaps seen) the horror stories and they fear the same befalling their children. That noble maternal instinct is often turned against them. The temptation is to *control*—to become a *Catholic* helicopter parent, haunting the child at every turn with reminders and corrections and questions… This meets with bad results. No one can live the faith for another, and the attempt to do so often drives them from the faith.

This wonderful book by Maribeth Harper takes a different tack: *prayer*. No, it is not about how to keep your child perfect in college. It does not contain the secret to getting them to go to Mass and Confession. Rather, it is about how to pray into each of the various situations that your child—and you—will encounter during those years. The goal is as simple as it is difficult: to surrender control to God. This is not a book about how to get control of your college child but about how to hand over control to God.

Prayer is the most important thing. Maribeth provides wonderful guides to the prayer that should be in place in each stage of this journey. Each chapter helps the reader learn to turn every event and situation into an occasion for prayer, trust, and intercession. Nor is this any kind of Pollyannish prayer. The guides to prayer are deeply rooted in Catholic doctrine, rich in passages from the Bible and the *Catechism of the Catholic Church*. In the course of intercession for her child, the pray-er is also being formed.

In crafting the book this way, Maribeth has side-stepped the most common error about prayer. Most of us begin praying out of need. And we would be fools *not* to pray when in need. Unfortunately, we typically do so in a mercantile manner: *God, if you give me that, I'll give you this…* In the end, however, prayer is not about changing things outside of us but about allowing *ourselves* to be changed as we approach each trial with faith. So, this book provides reflections and questions at the end of each chapter to ensure that the readers make an investment of self—that they will pray and not just say prayers, that they will be changed by prayer.

Prayer is the most important thing, but not the only thing. Pope Francis speaks often about "accompaniment." Sharing the faith means more than just praying and certainly more than lecturing. It requires walking with them, being with them in their struggles and searches. In keeping with that pastoral vision, this little book contains scripturally and doctrinally rich reflections on how parents can best accompany their children and witness the faith to them. And, just as importantly, it includes some cautions on what parents should *not* do!

…And So We Pray has grown out of *Praying College Moms* and is a tribute to that group. It displays a great trust in the power of prayer, in its scriptural and doctrinal

foundations, and its power to transform the one who prays. May this book help college moms make the transition from the active mother at home to the prayerful mother accompanying her child.

May our Lady, who perfectly lived this prayerful accompaniment, intercede for those moms.

Fr. Paul Scalia
August 4, 2016
Feast of St. John Vianney

PREFACE

The fervent prayer of a righteous person is very powerful.

To whom do you turn for parenting advice when disciplining your college-aged young adult? Lately, I've been struck by the sound advice of St. James. I can relate to his direct manner of speaking—double-barreled...no holds barred. Imagine reprimanding adolescents with these one-liners:

- For one who knows the right thing to do and does not do it, it is a sin. (James 4:17)
- You are a puff of smoke that appears briefly and then disappears. (James 4:14)
- The tongue is a small member and yet has great pretensions. (James 3:5)

Although his approach is one I wish I could have taken with my college-aged young adults, alas, I find "convincing" this generation of anything requires a bit more nuance than Saint James' straight-shooting approach. Instead of speaking my mind to the kids, I more frequently pray, "Set a guard, Lord, before my mouth, keep watch over the door of my lips" (Psalm 141:5). What I say or don't say, however, is less important than how I pray. And the same is true for every praying college mom. St. James reminds us that, "The fervent prayer of a righteous person is very powerful" (James 5:16).

In the pages of this book, I hope to convince you, college moms, that our prayer can assuage any situation in which we find ourselves or our children, no matter how desperate. By knowing deeply our beautiful faith, praying regularly to the Lord who loves us, and relying on the promises of Jesus found in Scripture, we raise up a protective shield around our children and draw Our Lord's peace into our lives and theirs.

This book is a compilation of three 11-chapter books, consolidated into one, written to accompany you through a year of college as you read and reflect upon one chapter per week while your kids are at school. Divided into three sections, the chapters cover themes suggested, for the most part, by the wonderful women of prayer with whom I have been privileged to speak. Their willingness to share intimate details of their relationships with their own young adults provides all of us with a true, concrete witness of how faith in the abstract can be applied every day.

In addition to reading the stories these generous women have shared, taking some time to contemplate the teachings of the Church can help us better understand what to say or do (or not say or do) during crises of any kind with our college-aged young adults. For that reason, every chapter highlights one or more teachings of the Catholic Church to help us better parent.

If you're a college mom looking for practical ways to have a positive influence on your children, stay tuned.

Through my research and the delightful women of faith who offer their testimonies here, I am encouraged, and I pray you will be too. Although each of the following chapters offers faith-based suggestions for parenting to help keep our kids Catholic, the practical tips are much more effective when the parent is holy, so I've included plenty of suggestions for drawing ever closer to Jesus Christ as well. God bless you, and I will be praying for you.

Section I

WHO IS GOD AND DOES HE CARE ABOUT MY CHILD?

CHAPTER 1:

WIT'S END AT SUMMER'S END

Janet planned for her family's transition from school days to summer break with logistical precision. She wanted hot, nutritious dinners, clean bathrooms (she has four boys), and a long-overdue family vacation. Five drivers competed for two cars, requiring the need for unprecedented familial cooperation. Paying for multiple college tuitions kept her and her husband at work for long hours, making her expectation for the "perfect" summer more than a little challenging. Nevertheless, it started off well. The oldest son, newly graduated from college, had begun a job in his field of interest. The family enjoyed a beach vacation, which was both relaxing and affordable. "Buster," a rescue dog, arrived, promoting teamwork among the siblings, making for lots of laughs and friendly arguments over whose turn it was to walk the dog. Janet managed her youngest child's time so that he was constructively occupied while the others found summer jobs that kept them coming and going…and cash flush. Yet, with the finish line in sight—the return of the children to their respective schools at the end of August—things began to unravel.

Buster didn't assimilate, as can sometimes happen with dogs who are fostered. To everyone's dismay, he unpredictably lashed out, alternating between sweet family dog and teeth-baring protector. It became clear he needed rehabilitation away from their home—permanently. Janet, the family's most avid dog-lover, arranged for his departure with a heavy heart. Next, Janet's oldest son left two weeks early for college, and Janet was conflicted by his parting criticism of how much time she spent away from home. Was he unappreciative of Janet's need to work hard to pay for college? Or was Janet, in fact, too committed to the office? Probably both. Sigh… The college junior asked once again if a couple of his friends could come over one night. "Sure," Janet said. Knowing him, she shouldn't have been surprised when fourteen hungry men gathered, ate pizza, and left the den in disarray…again. He would need "a talkin' to." Finally, their youngest was back home from a sleep-away camp and called Janet repeatedly at work to remind her he was now bored and "home alone." The chaos was building beyond tolerable levels.

Enough already…Janet wanted to cry. Despite all the hard work coordinating the vacation, job transportation, dog duties, and summer camps—not to mention keeping up with a demanding career—the summer still resulted in pandemonium and left Janet at her wits' end with fewer than two weeks to go before school started again. Janet wanted someone to listen…to offer advice…to understand! But who? She called on a best friend.

Available at a moment's notice, a best friend listens patiently and attentively to all kinds of troubles explained five different ways, upside down and backward. A best friend sorts through confusion and understands what is meant, not just what is said. A best friend offers wisdom that is perfectly tailored to the unique situation, knowing well the family history and the personalities involved. Full of compassion, a best friend embraces life's messiness and climbs into the trenches with you—every time.

Do you have a friend who fits this description? I do. In fact, we all do. God, our loving Father, listens closely to our every concern, acts wisely, and loves us unconditionally. True, we can't cry on His shoulder or lay our heads in His lap [not in this life, anyway] but His reassuring presence can be felt as tangibly. Our best friends are sometimes as busy as we are, but God is never too busy to listen and console us.

So often, our perception of God is what limits our ability to draw close and learn to trust Him as the friend He wants to be. Misperceptions abound! On the one hand, we imagine God as a magician, all sugar and spice and everything nice, showering His friends with every blessing, especially when they feel *good enough* and worthy of His attention. Or, we view God as a tyrant, shaking His divine finger at us when something goes wrong. This God-bully is relentless in His judgment and indifferent to our sorrow. In reality, however, God is our Father who constantly endeavors to befriend us, His beloved children. "Call to me, and I will answer you; I will tell you great things beyond the reach of your knowledge" (Jeremiah 33:3).

Is God's friendship *enough* when you find life overwhelming? That depends on how *you* think of God, doesn't it? Stop reading and take a minute or more to list five to ten words you would use to describe God. Write them down.

_____

_____

_____

_____

_____

_____

_____

_____

_____

_____

_____

_____

_____

_____

_____

_____

_____

_____

Is the God you described *strong enough, caring enough, attentive enough, or wise enough* to call on in a crisis or to ask for a favor? Do you trust Him to care for your college-aged child(ren)? Would you ask God to help you with something as simple as finding a parking space at the mall? Is He your best friend? Do you trust that He wants to be this kind of friend to you?

Getting to Know the Father as Friend

God, our Father, has bent over backward to help us learn to love and trust Him. He sent His Son, Jesus Christ, to redeem, reconcile and reunite us to the family. He gave us His Holy Spirit to enlighten and empower us after Jesus returned to Heaven. He left us His living Word in the Bible. For two thousand years, God has raised up saints who have radiated His glory so that we can learn from their example. And God built the Church, with its Sacraments, and the Magisterium, to guide and protect us until we rejoin Him for all eternity.

Most of us, so pressed for time, would appreciate "CliffNotes"—a quick and reliable way to get to know God so as to build up a real friendship with Him. Fortunately, He left us "love letters." Through Holy Scripture, God reveals Himself to us, so much so that the Catechism of the Catholic Church (CCC), a synthesis of all we believe as Catholics, teaches, "...such is the force and power of the Word of God that it can serve the Church as her support and vigor, and the children of the Church as strength for their faith, food for the soul, and a pure and lasting fount of spiritual life" (CCC 131).

What does Scripture say to us about Our Father? Here's a sampling:

God is love: "God sent his only Son into the world so that we might have life through Him. In this is love: not that we have loved God, but that He loved us and sent His Son as expiation for our sins" (1 John 4:9-10).

God is our creator: "Yet, Lord, you are our father; we are the clay and you our potter: we are all the work of your hand" (Isaiah 64:7).

7

God is merciful, forgiving us for every wrongdoing, big or small: "Merciful and gracious is the Lord, slow to anger, abounding in mercy. He will not always accuse and nurses no lasting anger; He has not dealt with us as our sins merit, nor requited us as our wrongs deserve" (Psalm 103:8-10).

God is our provider: "Therefore you are no longer a slave, but a son; and if a son, then an heir through God" (Galatians 4:7). "Do not be afraid any longer, little flock, for your Father is pleased to give you the kingdom" (Luke 12:32). "What eye has not seen, and ear has not heard, and what has not entered the human heart, what God has prepared for those who love him" (1 Corinthians 2:9).

God is our Father, *our Abba*. God's son Jesus lived and died so as to reveal His Father to us. "We have approximately 25,000 words that Jesus spoke recorded in the Bible. Of those 25,000 words, Jesus taught about the Father in Heaven at least 181 times. This means one out of every 140 words, Jesus was speaking about His Father. His central message and purpose was to restore us to a relationship with our Daddy in Heaven."[1] It is Jesus Christ who assures us that God is *enough*:

And I tell you, ask and you will receive; seek and you will find; knock and the door will be opened to you. For everyone who asks, receives; and the one who seeks, finds; and to the one who knocks, the door will be opened. What father among you would hand his son a snake when he asks for a fish? Or hand him a

---

1 "Top 10 Bible Verses about the Father," Monday Morning Review, March 08, 2010, accessed October 17, 2016, https://mondaymorningreview.wordpress.com/2010/03/08/top-10-Bible-verses-about-the-father/.

scorpion when he asks for an egg? If you then, who are wicked, know how to give good gifts to your children, how much more will the Father in Heaven *give the Holy Spirit* to those who ask him?" (Luke 11:9-13) [emphasis added]

Our Father answers our pleas for help by giving us His Holy Spirit. How is that *enough* when life gets us down? The Spirit's gift of patience kicks in when our homesick daughter calls for the third time in as many hours. We are given immeasurable kindness to deal with a son's disappointment over midterm grades. We surprise ourselves with a prudent response to a child's call from college asking for money...again. And, perhaps even more astoundingly, we react with faithfulness and peace when the unexpected happens—an arrest, an accident, or something worse. "With the Holy Spirit comes love, joy, peace, patience, kindness, generosity, faithfulness" (Galatians 5:22). In the Spirit's strength, we can find supernatural joy in every trial.

The Holy Spirit visited Janet in the weeks after two of her children left for college. The house was calmer, the laundry and grocery-shopping duties had eased. We would assume that she was relishing the relative quiet. But that's not what happened. Unanticipated financial pressures had arisen, there were surgeries, issues percolating with one child away at school, and the youngest unexpectedly needing more tutoring—a financial and emotional strain. Janet's circumstances had not substantially improved. Miraculously, however, even in the midst of these new challenges, she was peaceful.

"I have finally realized that things are so far beyond my control," she said, "that I have no choice but to trust God with all of this…and it's a good place to be." She wondered aloud whether God had placed her in difficult positions now and at other times in her life precisely so that she would learn to trust Him. "I'm a slow learner, but I think I'm finally getting it," she joked.

Janet hadn't suddenly found the time others have to pray before the Blessed Sacrament or say the rosary regularly. She hadn't seen visions or heard God's voice audibly. But she felt God heard her exasperated cry, "enough already," and answered as would a best friend. She was renewed in her determination to focus on God's love for her, trusting that God sees and appreciates her efforts to love Him back. And, as meager as she thinks they are, she now rests in the certain hope that her efforts are *enough*.

PRAYER

God, my Father, my *Abba*, I praise You for Your awesome power and might and for your gentle and attentive care of me. You are Almighty, Trinitarian, Creator of all things, but, as incredible as it seems to me, You also want to be my friend.

More than my husband, Lord, You are enough.
More than my children, Lord, You are enough.
More than my Earthly friends, Lord, You are enough.
More than my job, Lord, You are enough.
More than any of my life's circumstances, Lord, You are enough.

Only You fulfill me. Help me to realize Your gifts in my life. You give me breath and life, family and friends, talents, and many opportunities to share Your love with others. Praised be Your name!

Heavenly Father, bless my child _____ as he heads into the college years. Watch over him and draw him close to You.

Help me to treasure Your presence in my life and end each day with a heart overflowing with gratitude.

Questions for Reflection:

How does my image of God compare to what Jesus tells me about His Father in Scripture? Is He my friend or foe?

What words or phrases describing God do I find most meaningful in times of prayer, joy or sorrow?

Prayer Intentions:

Answered Prayers:

Prayer Practice:

I will be especially attentive while reading Scripture or listening to the Word at Mass for new insight into deepening the friendship God my Father wants to have with me. I will journal any words or phrases that touch my heart.

Have you not known? Have you not heard? The Lord is the everlasting God, the Creator of the ends of the earth. He does not faint or grow weary; his understanding is unsearchable. He gives power to the faint and strengthens the powerless. (Isaiah 40:28–29)

Lord, how can I love you more today than I did yesterday?

_____

_____

_____

_____

_____

_____

_____

_____

_____

_____

_____

_____

_____

_____

CHAPTER 2:

THEY'RE GONE…NOW WHAT?

We were standing in the circular driveway on a glorious September day at the end of a long weekend of hauling, stacking, sorting, and making beds with new linens (would they be regularly washed?); the time for good-byes had come. My two sons (the older a junior and the younger a freshman), towered over me, lanyards around their necks, laundry cards tucked away, dressed in new jeans and clean T-shirts. We had just shared Sunday brunch, and their father and I were preparing for the long drive home.

"Well, I guess this is it," I said as bravely as I could muster. In my mind I was imagining the stark, vacant bedrooms that would greet me at the end of the road. In fact, the whole house would be empty. "Don't go there…" I thought, fighting back my emotions to spare the boys. How could I be so incredibly proud of them and, at the same time, so very sad and…was it loneliness I felt? My husband was right there with me, after all.

As I reached up to embrace each of the boys, we shared a kind of group hug, and my tears began to flow. Drat! The boys began to stammer and pat my back the way I had patted theirs so very often as children. I was comforted by their awkward efforts to stop the tears. Just then, two young female students walked by and noticed that I was having a "moment."

"Aww…" one said to her friend, "Look at that mom crying." Her sing-song voice and pointing finger unknowingly mocked my hurting heart. It stung. Pulling myself together, I blew kisses to the boys (who were relieved the drama was about to end) and settled into the passenger seat of the car while my husband solemnly shook each boy's hand and bid his farewell. Deeply melancholic, I remembered how I was once young like those girls, oblivious to my mom's feelings as she dropped me off at college. I wondered if those girls would one day be kissing their sons good-bye in the same circle, bewildered by their own tears, heading home to an empty house…

Not all of us have an identical experience, of course, but every kind of sorrow can be assuaged by someone who understands—a loving husband who empathizes, a mother who consoles, a friend who supports. Our constant companion, however, is the One who loves us unconditionally and created us along with all of our intricate emotions. We are perfectly understood and loved by God who "has searched me and knows me" (Psalm 139:1). Our Father in Heaven is desperate to comfort His beloved daughters. (That's us!)

God the Perfect Parenting Partner

God the Father is a perfect parent—and our perfect parenting partner. God overflows with wisdom to help us advise our adult children, prudence to know what to say when, fortitude to embolden us during this time of transition, and all the tenderness and compassion our hurting hearts so desperately need. God begs us in the Scriptures to turn to Him and He wants to hear from us…regularly!

- "When you call me, and come and pray to me, I will listen to you." (Jeremiah 29:12)
- "Do not be anxious about anything, but in everything by prayer and supplication with thanksgiving let your requests be made known to God. And the peace of God, which surpasses all understanding, will guard your hearts and your minds in Christ Jesus." (Philippians 4:6–7)
- "Rejoice in hope, endure in affliction, persevere in prayer." (Romans 12:12)

When my first son went off to college, he surprised me with a framed picture of himself that he put on the kitchen counter. The frame played music when a button on the lower right corner was pressed. He had recorded himself playing "Blackbird" by Paul McCartney on the guitar, a song he had been playing around the house that whole summer. For weeks after he left for college, I teared up every time someone pressed that pesky button on the frame! My only daughter, who was then the oldest in the household and feeling her newfound privilege, used to delight in pressing the button to watch me tear up on the spot. It gave a whole new meaning to the phrase, "I know which button to press!"

The story serves to illustrate that I was a bit of a mess in the weeks following the departure of my oldest child. His college was a full day's travel away, and I worried constantly that, should he get sick or injured, we wouldn't be able to reach him in time. He didn't check in as he had promised in those first few weeks. I missed him terribly, and I was just about as equally furious with him for being so…well…independent.

One morning, alone in the kitchen, I sat at the table and turned my heart at last to my Father in Heaven. "Lord," I said, "I can't seem to pull myself together. I've got other kids to care for and lots of obligations. When will this sadness end? Help me!" After some time, I dried my tears and got up to go get the newspaper. Back at the same kitchen table, I was amazed to see that the *Washington Post*, our hometown paper, had run a front-page article in the Style section entitled, "This Man Who Just Left Me; My Son Heads to College, a Boy No More."[2] Here was another woman as sad as I was, missing her son. I was not alone. The feeling of accompaniment was overwhelmingly touching. I felt my Father's presence in a new way, and the first inklings of a profound new peace began to creep into my heart.

Our Father is perfectly attentive to our every need. He can be trusted—with our hearts and with the well-being of our children. He answers our cries for help with an awesome invitation to get to know Him better! He wants an intimate relationship with us, and that means really delving into what He has revealed about Himself.

---

2   Priscilla Dann-Courney, "This Man Who Just Left Me; My Son Heads to College, A Boy No More," Washington Post, September 19, 2005, Style.

Growing in Intimacy with the Father

When my husband and I met, we spent the early days getting acquainted. After some time, I learned what delighted him, and being young and in love, I spent time and energy dedicating myself to pleasing him. In the same way, God our Father desires that we spend time getting to know Him. Once we know Him, we can't help but love Him! He shows us how to please Him, too. These lines from the Bible and the Catechism were written for you and for me.

> God's very being is love. By sending his only Son and the Spirit of Love in the fullness of time, God has revealed his innermost secret: God himself is an eternal exchange of love, Father, Son and Holy Spirit, and he has destined us to share in that exchange. (CCC 221)

> See what love the Father has bestowed on us that we may be called the children of God. Yet so we are. (1 John 3:1)

> For you did not receive a spirit of slavery to fall back into fear, but you received a spirit of adoption, through which we cry, "*Abba*, Father!" The Spirit itself bears witness with our spirit that we are children of God... (Romans 8:15–16)

> Look at the birds of the air; they do not sow or reap or store away in barns, and yet your Heavenly Father feeds them. Are you not much more valuable than they? (Matthew 6:26)

Our Father is in an eternal exchange of love with the Son and the Spirit, and He invites us to join Him in that mysterious relationship. He is our *Abba*. We are family.

What is to fear when we have such a tender and loving Father?

Like many fathers, God delights in showering us with spiritual gifts of supreme value, but, like any human father, God does not give us everything we ask for. He is not a magic genie, nor does He run the lottery. He can't be bargained with. God is a loving *father*. Perfect, in fact. He exercises his "better judgment" where we're concerned and knows well what will do us good and what won't. He asks for our total trust.

Placing My Child into Loving Hands

Every time I drove away from college with an empty car and a heart full of raw emotion, my dear husband would remind me in whose hands I had placed my children. I would remember and would start to pray, seeking the peace that I knew would eventually come.

Have you ever imagined what the hands of the Father might look like? My father's hands are enormous, strong, and calloused. Over the years, he used them to build, to fix every broken thing in our house, and to squeeze me so tightly when we separated that it often took my breath away. I love his hugs! Our Father's hands must be larger, stronger, gentler and even more comforting. I place my child in those capable hands.

Ecclesiastes 3:1–8 says there is a time for everything under the sun. *Now* is the time to leave our children on the doorstep of their college experience. We acknowledge that it's appropriate, good for them, and ultimately good for us. We don't want to limit what God has in mind for their lives by clinging to them unnecessarily or covetously.

Instead, every time we worry, feel a little sad, or think "I wonder what he's doing?" we remember into whose hands we have placed him. Praising God, we release him, knowing that God can be everywhere we can't. God can parent him better than we can. Our Father has big, strong hands, and I've placed my own hand in one and my child's in the other. Ahhhh...peace at last.

PRAYER

Heavenly Father, *Abba*, You are Almighty, King of Kings, and Master of the Universe. By the Passion and Resurrection of Your Son, Jesus, You claim me forever as Your beloved daughter. I am a member of Your family by my Baptism. You desire my love and affection. Such knowledge is too wonderful for me; it is so high that I cannot attain it (Psalm 139:6).

Father, my child _____ is growing up, no longer under my roof 24/7, and is now able to make his own decisions. I place him into Your capable hands, knowing You are the best of parents. Guide him, lead him, inspire him, warn him, console him, and remind him, if You will, that he has a mother who loves and prays for him with all her heart.

Question for Reflection:

God is the perfect parenting partner, "attentive to our every need." When have I felt God's inspiration parenting my college-aged young adult?

Prayer Intentions:

Answered Prayers:

Prayer Practice:

I will remind myself each day that God my Father, my *Abba*, loves me limitlessly and that He loves my child more than I do. I will invite Him to co-parent my children.

The Lord's acts of mercy are not exhausted, his compassion is not spent; They are renewed each morning—great is your faithfulness! (Lamentations 3:22-23)

Lord, how can I love you more today than I did yesterday?

_____

_____

_____

_____

_____

_____

_____

_____

_____

_____

_____

_____

_____

_____

_____

_____

CHAPTER 3:

EQUIPPED FOR CHANGE

One of the first few days my son was away at school, he called to ask me where I put the Tylenol. I had no idea whether the little first-aid kit transferred from our car to his room before we left, but I knew where he could find Tylenol. We had run into a good friend and her freshman daughter at a big-box store while we were getting settled. They had loaded up two carts with matching…everything, while my son was purchasing deodorant, a set of sheets, and a shower caddy (at my insistence). As fate would have it, my friend and her daughter had to cram two cartloads of necessities into the tiniest room on campus, while my son and his roommate shared a veritable mansion across the street. He had floor space and air conditioning. She had everything else. She was sure to have extra Tylenol. I laughed at the memory and encouraged him to seek her out.

Within our means, moms do all we can to make the transition to college as smooth as it can be for our children. But the transition happens on our end too, so how well do we prepare ourselves? Ali jokingly says she didn't notice her oldest was gone until she was looking for an extra carpool driver back home. Julia, however, grieved all summer before her only daughter left for college. Everyone experiences a change in the family dynamics as a child leaves for school, but we cope very differently.

What best equips us for this change (or any major life event)? We know that God wants to be our friend. We have learned that He is the perfect parenting partner. To best cope with whatever comes our way, we need His help and we call on Him when we pray.

What Is Prayer?

Is there a right or wrong way to talk to God? What's the best way to get Him to listen to us? Should we consult an expert? Read a book? Is there a test we have to pass? Every spiritual master would tell us the same thing...talking to God is called "prayer," and any honest words from the heart will do. There are many forms of prayer, and lots of prayers have been composed to help us pray well. But, in essence, *Abba* wants to hear from us, and there's no "should" when it comes to the "how."

When we're sad or worried, as we can be about our college kids, prayer might sound like a long series of requests, right? And that's OK—even beautiful—because God the Father hears and treasures every word, and more importantly, the longing of our hearts. God wants to draw us close when we pray, so our prayer can be much, much more fulfilling than a long list of requests. God wants to reveal Himself to our hearts and minds. He wants to work through us to affect change in the world, starting with those we love the most—our children.

When we come to a moment of prayer, let's try to remember who it is we are talking with and what He wants from us in exchange.

- He is *Abba*. He wants intimacy.
- God is Father. He wants to protect us (sometimes from ourselves).
- God is omniscient. He has the Big Picture, and we do not. He wants our trust.
- God is giver of every good gift (James 1:17). He wants our gratitude.
- God is powerful and creative. He wants to share these qualities with us.
- God is Almighty. He wants our heartfelt praise.

The only "right way to pray" is to know who we're talking to and how precious we are to Him. In the weeks ahead, we'll be adding to this list our own experiences of God, the gifts He has given to us, and the fruits of the Spirit we employ for the good of our family, our prayer group, our community, and the whole world.

Kickstarting Your Prayer Life

When my next two sons prepared for college, one of them carefully boxed, folded, taped, and wrapped his belongings to fit in the trunk. The other threw everything into green garbage bags. When it comes to talking with God, some thrive by praying with an "anything goes" disposition, while others prefer a little bit of structure to help them express their innermost thoughts.

We are equipped to be prayer warriors when we imitate Jesus' perfect example and prayerfully read His Word recorded in Scripture. Jesus taught us that the words of Scripture powerfully deflect the enemy. After His baptism, during which the Father audibly acclaimed, "This is my beloved Son in whom I am well pleased" (Matthew 3:17), Jesus went into the desert, led by the Spirit, for forty days of fasting and prayer to prepare for his active ministry. At the end of this period, he was tired and hungry. There, three times, Jesus was tempted by Satan. Three times, Jesus rebuked him by quoting Scripture.

"Turn the stones to bread," Satan demanded.

Jesus said, "It is written, 'One does not live by bread alone but on every word that comes from the mouth of God.'" (Matthew 4:4)

"Worship me," Satan tempted.

Jesus said, "It is written: 'You shall worship the Lord, your God, and him alone shall you serve.'"

For his third temptation, Satan himself used the words of Scripture to entice Jesus. "If you are the Son of God, throw yourself down from here, for it is written: 'He will command his angels concerning you, to guard you,' and: 'With their hands they will support you, lest you dash your foot against a stone.'" Luke 4:8-9)

Jesus would have no more of it! "It [Scripture] also says, 'You shall not put the Lord, your God, to the test.'" (Luke 4:11) The devil fled.

The power of praying with Scripture is unparalleled. A friend of mine, Lisa Brenninkmeyer,[3] has the habit of

---

3   Lisa Brenninkmeyer is founder of a Catholic Women's Bible Study, Walking with Purpose, and a wife and the mother of seven.

praying Scripture aloud for encouragement when she is down, to chase away Satan, and to pour out every grace and blessing on her family. She told this story recently:

I was beyond distraught. My heart was so sad about my son, who was in the midst of a serious medical crisis, and my husband and I were not communicating well. On top of that, someone whose opinion I respect told me I was a fake because of the way in which I guarded my feelings. There's not much worse you can say to me! All sorts of thoughts began to swirl in my head—some true, and some that were distortions, exaggerations, or downright lies. When I started to feel that the enemy was messing with me, I went to the privacy of my car, and I spoke aloud truth of Christ into the mire of lies. I call these the I DECLARES.

This is what I say:

I DECLARE that I serve a God who makes all things new.

I DECLARE that my child is not beyond the reach of redemption.

I DECLARE that God loves me and wants what is best for me.

I DECLARE that God's arm is not too short to save. It can reach into my child's heart and mine and work miracles.

I DECLARE that I am a fighter and that I do not give up.

I DECLARE that He who is in me is stronger than he who is in the world.

As Lisa shows us, praying aloud can be very liberating. The Church also recommends the recitation of "vocal prayers." Many of them we know well: the Hail Mary, the Glory Be, and the prayer Jesus Himself gave to us in the Gospel of Matthew (6:9-13)—the Our Father. The best resource for appreciating the beauty, depth, and significance of the Our Father is the Catechism, part four on Christian prayer. Section two is devoted to the seven petitions of the Our Father. We imitate Jesus in His love for the Father when we say this prayer reverently.

The Rosary is another familiar vocal prayer, which can be said in a group or quietly as a meditation on each mystery. Praying College Moms gathers monthly and speaks aloud the name of each child for whom they pray, while saying the Rosary. (See chapter 33 for more about the rosary.)

Whether we pray for our children in the name of Jesus or with the words of Scripture or by reciting vocal prayers, we are making an effort to talk to God and invoke His power in our lives. In moments of grace, conversation with God can flow naturally, full of sweet consolation and assurances of being heard and loved. But when we're stuck, there's yet another way to enkindle some fervor—prayers of praise.

The Psalms and countless other prayers are full of praise for God, but sometimes the most effective can be the praise that rises from your heart, inspired by a beautiful sunset or an infant's smile. Praising God is so, so beneficial for our souls! We take our minds off of the problems at hand and draw our thoughts back to God, who has the power to fix everything. By praising God, we acknowledge what He told Saint Catherine of Siena: "You are she who is not and I am HE Who Is."[4]

Prayers of praise require faith, and faith always paves the way for miracles. Think of the New Testament healings Jesus granted to those who expressed their faith in Him: The leper in Galilee (Matt. 8:1-4), the paralytic at Capernaum (Mark 2:3-12), the man with the withered hand (Luke 6:6-11), the woman with the hemorrhage (Luke 8:43-48), the man born blind begging outside the temple in Jerusalem (John 9:1-12), the ten lepers (Luke 17:11-19), blind Bartimaeus (Mark 10:46-52)…and the list goes on. They received healings, and we can too!

Finally, our praise gives God the glory He is due, which is also very good for us psychologically. Praise is the opposite of negativity and complaining. It forces us to reorient, and that's usually a good thing!

A priest-friend of ours told our moms' group one time that praise should be the first thing that comes out of our mouths, even when we're in pain. "Praise God in all circumstances,"[5] he told us. That afternoon, I smashed my finger in the kitchen drawer. Ouch…"Praise God!" I yelled out in an angry tone. My son in the next room thought he had heard me incorrectly. He laughed when I told him what I was doing, and then he recommended that next time I change my tone of voice, because after all, I was talking to God.

Because praising God is so valuable and such a good habit, we begin the prayer that follows each chapter with

---

4   Thomas McDermott, Catherine of Siena: Spiritual Development in Her Life and Teaching (New Jersey: Paulist Press, 2008), 119.
5   He was referring to 1 Thessalonians 5:18: "In all circumstances give thanks, for this is the will of God for you in Christ Jesus."

praise. Hopefully, these written prayers will springboard us into praying spontaneously from the heart for our child and for all college students and their families.

The Best Prayer of All

Praising God is so fulfilling because we were made to worship. "Our heart is restless until it rests in You,"[6] Saint Augustine famously said. One prayer stands out as the highest form of praise and worship: The Holy Mass. This community prayer is considered by Church fathers to be the "source and summit of the Christian life" (CCC 1324). At Mass, we receive the body and blood, soul and divinity of Jesus Christ in the Eucharist. When we receive the Eucharist, we become "Christ bearers," as was Mary, who carried her son for nine months. We turn into living tabernacles, carrying our Lord out into the world.

We are obligated, as Catholics, to go to Mass every Sunday,[7] but we are *invited* to go more often. Mass attendance supercharges our prayer life. According to the Catechism, at every Mass we are drawn into union with the Lord, who forgives our venial sins and preserves us from grave sin (CCC 1416). We always get much more than we give, because our Father is pleased to shower His grace upon us, especially when we praise Him as He deserves.

Pleading for grace for our children at Mass will yield results! "Without doubt, the Lord grants all favors which

---

6   Saint Augustine, The Confessions of St. Augustine, trans. Henry Chadwick (New York: Oxford University Press, 1991), 3.

7   "Remember to keep holy the Sabbath day" (Exodus 20:8). This is the third commandment.

are asked of Him in Mass, provided they be fitting for us; and, which is a matter of great wonder, ofttimes He also grants that also which is not demanded of Him, if we, on our part, put no obstacle in the way,"[8] says Saint Jerome, a doctor of the Church. (See chapter 11 for more about the Mass.)

So You're Not a Perfect Pray-er? Who Is?

Kathy relished her time at home with her six kids, but as the college years approached, she felt compelled to return to work to pay the tuitions. After seventeen years at home, she landed a directorship with a small association, which she leveraged into a well-paid position as chief of staff in a multinational company two years later. Suddenly, she was fulfilled at the office but working fifty-plus hours a week, on call around the clock. She now feels chronically overwhelmed, incapable of balancing the needs of her three sons at home, the three away at college, and her eight direct-reports at the office—not to mention her husband, who holds a demanding full-time job. She's frustrated and exhausted a lot of the time.

Kathy desperately wants her kids to be happy, productive, successful, and...saved. But the idea of adding one more "to do"—like prayer—to her plate is out of the question.

"Prayer?" she asks. "It's a luxury." There's little time for quiet reflection, and she volleys between guilt and worry when it comes to her kids' well-being. Instead, she

---

8   Lorrie McNickle9/20/2015, "Mass: The Ultimate Hour of Power," Catholic365, accessed March 15, 2016, http://www.catholic365.com/article/2388/mass-the-ultimate-hour-of-power.html.

snatches sound bites on her iphone riding the metro, reads the headlines of spiritual blogs, and sometimes listens to Christian music, finding encouragement in the nooks and crannies of her hectic days.

Pope Francis has some words of encouragement for those of us who feel like Kathy: "God waits; He waits for us to concede him only the smallest glimmer of space so that He can enact His forgiveness and his charity within us…"[9]

Our loving Father doesn't expect perfection. He is satisfied with our efforts, no matter how seemingly insignificant. To our weakness and brokenness (aren't we all somehow broken, after all?), God brings His strength! Saint Paul says, "I will rather boast most gladly of my weaknesses, in order that the power of Christ may dwell with me. Therefore, I am content with weaknesses, insults, hardships, persecutions, and constraints, for the sake of Christ; for when I am weak, then I am strong" (2 Corinthians 12:9-10).

What's important is that we're real with God. He sees right through it when we put on false "prayer faces"— when we try to pretend we're more capable, more loving, or more spiritual than we are. It's even OK to say, "Lord I don't feel like praying right now, but here I am." A friend of mine, a spiritual coach, says, "Pray as you can, not as you can't." We are to approach God with confidence and state our needs, remembering that we are beloved daughters, no matter what choices we've made or how we see ourselves. He sees and loves us unchangingly and eternally.

---

9   Pope Francis, The Name of God is Mercy, trans. Oonagh Stransky (New York: Random House, 2016), 35.

God doesn't want us wrapped up in guilt or worried out of our minds about our kids. (Would you want your child to feel that way about you?) So relax into those brief moments of prayer, if that's all you have to give. Know that your loving Father sees and hears you in every moment. And whether you or your children are making good choices or bad ones, God the Father has you covered. With childlike trust, and sometimes with a bit of patience, we can rest assured that all things work for good for those who love God (Romans 8:28). And we love Him, or we wouldn't be reading this book.

May the God of peace...Jesus our Lord, furnish [equip] you with all that is good, that you may do his will. May he carry out in you what is pleasing to Him through Jesus Christ, to whom be glory forever and ever. Amen. (Hebrews 13:20–21)

PRAYER

Lord, I know that my conception of You is dim and partial (1 Corinthians 13:12). I want to love You more, so help me to know You better! Grant me the grace to pray regularly, to make the time for prayer even when I don't feel as if I have any to give. You are the master of time. Help me to trust that my effort to pray blesses me, my child _____ and my entire family more abundantly than I can imagine.

Question for Reflection:

I can do nothing without God (John 15:5). Am I prepared to dedicate myself to support my child by growing in my relationship with God? What concrete changes will I make to my routine so that prayer is an integral part of my day going forward?

Prayer Intentions:

Answered Prayers:

Prayer Practice:

I will commit myself to one new form of prayer this week.

With all prayer and supplication, pray at every opportunity in the Spirit. (Ephesians 6:18)

Lord, how can I love you more today than I did yesterday?

_____

_____

_____

_____

_____

_____

_____

_____

_____

_____

_____

_____

_____

_____

_____

CHAPTER 4:

───────── ⌒ ─────────

GETTING TO KNOW THE SON

When Barbara and her husband bade farewell to their oldest daughter, Cara, she headed off to college with a natural self-confidence, an outgoing manner and a fierce independence. Throughout the four years, Cara chatted regularly with her mom, sharing ups and downs, but rarely asked advice. That was fine with Barbara who relished the opportunity to touch base so frequently and "listen in" on her daughter's college years. Cara's college experience met all of Barbara's expectations.

Several years later, Barbara's son, Bobby, was ready for college. Barbara anticipated a slightly different experience with Bobby, who was much quieter than his sister, but nothing prepared her for the angst she felt when Bobby chose to attend a nearby "commuter school" over the two top-tier colleges that had accepted him.

"I wanted the best for Bobby and for some crazy reason thought he should be going away," Barbara shared. "I was convinced about it," she added, "and I suppose I was projecting my own ideas about what would make for an exciting college experience—a city with a lot to see and do, not necessarily a party school, but something more exciting than what he chose…"

Barbara and her husband had always been a prayerful couple—solidly grounded in faith and well-formed as Catholics. Barbara allowed her anxiety over Bobby's decision to draw her to Christ in prayer. "I made his college choice the intention for my weekend retreat," she explained. Our Lord did not disappoint her. "I heard the Lord say in my heart, 'This is where I want him,'" Barbara said.

God became man in Jesus to bring us into His family as adopted daughters of the Father. In spite of this loving reality, we often seek solace and comfort from more familiar sources…a glass of wine or two, a shopping spree, internet browsing, or relationships that can provide more immediate interpersonal satisfaction than does prayer. What drew Barbara to Jesus? Barbara has had years of experience in daily prayer with Jesus.

No matter where we are in our faith journey, it is possible to fall more in love with Jesus. His reality is fathomless. Right here, right now, let's take a moment to place ourselves around the campfire described in the New Testament Gospel of Matthew, chapter 16. As we warm our palms by the fire, shoulder-to-shoulder with Jesus' disciples, allow Him to ask us, "Who do *you* say that I am?" (Matthew 16:15)

Jesus' disciples had plenty to say just minutes before when they were asked, "Who do *people* say that I am?" (Matthew 16:13-14) "Some say John the Baptist, others say Elijah; and still others Jeremiah or one of the prophets," they offered unselfconsciously. We, too, can find that question easy to answer. We know that believers say Jesus is God. They say Jesus is the Eucharist. Or, Jesus is their personal Lord and Savior. Non-believers—so many of our millennial "nones"—reject Jesus in favor of science, common sense, or logic.[10]

When Our Lord asked his disciples that night, "Who do *you* say that I am," perhaps a moment of uncomfortable silence hung in the air. What were their thoughts before Peter spoke up? What are our thoughts? Our answer to the question posed by Christ has the power to change every aspect of our lives—and our deaths, for that matter. Is Jesus an historical figure, nothing more, or is Jesus Christ *alive*? In other words, do we, like Barbara, take our concerns to Him asking for clarity and consolation?

The apostle Peter, destined to be the leader of the newly formed Church, was prompted by the Holy Spirit to answer Jesus' fireside question by proclaiming for the first time in human history, "You are Christ, the Son of the living God." At some point, we either accept Christ and his teachings, reject him outright, or neglect to make a decision, which is essentially a rejection. Contemporary Christian writer C.S. Lewis offered this insight...

"A man who was merely a man and said the sort of things Jesus said would not be a great moral teacher. He would either be a lunatic—on a level with the man who says he is a poached egg—or else he would be the Devil of Hell. You must make your choice. Either this man was, and is, the Son of God: or else a madman or

10 Michael Lipka, "Why America's 'nones' Left Religion behind," Pew Research Center, August 24, 2016, , accessed March 16, 2018, http://www.pewresearch.org/fact-tank/2016/08/24/why-americas-nones-left-religion-be-hind/.

something worse. You can shut Him up for a fool, you can spit at Him and kill Him as a demon; or you can fall at His feet and call Him Lord and God. But let us not come with any patronizing nonsense about His being a great human teacher. He has not left that open to us. He did not intend to."[11]

Scriptures make it clear that Jesus is our Lord and *Master*, the One to whom we must completely submit our personal freedom. We would be wise to follow Barbara's example and surrender…abandon ourselves completely… hand over control of our lives to our Master, Jesus the Lord. When we allow Him to be our master, we are able to do any number of ordinary or extraordinary daily works with a special pizzazz, by His strength. We see in the lives of so many saints how Jesus our Master intercedes on their behalf. A charming account of Saint Scholastica and her twin brother, Saint Benedict, proves that honoring Christ as "Master" pays off. [12]

In the sixth century, Scholastica was a faithful nun and a loving sister to St. Benedict. He ran a monastery five miles from her own and they would visit each other once a year at a pre-arranged spot. They enjoyed each other's company immensely. One evening, as the time for their visit drew to a close, St. Scholastica begged her brother to stay. He refused, reluctant to break his own rule by spending the night away from the monastery. In response, she quietly

---

11 C. S. Lewis, Mere Christianity (London, England: William Collins, 2017), p.53.
12 "Lives of the Saints - St. Scholastica," St. Scholastica Catholic Church, accessed March 16, 2018, https://stscholastica.org/lives-of-the-saints---st-scholastica.

bowed her head in prayer. Soon, a terrible thunderstorm moved in and prevented her brother from returning.

Benedict cried out, "God forgive you, Sister. What have you done?"

Scholastica replied, "I asked a favor of you and you refused. I asked it of God and he granted it." It was to be the last time Scholastica would see her brother, for she died three days later. How tender was Our Lord to grant Scholastica's request! He's eager to do the same kinds of favors for us.

Like Scholastica, Barbara, also experienced the Lord's favor. "Bobby wasn't two semesters into school when I realized what a blessing it was going to be to have him so close by," Barbara said. It had been a difficult transition into college for her son. Shortly after he got there, Bobby was diagnosed with depression. Barbara was able to pair him with a trusted doctor the family knew close to college. Barbara's husband, who works 15 minutes from the school, began to meet his son weekly for dinner. These dinners became a life-line for Bobby. "In those first few weeks, there were things that Bobby didn't want to talk to me about, and the telephone wouldn't have worked, but he was able to draw close to his father and share what was on his mind," Barbara explained. "These dinners have been an emotional anchor for both of them. I don't know how we would have managed if Bobby had gone away to school!" she exclaimed.

Jesus Christ is the Lord and Master of our lives. When we explore answers to life's million dollar question, *Who do you say that I am?,* there's literally no end to the discoveries we can make. Perhaps you're feeling a little, well, lukewarm about knowing Jesus better. There's a great model for the individual who *kinda sorta* wants to know Christ, wants to have a spiritual life, however that might evolve, but just can't seem to find the will to make it happen. The Evangelist Mark writes of a father whose young boy was ill. (Mark 9:14-25) This devoted father pleaded with Jesus, "If you can do anything, take pity on us and help us." Notice, the father didn't declare his abiding faith in Jesus as he asked for a cure. He merely asked, "if you can…"

Jesus responds, "If you can? Everything is possible for him who believes."

And here is the moment so worthy of our imitation. "Immediately," Scripture says, the poor father exclaimed, "I do believe; help me overcome my unbelief." His son was cured. It's the perfect prayer for those of us who struggle to know Christ when all we have is a mustard seed of faith. To get to know Christ, we need only recognize that we don't know how, and, at the same time, beseech His help saying, "increase my faith. Help me!" It's a prayer our Lord can't resist.

PRAYER

Jesus Christ, you are the Master of my life. I praise Your almighty power. Deepen my understanding of this awesome reality in my life. Allow me to answer the question, *"Who do you say that I am?"* with more intention each and every day.

As I become open and receptive to Your grace and love, may I grow in peace and joy—two fruits of Your Spirit. May my life increasingly radiate Your love toward _____, and the rest of my family so that they perceive some slight semblance of Your love for them in me.

You know I am weak, that I worry, and I see things only dimly through the eyes of faith. "Help my unbelief!" Strengthen my faith. Allow my fears to draw me to you in prayer where I can more clearly understand Your will for me and my family.

Help me to treasure Your presence in my life and end each day with a heart overflowing with gratitude.

Your faithful servant and friend,

_____

Question for Reflection:

Our Lord knows better than we do how difficult it can be to trust Him with our children's futures. When I struggle to believe that all will be well, where do I first turn? To a friend, a glass of wine, a catalog, the internet... When have I said to the Lord, "Help my unbelief?"

Prayer Intentions:

Answered Prayers:

Prayer Practice:

I will reflect on the question, "Who do you say that I am?" every day for the next week and journal what I learn about Jesus.

Great and wonderful are your works, Lord God almighty. Just and true are your ways, O king of the nations. Revelation 15:3

Lord, how can I love you more today than I did yesterday?

_____

_____

_____

_____

_____

_____

_____

_____

_____

_____

_____

_____

_____

_____

_____

_____

CHAPTER 5:

BETTER THAN THE MOVIES– REAL LIFE WITH JESUS

Nothing prepared Veronica for the grief she felt when her only son left for college, so she hid in the dark—literally. She took her Costco Skinny Pop popcorn to the movie theater. "I had a lot of time, more than I expected to have or would have liked. Being at home reminded me that I should be cleaning, something I hate with a passion and had been ignoring," she explained. "I was depressed so I went to see nine movies by myself in three weeks. Often, I was the only one in the theater," Veronica recounted.

Veronica says she chose to distract herself with movies because it was something she and her son always enjoyed together. "I would finish the popcorn and then splurge on Snow Caps because I felt so sorry for me," she laughed. "I told the Lord I just needed to do this until I could get a grip on my life and work through the transition."

When Veronica finally emerged from the dark, she made a beeline for the light, resolutely deciding that her faith in God, which had cooled when prayer slipped from her highest priority, would see her through this tough time. "I began to recognize that I had a golden opportunity to get my spiritual life in order. I've tried before but didn't stick to it," she explained. Buoyed by renewed fervor, Veronica began attending Mass more frequently. She found a spiritual director to help her remain accountable to her new resolve. Slowly but surely, Veronica stopped procrastinating and tackled the deep cleaning and reorganizing she had promised herself she would do, finding strength in her deepening spiritual life. She also committed to praying at the adoration chapel in her parish twice a week for ten to thirty minutes. Spending time before the Blessed Sacrament helped Veronica more than any other devotion at this time in her life, she said.

What does she do there? "I often go in anxious, and I try to spend time in praise and worship, rather than list all the problems I'm having. That helps reset my mood," she said. "Then I tell the Lord, 'Here I am; let's go through this again…' He must be bored with my repeating myself, but I hand it all over the altar to Him. Usually, when I leave, I feel like I really have left my sadness there. Three days later, it's kind of back so I return to the adoration chapel."

"I'm not accustomed to praying in silence and get fidgety," Veronica shared. "It's difficult, but I also find great peace there. By forcing myself to sit, focus, rest, and listen, my prayer time has become really fruitful. I am aware that the Lord is handling everything. He's got it all—my son's college career, my daughter's professional life, and my marriage—so I can walk away and feel better."

Veronica roused herself from binging on Hollywood movies at the theater to kneeling on a pew at the adoration chapel, but how did she manage to exchange anxiety and

...AND SO WE PRAY

depression for rest and peace? She was called by the light, Jesus Christ. "I am the light of the world. Whoever follows me will not walk in darkness but will have the light of life" (John 8:12). Of course, not everyone becomes depressed when their children leave for college, nor do we all find time to spare for movie watching. But no matter what our circumstances, the Lord calls us all out of "darkness"—anxieties about the kids, pressures at work, difficult relationships, health issues—and into His restorative light and a "peace that surpasses all understanding" (Philippians 4:7).

The Call into Light and Our Response

When you hugged your freshman for a final goodbye, did he return your affection with a manly bear hug? Or cringe and stiffen in embarrassment at the public spectacle? Or was it something in between? God, our Father, reaches out to us with this kind of intense parental love. He prompts our soul interiorly to pray or to act, and He uses all of our surroundings to do so: the beauty of nature, the kindness of others, and sometimes, mysteriously... even our suffering. According to the Catechism, "God, infinitely perfect and blessed in himself, in a plan of sheer goodness freely created man to make him share in his own blessed life. For this reason, at every time and in every place, God draws close to man. He calls man to seek Him, to know Him, to love Him with all his strength..." (CCC 1).

Prayer is one way of responding to God's spiritual hugs. Our greatest treasure in this age of technology and perpetual busy-ness is the very gift God seeks from each of us: our undivided time and attention. A very special kind of prayer the Masters call "mental prayer" requires our full attention and concerted effort. This quiet solitary prayer is an intimate exchange between two: the humble, needy soul and her God. As Veronica discovered, when we sit quietly, fight off distraction, and try hard to *pay attention,* the Lord makes Himself known—what an awesome reward!

Prayer: An Act of Love

Any desire we feel to pray has already been placed in our hearts by God who loves us. He inspires us to want to thank Him, praise Him, and, of course, to regularly ask His blessing on our college kids. We correspond to His grace when we commit to consistent daily prayer. Modern Psychology touts the emotional benefits of prayer: stress relief, better overall health, faster post-surgical healing, and a happier disposition.[13] But it's the spiritually restorative properties of daily mental prayer that bring lasting peace.

Five hundred years ago, the Lord sent us a messenger to encourage us in prayer. Her name is Saint Teresa of Avila, and she was a nun, a reformer, and doctor of the Church (a trusted expert) on the topic of prayer. She describes prayer this way:

---

13 "5 Scientifically Supported Benefits of Prayer," Psychology Today, June 23, 2014, accessed October 19, 2016, https://www.psychologytoday.com/blog/more-mortal/201406/5-scientifically-supported-benefits-prayer.
"10 Ways Praying Actually Benefits Your Health!" Health, Fitness, Beauty & Diet, March 20, 2015, accessed October 19, 2016, http://www.thehealthsite.com/diseases-conditions/10-ways-praying-actually-benefits-your-health-p114/.

- Mental prayer in my opinion is nothing else than an intimate sharing between friends; it means taking time frequently to be alone with Him who we know loves us.[14]

- However quietly we speak, He is so near that He will hear us: we need no wings to go in search of God, but have only to find a place where we can be alone and look upon Him present within us… we must talk to Him humbly, as we should our father. [15]

- The important thing is not to think much but to love much. [16]

We're All Beginners

Resolving to set aside a daily time of prayer can be daunting for the beginner, but even the seasoned pray-er—a woman with five to ten years of relationship with God—can feel like a toddler as she finds herself needing to recommit over and over to preserve her sacred prayer time. In the simplest of terms, becoming a regular daily pray-er requires that we *set the date, educate,* and *meditate.*

Set the date

How do you prioritize each day? At the top of the list are life's essentials: sleeping, eating, showering, but what comes next? Care of the family? Work at an office?

---

14 Teresa of Avlia, The Collected Works of Saint Teresa of Avila, vol.1, trans. Kieran Kavanaugh, OCD and Otilio Rodriguez, OCD (Washington, DC: Institute of Carmelite Studies, 1976), 96.

15 Teresa de Jesús (Teresa of Avila), The Way of Perfection (New York: Doubleday, 1991), 184.

16 Teresa of Avila, The Interior Castle (New York: Paulist Press, 1979), 70.

Exercise? If the list is much too long for a single day, then perhaps your list is longer than the one God has written for you. How would you know? —By beginning each day with a dedicated ten to fifteen minutes of prayer.

We know that date nights with husbands, coffee klatches with "the girls," and FaceTime with our college kids build relationships. Friends and spouses share a history that builds mutual trust and loyalty. God invites us to "set the date" so He can build with us a reservoir of memories—a history—so that we will look back at the times He has helped, big and small, and learn to trust Him, especially when life gets tough.

"Oh, I pray all day long," my friend Linda said. "I offer little thoughts to God whenever I think about it."

"That's great, but do you commit to a regular time of prayer?" I asked.

"Nope," she admitted. "Is that important?"

We talk to husbands or good friends multiple times a day… "Honey, what time will you be here for dinner? I'm going to the store. Can I get you something? Could you drive Tom to practice today?" Those kinds of conversations happen, but they're not soul building. God wants to superabundantly bless us when we pray with focused attention. Listen to the list of spiritual goodies God gives to the woman [or man] who prays:

In mental prayer, the soul is purified from its sins, nourished with charity, confirmed in faith, and strengthened in hope; the mind expands, the affections dilate, the heart is purified, truth becomes evident; temptation is conquered, sadness dispelled; the senses are renovated; drooping powers revive; tepidity ceases;

the rust of vices disappears. Out of mental prayer issues forth, like living sparks, those desires of Heaven which the soul conceives when inflamed with the fire of divine love. Sublime is the excellence of mental prayer, great are its privileges; to mental prayer Heaven is opened; to mental prayer Heavenly secrets are manifested and the ear of God [is] ever attentive. (Saint Peter of Alcantara, spiritual director to Saint Teresa of Avila[17])

Still, making this commitment to daily prayer takes great faith, doesn't it? We have to believe that when we sit each morning in our comfy chair, perhaps with a cup of coffee and a Bible or prayer book, God is really present and that He wants to talk with us. When life is especially harried and overwhelming, stopping for fifteen minutes to pray can feel like too much to ask. We can fall prey to "the urgent" which overtakes "the important." The enemy can also convince us that prayer really doesn't matter and won't help. Even Saint Teresa succumbed to that temptation. At one point during her years at the convent, she had become so preoccupied with social life in convent's visitor lounge that, convicted by a false humility, the saint resolved to refrain from mental prayer. This was a big mistake, which she rectified with the help of her spiritual director. "This excuse of bodily weakness," she wrote afterward, "was not a sufficient reason why I should abandon so good a thing, which required no physical strength, but only love and habit."[18]

---

17 Saint Peter of Alcantara, Treatise on Prayer, part 1, in Conversations with Christ: An Introduction to Mental Prayer, Rev. Peter-Thomas Rohrback, OCD (Chicago, IL: Fidels Publishers, 1956), 13.

18 "Saint Theresa of Avila," accessed April 13, 2017, http://www.ewtn.com/library/MARY/AVILA.htm. Taken from Father Vann Joseph, Lives

We need love and habit, says Saint Teresa! We are called to set the date "…with a firm determination not to give up, no matter what trials and dryness one may encounter" (CCC 2710).

Educate

When my first son left for college, I began sending care packages of chocolate chip cookies because I knew they were his favorite.[19] Now three of my four children live far away, and I continue to mail care packages occasionally, full of their favorite things. I know what they like because I have spent a lifetime learning their preferences. Similarly, God encourages us to get to know Him. What pleases Him? What does He desire for us? What does He have in store for us for all eternity? He has sent us some love letters to read—His Living Word in the Scriptures. By praying in little increments using the Scriptures, especially the Gospels, God reveals Himself to us through Jesus Christ, and teaches us plenty about ourselves! We are also blessed with more than two thousand years of Church tradition, treatises such as the Catechism of the Catholic Church, and the living witness of the saints to help us learn about God.

Does it seem odd that God would "desire" us to *educate* ourselves about spiritual things? Why doesn't He just infuse this knowledge into our souls? The simple answer is "love." By setting the date, and educating ourselves about

of Saints with Excerpts from Their Writing, 1954 ed. (New York: John J. Crawley & Co., Inc., 1954).

19 Praying College Moms Care Packages are delivered every November to hundreds of college students all over the country. For more information or to order, see prayingcollegemoms.org.

who God is, we are exercising our free will which is the single greatest gift God gives us. By choosing God over worldly distractions, by carving out precious moments reading His love letters, and by thinking about Him, we prove our love for Him...which brings us to the next point...

Meditate

The practice of meditation has become popular, newsworthy, and mainstream. "We all need to get a little head space," says Headspace founder Andy Puddicombe.[20] Headspace is among the top five smartphone apps, with an alleged six million subscribers.[21] Yogis encourage meditation, as do tai chi and qi gong instructors. A Harvard Medical School blog post references a study providing evidence that meditation is more beneficial than vacation.[22]

Citing unprecedented anxiety among college students,[23] a web search reports these top five of fifty

---

20 "Man behind meditation app goes from monk to millionaire," Telegraph, accessed October 31, 2016, http://www.telegraph.co.uk/men/the-filter/11154773/Man-behind-meditation-app-goes-from-monk-to-millionaire.html.
21 "How Andy Puddicombe, Monk-Turned-Entrepreneur, Brought Meditation to the Masses," Huffpost, accessed October 31, 2016, http://www.huffingtonpost.com/entry/andy-puddicombe-headspace-meditation_us_570bbb68e4b0836057a1ac66.
22 Editor-in-Chief, Harvard Health Publications et al., "Regular Meditation More Beneficial than Vacation," Harvard Health Blog RSS, October 27, 2016, accessed November 02, 2016, http://www.health.harvard.edu/blog/relaxation-benefits-meditation-stronger-relaxation-benefits-taking-vacation-2016102710532.
23 The American College Health Association found in a 2015 study that 85.6 percent of respondents felt overwhelmed by their responsibilities. American College Health Association, American College Health Associa-

leading campuses have designated space for student meditation:

- The Bartlett Reflection Center at DePauw University
- Skidmore College—Gazebo on Haupt Pond
- The Cornell Plantations in Ithaca, New York
- Colgate University—Chapel House
- The Danforth Chapel at the University of Kansas[24]

While contemporary culture may acknowledge that meditation is good for us, an important distinction must be made between present-day "meditation" and Christian meditation. By Christian meditation, we are referring to the sacred appointment we carve out each morning to meet with Our Lord in our prayer chair. All Christian meditation is oriented toward God, as revealed to us through the Scriptures. Christians give their great treasure of time and attention to God who loves them personally and universally. Christians strive for interior silence, not in an effort to empty the mind for its own sake, but to make room for the Holy Spirit. Christians seek interior silence to hear the voice of God who whispers (1 Kings 19: 11-13).

In Christian meditation, no mantra is chanted, nor does the pray-er necessarily sit or stand a certain way. How do Christians meditate? Fifteen minutes can feel like an eternity for a soul learning or struggling for any number of

---

tion-National College Health Assessment II: Reference Group Executive Summary Spring 2015 (Hanover, MD: American College Health Association, 2015).

24 "The 50 Best Campus Meditation Spaces.," Best Counseling Schools, October 2015, accessed November 01, 2016, http://www.bestcounseling-schools.org/best-campus-meditation-spaces.

reasons to pray. Because we are only human and prone to distraction, applying a little structure to the time set aside for prayer can help. One of the best guides for spending prayer time well suggests that we Concentrate, Consider, Converse, and Commit.[25]

Using a short passage from the Gospel,

- Concentrate: Quiet your mind, relax, and speak to God. Ask for grace to hear Him.
- Consider: Read and reread the lines from the Gospel you chose, asking for inspiration.
- Converse: When a line of the Gospel moves you, praise God, adore Him, express your sorrow for sin, thank Him, and/or ask for what you and your family need.
- Commit: Renew your commitment to God, to prayer, and to whatever inspirations and resolutions He has given you in your time of prayer.

God shows up whenever we pray, no matter how we pray, as long as we make the effort. As Veronica learned during her time at adoration, even if our senses don't perceive Him, the "peace that surpasses all understanding" (Philippians 4:7) is a sure sign God has visited us. Which one of us can afford to miss out?

---

25   Father John Bartunek, LC, *The Better Part* (Hamden, CT: Circle Press, 2007). Front and back cover flap.

PRAYER

Dear Lord, I am humbled, awed and grateful that you invite me to meet You whenever I pray. I want to commit myself to praying regularly, with great fervor, because I know it pleases You, and prayer changes me, transforming me more closely to Your image and likeness. Please give me this grace.

Help me, with a better understanding of your personal love for me, to weather the transition of sending my child _____ into the next phase of her life. With your grace, I will be a cheerful, peaceful witness to my child and her friends, as well as to everyone you place in my path from this day forward.

Questions for Reflection:

What kinds of emotional factors keep me from praying regularly (or if I'm praying daily, more intentionally)? Fatigue? Melancholy? Lack of faith? What steps can I take to deepen this commitment to God?

The Lord works through our memories and experiences. I will share with the group and/or journal about times God has answered my prayers, surprised me with an unexpected gift, or lifted my spirits in suffering.

What is my favorite way to pray/meditate? I will share with the group and/or journal about what works well for me and what kinds of obstacles I experience.

Prayer Intentions:

Answered Prayers:

Prayer Practice:

"We live in a society in which it seems that every space, every moment must be ‹filled› with initiatives, activity, sound; often there is not even time to listen and dialogue. Dear brothers and sisters! Let us not be afraid to be silent outside and inside ourselves, so that we are able not only to perceive God's voice, but also the voice of the person next to us, the voices of others.» --Pope Benedict XVI, July 4, 2010

Setting up a prayer corner can help women at any stage of prayer to "make the date." My prayer chair is in my bedroom with bookshelves to my right and left. They are filled with inspiration to help me settle into prayer the moment I arrive.

Coffee, candles, music, or silence…whatever sets the mood is welcome in the prayer corner. Once I am seated, I try to quiet my mind and block out all distractions. When distractions come, which they do, I give them over to God. I ask the Holy Spirit to help me stay focused and seek the Lord.

Each day I will:

- Read a passage or two from the Bible or other spiritual book, then put it down and quietly meditate on what I read.

- Spend a couple of minutes or so in silence. Encounter the Lord by listening for His voice.

- Give thanks and, perhaps, journal about inspirations He sent.

Seek out the Lord and his might; constantly seek his face. (Psalm 105:4)

Lord, how can I love you more today than I did yesterday?

_____

_____

_____

_____

_____

_____

_____

_____

_____

_____

_____

_____

_____

_____

_____

CHAPTER 6:

SURPRISED BY GRACE

If she were an actress, Brooke would have received an Academy Award. At her parents' last visit to campus, she appeared to be a thriving, communicative, and happy college sophomore. No clues existed for the dramatic turn of events that lay ahead. They excitedly welcomed her home for Christmas vacation, but as their time together drew to a close, everything changed in an instant. She flatly refused to return to school, offering no explanation. Shocked and bewildered, her parents complied. Brooke withdrew from school.

As the youngest child in a large family and student athlete, her sudden departure from school left her empty-nesting parents anxious but prayerful. Patty, Brooke's mother, stayed at home while Brooke and her father retrieved belongings from school. Patty attended Mass to pray for insight. Suddenly, like a lightning bolt, the answer struck her as she sat in the church parking lot after Mass. "Could Brooke be pregnant?" She was altogether certain of it. Having no details and numb with pain, she wanted to cry. However, she recalls that, by God's grace, within moments her raw emotions were replaced by a strange and immediate sense of gratitude. "Thanks be to God she hasn't had an abortion. I want to be supportive of this brave decision," she thought. "What a blessing God gave me to know for sure that Brooke is pregnant, so that I can reflect and pray before reaching out to her," Patty thought.

Perhaps it was the unwavering faith of Patty's elderly Irish Catholic grandmother, or the nuns who taught her in school about the preciousness of life. Patty's own medical background working with terminal patients undoubtedly also influenced her conviction that all life is a gift. Patty was determined to see Brooke safely through the birth of this child, no matter what the physical, emotional, or spiritual costs to the family.

Shortly after Brooke and her father returned from getting her things at school, Patty and her husband sat down with Brooke in the library. Patty's suspicion was confirmed by Brooke who admitted to her parents that she was indeed pregnant, apologized profusely, and told them they had been good parents and didn't deserve this. Brooke's father was understandably disappointed, but also overwhelmed. He knew well the responsibilities involved in raising a child and felt riddled with fear about his daughter's future. He sought out advice from his brother who told him, "Brooke needs you now more than ever." From that moment, he was "all in" emotionally and financially.

Patty and her husband supported Brooke through the pregnancy and for several years afterwards, enabling Brooke to complete her degree at a university closer to home and attain a master's degree as well. "I took care of my grandson all day," Patty said. "The hardest part was that I wanted to raise him the way I wanted to. And then I became so attached that it was really difficult when he left. I also had to exercise self-restraint not to say to Brooke, 'Please. Take some of this advice. I know so much more now than I did at your age,'" she said. Although it was difficult, Patty felt she was never alone in caring for her grandson. "So many prayer warriors took me under their wings," she said. Her faith and those of her praying friends armed Patty with the grace she needed to do the job she felt called to do.

One of the most moving episodes from Patty's experience helping to raise her grandson came one day from a caller she barely knew. A woman contacted Patty and told her that she had become pregnant, but she ended the pregnancy. She could not tell her parents out of fear she would disappoint them. This grieving soul was incredibly touched by Brooke's bravery and Patty's outpouring of loving support. Her call was a grace that fortified Patty to continue on.

How Does Grace Work?

Patty suddenly knew Brooke was pregnant. Was that a grace? Our faith teaches us that inspirations like that are actual graces[26], extended by God to us for our good and His glory.

---

26 Temporary supernatural intervention by God to enlighten the mind or strengthen the will to perform supernatural actions that lead to Heaven. Actual grace is therefore a transient divine assistance to enable man to obtain, retain, or grow in supernatural grace and the life of God. Catholic Dictionary/Catholicculture.org, accessed June 18, 2018. https://www.catholicculture.org/culture/library/dictionary/index.cfm?id=31646

God first takes up residence in our souls through a more permanent type of grace called "sanctifying grace," which we receive at Baptism. All of the sacraments, in fact, channel sanctifying grace into our souls until we overflow with its abundance and are made holy. To help us *stay* holy, we receive actual grace at the Lord's discretion. He always has our "personal best" as his single goal. These bursts of actual grace are meant to dispose us to take on even more of the permanent sanctifying kind of grace.

Can you envision how much water flows over Niagara Falls on average, every minute of every day, seven days a week, year after year? Four million cubic feet! How fruitless would it be to stand below trying to fill an empty soda bottle! Niagara Falls would have to slow to a trickle to accommodate the narrow neck of that bottle. God's grace, however, flows toward us at an infinite rate. To make room for His Grace in our souls, we strive to widen our perspective, stretch our hearts, and expand our capacity to receive. We cannot now, nor will we ever be able to fill *ourselves* with grace. That is God's work. We simply receive.

What does Grace *Feel* Like?

A parish priest came to my home one evening many years ago to address a group of moms on topics of faith. The questions ranged from the theological to the practical, on matters of marriage and parenting as well as Heaven, Hell, and everything in between. Most memorable, though, was a question whispered from the back of the room by a friend who rarely spoke up. She timidly raised her hand and, when recognized, asked the priest, "What does grace feel like?" The question brought everyone to silence. All eyes fell expectantly on our visiting priest. He simply responded, "I don't exactly know."

One easy and truthful answer would be that grace feels good. Grace feels like the welcome recognition of God's presence on freshman move-in day…the assurance of having said the right thing to a child wrestling with a serious dating relationship…or supernatural calm in the face of a surprise pregnancy. To use St. Paul's analogy of putting on the armor of Christ (Ephesians 6:10-17), grace feels safe. Since we're placing our security in Christ, earthly dangers fail to overwhelm us. We feel equipped! We are armed with the shield of faith, the helmet of salvation and the sword of the Spirit to feel powerful in the face of evil and ready to battle our own concupiscence.

Since grace is the life of Christ in our souls, having grace ultimately helps us to be more loving. We are more capable of sharing our gifts with others in positive and affirming conversations, little or big acts of service, tokens of affection, or in the willingness to testify to the One within who radiates through our smiles, our words and our actions.

There's something irresistible about a waterfall. We're attracted to it, but we hesitate, standing first in awe of the torrent of grace that is Niagara…filled instead with our insecurities, certain of our unworthiness, seeing only our limitations and failures. Yet, God beckons us nearer to feel the refreshing mist on our faces. We approach until we are showered upon so that grace rinses clean our sins, fills us to overflowing and re-hydrates our withering soul. The more grace we absorb, the more grace-filled and God-like we become. Our little souls are cleansed and stretched to well beyond our human capacity, all according to God's holy will. We know well that our bodies can't be sustained longer than a few days without water. Similarly, our souls thirst for and require the life of Christ, His grace, to thrive. Fortunately, God's grace is our gift without limit, flowing infinitely faster than four million cubic feet per minute.

PRAYER

Almighty Father, I praise you for generously sharing your life of grace with me. I am grateful to have such a benevolent Father caring for me and my child _____. Grace is a wonderful mystery. Help me to grow in appreciating for your grace-filled actions in my life and the lives of those I love. May you shower all of us with more…and more…and more grace, so that we recognize You in joy-filled times and, when life gets difficult.

Questions for Reflection:

If the Lord is showering us with grace at an infinite rate, there must be numerous instances of actual grace in each of my days. How often do I stop to recognize God's presence in my day? Discuss and/or journal about a time when you felt "inspired" or "empowered by grace" to do something beyond your ordinary strength.

Prayer Intentions:

Answered Prayers:

Prayer Practice:

I will take a few minutes each night to reflect back over my day and look for moments of grace: little God-winks; inspirations; promptings to help others... I will thank God for His grace-filled presence.

For by grace you have been saved through faith, and this is not from you; it is the gift of God; it is not from works, so no one may boast. *(Ephesians 2:8-9)*

Lord, how can I love you more today than I did yesterday?

_____

_____

_____

_____

_____

_____

_____

_____

_____

_____

_____

_____

_____

_____

CHAPTER 7:

———⟨——⟩———

LIVING WITH THE HOLY SPIRIT

We learned from Patty's experience with Brooke in the previous chapter that grace can surprise us and inspire us to be good and wise parents. We talked about how grace works and what it feels like, but not how to get it.

You can't purchase grace; it's not a commodity for sale at Amazon. Grace can't be earned. The initiator of all grace is the third person of the Trinity: The Holy Spirit, also known as The Sanctifier. Praying through the Holy Spirit is very much like experiencing life in high definition. With anointing by the Holy Spirit, the brilliant hues of an ordinary sunset fill us with awe, as if seeing it for the first time. Everyday sounds delight us anew—from the dark, quiet hush of an early winter's morning, to the thunderous din of migrating birds in the neighbor's tree. The familiar smell of baking cookies may bring unexpected tears of gratitude for family. We develop a taste for the things of Heaven in the midst of life right here on Earth. All reality is as if viewed in surround sound with plasma-screen clarity for a soul who has been touched by the Holy Spirit. The Spirit is presence, warmth, joy and motion.

We find the Holy Spirit in the most astonishing place—within each one of us, at the center of our very soul. As St. Paul reminds us, "Do you not know that you are the temple of God and that the spirit of God dwells within you?" (1 Corinthians. 3:16). It's the Spirit that lives within us, not stagnantly, not awaiting our acknowledgment, or even our worship. The Spirit acts in our souls, performing very beautiful, entirely necessary renovations to our spiritual temple so that we become holy.

The Back Story

We have some understanding of God the Father, since we all have fathers to provide a frame of reference. Jesus Christ became man, lived in our history, and left behind his words and deeds for us to ponder and pray over. But, for many of us, the Holy Spirit is more of a mystery. Technically, in fact, knowledge of the Spirit is infinite. The Spirit has depths we can never hope to plumb. Reading about Him in the Bible or the Catechism will tell some of His story. Talking about Him with teachers, preachers and spiritual friends might reveal more of His truth. But the best way to get to know the Holy Spirit is to invite Him into our personal lives as a close companion and constant source of comfort. And even then, His mystery will remain. "If you understood Him, it would not be God," says St. Augustine.[27]

Our Church teaches that there are important distinctions among the three persons of the Trinity. There is "one God and Father *from* whom all things are, and one Lord Jesus Christ *through* whom all things are, and

27 St. Augustine quoted in CCC 230

one Holy Spirit *in* whom all things are."[28] And these three persons specialize in the following ways: "To the Father is attributed the creation, to the Son redemption, to the Holy Spirit the sanctification of our souls."[29] It's the Holy Spirit's self-ordained job to help us grow in love for God and others.

Drama, majesty, fire-power… We first read of the Holy Spirit floating over the waters of the Earth before the creation of the world, when the planet was a dark, formless void (Genesis 1:2). He was "in the beginning, is now, and ever shall be" as we often pray in the *Glory Be*.

The same Spirit, through Moses, motivated the Israelites to contribute more wealth than they could even use to build a beautiful place of worship (Exodus 35,36). Samson was strengthened by the Spirit to slay a lion with his bare hands (Judges 14:6). More than 12 times, the Old Testament chronicles the actions of the Holy Spirit who prompts, inspires, encourages, and empowers the people of Israel.

In a stroke of divine intervention, the Holy Spirit forever altered human history when he overshadowed the Virgin Mary so that the Messiah, the second person of the Trinity, Jesus Christ, could grow in her womb. Jesus, who, like the Holy Spirit, is eternal, was born into time for our sakes by the movement of the Spirit. St. John the Baptist preached to the Jews of Jesus' time about the Holy Spirit, predicting just before Jesus' public ministry that

28 CCC 258, footnote 98
29 Luis M. Martínez, The Sanctifier (**Boston, M**A: Pauline Books & Media, 2004), 119.

Jesus would soon baptize with "the Holy Spirit and fire" (Matthew 3:11).

The Holy Spirit appeared in human history as a dove hovering over the newly baptized Jesus in the Jordan River,[30] accompanied by the rumbling voice of the Father [some thought it was thunder] who announced that He was well pleased with Jesus, his son. In fact, this is the only time that all three persons of the Holy Trinity were revealed together in a singular moment. Three eternal persons, one Trinity, in one place at one time.

Jesus made formal introductions to the Spirit just before the Last Supper when he told the disciples, "I will ask the Father, and he will give you another helper, that he may be with you forever; that is the Spirit of truth, whom the world cannot receive, because it does not see him or know him, but you know him because he abides with you and will be in you" (John 14:16). This advocate, Jesus told them, and us, is sent to teach us and help us to remember all that Jesus himself taught (John 16:26).

The apostles were probably very thankful to have had this reassurance from Jesus when the Holy Spirit finally made himself known personally to each of them. Locked away in a "safe house" after the death and resurrection of Jesus for fear of further retribution by the Jews, the disciples were praying, accompanied by Mother Mary, when the Holy Spirit descended upon them in all his formidable power. Flames of fire hovered over each of their heads. They spoke eloquently in foreign tongues to thousands of Jews who assembled, converting them all. What surprise, confusion, wonder, and fear…how overwhelmed must

---

30 Matthew 3:16; Mark1:10; Luke3:22; John1:32; Acts7:56

these fishermen have been by this awesome visitation of the Holy Spirit!

The Holy Spirit is the very same these days as he was 2,000 years ago, and He can make His presence known in our lives in equally dramatic ways. He permeates our senses, directs our actions, widens our capacities, and helps us to see more clearly every day the spiritual realities of our earthly lives. Come Holy Spirit!

The Guest of Our Soul

When the Holy Spirit visits us, He brings gifts, fruits, and charisms...lots of them. And, in His omniscience, the Holy Spirit knows exactly how to shower us with gifts perfectly suited for us. It's as if He places His graces in our lives strategically so that we come upon each one at just the right time, according to his perfect plan for our personal sanctification.

There are seven gifts, treasures really, that the Holy Spirit wants to bestow on us: wisdom, understanding, knowledge, counsel, fortitude, piety and fear of the Lord. These gifts, if opened and cherished, have a permanent and eternal effect in our souls. "They complete and perfect the virtues of those who receive them" (CCC 1831). Slowly but surely, they help us to become more docile to God's Will in our lives. Using these gifts, we can more easily recognize the subtlest of the Holy Spirit's promptings.

The Scriptures also describe fruits we receive from the Holy Spirit (Galatians 5:22-23). According to the Catechism, these fruits are "perfections that the Holy Spirit forms in us as the first fruits of eternal glory" (CCC 1832). Church tradition lists twelve: charity, joy, peace, patience, kindness, goodness, generosity, gentleness, faithfulness, modesty, self-control, chastity. Just as red juicy apples are fruits of a healthy tree, the fruits of the Holy Spirit are manifest in people with a regular prayer life who strive to live virtuously and who recognize and nurture the gifts of the Holy Spirit within their souls. The fruits are side effects, so to speak, of the presence of the Holy Spirit's gifts. Imagine living with a heart void of fear, hatred, mean-spiritedness, cynicism, sarcasm, or any of the other very human traits that so often rule our will. The fruits of the Holy Spirit are sweet and delectable to our souls. They bring a slice of Heaven to our lives while we're still here on Earth.

Saint Paul refers to yet more manifestations of the Holy Spirit in his first letter to the Corinthians (v. 28), "Some people God has designated in the Church to be, first, apostles; second, prophets; third, teachers; then, mighty deeds; then, gifts of healing, assistance, administration, and varieties of tongues." Again, in the letter to the Romans 12:6-8 Paul teaches, "Since we have gifts that differ according to the grace given to us, let us exercise them: if prophecy, in proportion to the faith; if ministry, in ministering; if one is a teacher, in teaching; if one exhorts, in exhortation; if one contributes, in generosity; if one is over others, with diligence; if one does acts of mercy, with cheerfulness."

In our day, we understand that the Holy Spirit infuses us with "charisms" as well as gifts and fruits. Although the notion of charisms is not a new concept within the Church, Catherine of Siena Institute[31] co-founder Sherry

---

31 www.siena.org

Weddell created the first charism discernment process specifically designed for Catholics in 1993.[32] The Institute distinguishes between the traditional gifts and fruits of the Spirit, which are meant to be kept since they help to make us holy, and charisms, which are meant to be given away to others so as to enrich the whole world, starting with our own families. The Institute's Spiritual Gift Inventory identifies 24 charisms and encourages each of us to discern which we have been given so as to make good use of them for the glory of God. (See Chapter 19 for a discussion of how gifts and charisms appear in our children.)

Overwhelmed or confused yet? Suffice it to say, the Holy Spirit can equip us with all we will ever need to get to Heaven and bring those we love along with us. The Catechism sums up God's gracious benevolence toward us:

> The Holy Spirit is the principle of every vital and truly saving action in each part of the Body (of Christ). He works in many ways to build up the whole Body in charity:
> - by God's Word, which is able to build you up;
> - by Baptism, through which he forms Christ's Body;
> - by the sacraments, which give growth and healing to Christ's members;
> - by the grace of the apostles, which holds first place among his gifts;
> - by the virtues, which make us act according to what is good;

---

32 According to siena.org

- finally, by the many special graces (called charisms), by which he makes the faithful fit and ready to undertake various tasks and offices for the renewal and building up of the Church (CCC 798).

Practically speaking, these gifts, fruits and charisms of the Holy Spirit are as obvious in a person as is a stylish new haircut. They look good on us. Gifted with these spiritual goods we become mothers with legitimate influence over our children because our faith is attractive. Below are some examples of the Spirit in action in the lives of praying college moms.

"When my son and I have had the chance to talk about faith, I am grateful that I have felt the Holy Spirit inspiring me and giving me wisdom," says Sarah. "I know at college he is not going to Mass, and that upsets me a lot, and there are times when I want to say something but, instead, I'll ask a different question, or say something I hadn't planned, and just know that the Holy Spirit is at work helping me to relate to my son in the best possible way," she shares. "I pray for him every day and it is God's doing, not mine, that will bring him back," she adds.

Jolie, a working mother of seven, has always felt strange promptings to pray for her children, often waking in the middle of the night with a sense of urgency to pray for one or the other. "It comes upon me...and I just feel really connected in prayer to the Holy Spirit," she explains. "I have prayed for all of my children, and other times I don't even know who I'm praying for. God gives me very specific things to pray about even when I don't know the people," she says. "I never knew what those feelings were, but I recently heard about spiritual gifts and it seems like I have a gift for intercessory prayer," she concludes. "The promptings are strong, and I always obey them. It's weird to have this gift because it's not like I'm good at praying in other ways," she laughs. Jolie believes that her "midnight prayers" were especially effective when her oldest daughter, who had chosen a secular school, faced the typical dormitory chaos of freshmen life: alcohol, sex, and sleeplessness. "I sometimes woke up and felt like there was a safety issue, so I would pray for her then and there," Jolie admits.

Tammy, mother of four teens, has some measure of the gift, *Fear of God*. She clings to God's majesty and power like a baby clings to his mother when life is scary. "When my oldest is away at college, I can't be there next to him, so I trust in God Almighty who knows better than he does," she says. For her other children, whether it's filing more college applications, monitoring academics, or supervising weekend activities, Tammy says that she's always fighting her tendency to want complete control. She's consoled when she remembers that God is so much bigger and more capable than she is, and she fears offending the Almighty Father because she loves him as a daughter. From Tammy's perspective, she says it's a wonder that life with four teens ever runs smoothly. But how much more wonderful is it that God Almighty involves Himself in her daily worries and concerns, simply because his daughter asks?

Patricia says that she felt the power of the Holy Spirit when her only child first stepped out of the car as they visited the college he would eventually attend. "My husband had done a lot of research and planning, but I hadn't really focused yet on where he would go to college," Patricia says. "I just knew it was the right place the minute he got out of the car. Holy Spirit has often given me a premonition about these kinds of things, and I was immediately at peace," she explains.

If the wonders of the Holy Spirit were for sale on the grocer's shelves or available in a prescription bottle, would they be easier to access than they seem to be? As baptized Christians, we have each been given gifts, fruits and charisms in some measure. They rest dormant until we activate them. It's our job every day to ask the Spirit to help us recognize our need for Him, find His gifts within, then open and use them.

Further Thoughts

The Holy Spirit is light, breath, consoler and advocate. He is also, however, fire that purifies our desires and the wind that wears away our rough edges. If we could gaze upon the face of the Holy Spirit, we would see only gentleness and love but, because of our human nature, making room for the Holy Spirit can feel uncomfortable at times as He stretches our soul's capacity to love, re-directs our steps toward the narrow road when we stray and helps us to guard our passions, reign in our selfishness, and sharpen our attentiveness to the needs of others. His ultimate goal, after all, is no less than our complete transformation. Through His gifts, fruits and charisms, the Holy Spirit empowers us to become the women he created us to be. How blessed are we to have his almighty, awesome, supernatural help.

Do you want to experience more of the life of the Holy Spirit within? The only prerequisite is a sincere desire to know Him, and the making of a daily sacrifice of time and effort in prayer... Come, Holy Spirit! Fill our hearts with the fire of your Love. Send your spirit to renew the Earth. Grant that we may be truly wise and enjoy your consolations.[33]

---

33 Adapted from traditional prayer "Come Holy Spirit."

PRAYER

A Praying College Moms Litany to the Holy Spirit

Most Holy Spirit, third person of the Trinity, reign in my heart and the hearts of my family, especially _____.

Holy Spirit, Advocate, pray within me so that my words and actions reflect only my love for _____.

Holy Spirit, Counselor, advise me so that I may be a responsible, loving and holy parent.

Holy Spirit, Breath of Heaven, instill in me a strong eternal perspective so that I may increasingly see my worldly activities with Your eyes.

Holy Spirit, Protector, guard my child at college, sheltering her from all temporal and spiritual danger.

Holy Spirit, Giver of every good gift, shower me and my family with all of the natural and supernatural gifts we need to glorify you with our lives.

Holy Spirit, Fire, purify my soul of everything not pleasing to You and bless _____so that she may also be pure and chaste, according to your divine plan for her.

Holy Spirit, Sanctifier, make me holy, and bless with your infinite power my child in college _____.

Come Holy Spirit, fill my heart with your love!

Questions for Reflection:

Which of the gifts of the Holy Spirit do I recognize in myself? Which do I most desire at the moment? Why? Journal and/or discuss.

Gifts and fruits are for our own interior transformation while charisms (also known as spiritual gifts) are given to us to be used to build up the kingdom of God. What kinds of faith-sharing activities do I most enjoy? Speaking? Singing? Organizing? Hospitality? Am I a natural leader? An administrator? List at least four of your natural strengths (if you need help, ask a trusted friend). How have I used these talents to bring glory to God? To assist those around me? To spread the Gospel message?

(If there is interest in your small group or parish, contact the Saint Catherine of Siena Institute to arrange a "Gifted and Called" seminar where you will learn how to discern your spiritual gifts and put them to use.)

Prayer Intentions:

Answered Prayers:

Prayer Practice:

The Holy Spirit is eager to shower us with gifts, fruits and charisms! Each morning in prayer, ask the Holy Spirit for comfort, consolation, enlightenment, and guidance. Any prayer to the Holy Spirit will do. Here's one that St. Augustine prayed:

Breathe into me, Holy Spirit, that my thoughts may all be holy. Move in me, Holy Spirit, that my work, too, may be holy. Attract my heart, Holy Spirit, that I may love only what is holy. Strengthen me, Holy Spirit, that I may defend all that is holy. Protect me, Holy Spirit, that I may always be holy.

But when he comes, the Spirit of truth, he will guide you to all truth. He will not speak on his own, but he will speak what he hears, and will declare to you the things that are coming. (John 16:13)

Lord, how can I love you more today than I did yesterday?

_____

_____

_____

_____

_____

_____

_____

_____

_____

_____

_____

CHAPTER 8:

OUR TWO-EDGED SWORD

Melissa Overmyer[34] is an author, speaker, artist, teacher, and a devoted wife and mother of four daughters, but the role that she finds most intensely demanding of late is that of a praying college mom. Fortunately, she is well armed for the task. "My pocket Bible, the one I keep in my purse, I call 'Sting,' after Bilbo Baggins' small dagger in *The Lord of the Rings*," Melissa explains. "The one in my home I call 'Excalibur' like the sword that belonged to King Arthur," she laughs. The creative nicknames were inspired by Hebrews 4:12, "Indeed, the word of God is living and effective, sharper than any two-edged sword, penetrating even between soul and spirit, joints and marrow, and able to discern reflections and thoughts of the heart."

The dog-eared, underlined, well-worn state of Melissa's Bibles reflect her affection for the Word of God, and her utter dependence on Scripture to guide her life and the lives of her husband and children. Her reliance on Scripture began at age 12 when she committed to God to read His Word every day. "The Lord told me that He would never leave me or forsake me (Hebrews 13:5), so

---

34 Melissa Overmyer is her actual name and used with permission.

I wasn't going to leave Him either," she explains. "I can literally count on one hand the days I have missed praying with Scripture before closing my eyes at night," she says.

Tried and True

Over the years, God's word gently led Melissa from Protestantism to Catholicism via the Baptist, Presbyterian, Episcopal and Anglican Churches until she finally came happily to rest at home in the Catholic Church. You can read about her journey in *Metamorphosis of a Soul, One Woman's Testimony* or on her website.[35] In her work as a writer and speaker, Melissa readily witnesses about the power of Scripture in her life. But a true test of her love for the Word came when her daughter, a sophomore in college, broke her neck while surfing on the west coast during the fall. "She was literally 3,000 miles away when she had the accident," Melissa said. "We had to bring her home on a medically assisted flight to be treated, because it was faster than my going to get her. The whole episode was terrifying," she recalled.

While her daughter was recuperating, Melissa found peace by diving head-long into the Scriptures. "I called all the time on the Lord's sovereignty and His authority," Melissa explained. "I didn't understand why all this was happening, but I kept repeating to myself 'Great is Thy faithfulness,'" she said. Melissa was confident that God would bring good from this situation because of His promise in Romans 8:28. Throughout the ordeal, she especially prayed parts of Psalm 34 for herself, "I sought

---

35 Take a look at Melissa's ministry at Melissaovermyer.com or something greaterministries.com.

the Lord and He answered me, And delivered me from all my fears…This poor man cried and the Lord heard him, And saved him out of all his troubles. The angel of the Lord encamps around those who fear Him and rescues them," v. 4-6. Over her daughter's injuries she prayed, "The Lord is close to the brokenhearted, saves those whose spirit is crushed. Many are the troubles of the righteous, but the Lord delivers him from them all. He watches over all his bones; not one of them shall be broken," v. 19-20.

"I asked that all of her bones would grow back together correctly, and praises be to God, they did," Melissa said.

Psalm 91 also consoled Melissa. "The Psalm says that God shields and shelters us under His wings (v.4) so I pictured my daughter nestled in feathers, safe and secure while she was healing. I still pray that way for my girls," she says. "I sleep with a down comforter and feather pillow and often little feathers will escape into my hair. I feel like that's God's little wink. He is telling me that even while I sleep he covers us all in feathers!"

Her daughter's dangerous fall reminded Melissa that life can change in an instant. "I became aware of our fragility and far more acutely aware of the goodness of God, realizing that my life has been enormously blessed," she says. "Each and every breath I take is because He wills it," she adds.

Miraculously, Melissa's daughter was able to return to school to finish the semester, despite debilitating headaches. Today she is cured. "Looking back, we can joke now that she took the words 'fall break' a little too seriously," Melissa giggles.

Bible "School" – Life Lessons

Melissa's grandfather was a Baptist preacher and she grew up reading the Scriptures with her mom every morning, so she is well accustomed to praying the Scriptures. Sadly, many cradle Catholics are not. What are some of us reading instead of the Bible? A quick survey of bestselling self-help books includes titles about esteem, anger management, marriage and sexuality, parenting, depression, anxiety, and much more.

Let's see what kind of practical wisdom the Bible holds for modern readers of the more than 250,000 self-help titles.

Self-esteem

Lord, you search me and you know me. You know when I sit and when I stand...I am beautifully, wonderfully made (Psalm 139).

For I know the plans I have for you, declares the Lord, plans to prosper you and not to harm you, plans to give you hope and a future (Jeremiah 29:11).

Anger Management

Be angry, yet do not sin. Do not let the sun go down on your anger and give the devil an opportunity (Ephesians 4:26-27).

Cast your burdens on the Lord and he will sustain you (Psalm 55:23).

Marriage and sexuality

Marriage is to be held in honor among all, and the marriage bed is to be undefiled (Hebrews 13:4).

Your adornment must not be merely external—braiding the hair, and wearing gold jewelry, or putting on dresses; but let it be the hidden person of the heart, with the imperishable quality of a gentle and quiet spirit, which is precious in the sight of God (1 Peter: 3:3,4).

Parenting

Children are a gift of the Lord. The fruit of the womb is a reward (Psalm 127:3).

[Parents,] do not provoke your children to anger, but bring them up in the discipline and instruction of the Lord (Ephesians 6:4).

Anxiety—there are so many lines of encouragements in the Bible, it's hard to choose. Here are some of the most widely read.

Do not be anxious about anything, but in everything, by prayer and petition, with thanksgiving, present your requests to God (Philippians 4:6).

I can do everything through him who gives me strength (Philippians 4:13).

Trust in the Lord with all your heart and lean not on your own understanding. In all your ways acknowledge him, and he will make your paths straight (Proverbs 3:5,6).

Come to me, all you who are weary and burdened, and I will give you rest (Matthew 11:28).

What's on your bookshelf right now? How do you cope with life's challenges? When you're in need of advice about a complicated family matter, do you turn to a self-help book, call your sister to vent, or pick up a Bible? Why, so often, is the Bible our last recourse? Let's take an honest look at why we can sometimes resist becoming "fluent" in the love language of our Lord found in the Bible.

Is the Bible Inspired?

MD, PhD, DDS, CPA, MBA…these letters automatically boost credibility and instill confidence when they appear behind someone's name. We place our trust in their expertise and presume on their qualifications. The Bible, however, was not authored by credentialed professionals. St. Luke was a doctor, but he didn't leave us medical advice. What could the evangelist Matthew, a tax collector, or Mark, a friend of Peter the fisherman, have to say to us in the 21st century? John wrote his Gospel in his old age, sequestered on a deserted island, Patmos. How can we be sure that these messengers who wrote so long ago are reliable?

What proof we do have comes from recorded history. (See Appendix 3 for proof of the Bible's historical authenticity.) Secular historians repeatedly corroborate with biblical accounts of Old and New Testament stories. Historians have located more than 5,000 early archeological finds, such as the inscription "Pontius Pilate" found on a tablet in Caesarea, Maritima, in 1962, which have lent great credence to the accuracy of Scripture. The evangelists themselves repeatedly assert that they were eye-witnesses of the death and resurrection of Jesus. "We did not follow cleverly invented stories when we told you about the power and coming of our Lord Jesus Christ, but we were eyewitnesses of his majesty" (2 Peter:16). The apostle John says of his own experience, "The man who saw it has given testimony, and his testimony is true. He knows that he tells the truth, and he testifies so that you may also believe" (John 21:24).

The Church has always taught that the Bible is the word of God and that its writers were inspired by the Holy Spirit. "God is the author of sacred Scripture," says our Catechism (CCC 135). All other Christian denominations also hold to the belief that the Bible is true. Additionally, countless saints have attested to the Bible's validity. For 2,000 years, the Bible has inspired lives of holiness. These are observable facts. Yet, we can still doubt.

Faith in God and his Word takes our active assent. We don't just say, "I believe," once and for all. We proactively reaffirm our belief every single day by asking Our Lord, as did the Apostles, "Lord, increase our faith." Faith is a gift we are to ask for from the Lord and he encourages us to do so! Seven times in the Gospels, Our Lord implores us to have "ears to hear," his words in Scripture.

Isn't it too Hard to Read?

As we know, every September students head off to college and parents fall into the school-year routine with the expectation that students will learn if they study well and apply themselves. We expect our children to work hard but, quite often, maybe even subconsciously, we assume our study of God's word should be easy. A friend always used to say in jest, "If God wants to talk to me, why doesn't he just text me?" Our Lord invites us to become students of His Word—to read, re-read, ponder and pray over the Scriptures. We are blessed in these days because reading Scripture has never been easier!

The Bible was originally written in ancient Greek and Hebrew, accessible only to specially trained scribes who translated it for a small elite community. Then, in about 380 AD, St. Jerome provided the Church with a Latin version which was more widely read by the faithful for the next 1,500+ years. These days, students of Scripture need not know Greek, Hebrew or Latin. The Bible can be read in any language. Though parts may still be difficult to understand, there are many resources at our fingertips to assist us with our study, thanks to the internet.

Claire, a praying college mom, has arranged her entire day so that she is never too far from what she, like Melissa, calls her "secret weapon." Most mornings she makes a cup of coffee and heads straight to her prayer corner to read the Scripture of the daily Mass. She reflects on these words, talks with the Lord, and journals. While in the kitchen, making breakfasts and lunches, her computer screen saver flashes her favorite Scripture verse, "My grace is sufficient for you." After the younger kids head off to school, Claire checks her email where she can skim the daily reflection she had sent to her by a Catholic online service. On occasion, she also scans the headlines she receives via email from a Catholic news organization that reports daily from Rome. She keeps a tiny Bible in her car and a rosary in her pocket to remind her that she is never alone. At night, Claire tries to read a line or two of Scripture before she picks up her current novel. Before she turns out the lights, she thanks the Lord for what went well that day and asks His blessings on her children. Her last waking thought is a simple "good-night" to the Lord. By living with the Word, as Claire does, our hunger for intimacy with Christ overcomes our reluctance to pick up a Bible. Eventually, we progress from wanting to know Christ in Scripture to *needing* to find him there. "Reading His Word becomes our delight," Melissa says. Our Lord, himself, made us this promise when He said, "Ask and you shall receive. Seek and you shall find. Knock and the door will be opened to you" (Matthew 7:7).

Some Say It's Old-Fashioned

Cleaning out my attic recently, I found some old love letters and brought them downstairs to show my children. In their texting techno world, these old yellowed letters full of mundane news and occasional silliness were a novelty. Our Bibles are love letters from God. Wouldn't it be wonderful if they were dog-eared, yellowed and pondered over endlessly?

We are all brides of the Eternal groom. Cultivating the habit of praying with the Scripture guarantees our connection to the bridegroom whenever we need Him. Reading Scripture—praying this way—never goes out of style. We are forming a relationship with God and acknowledging the sacred pledge he made to us. Through the Scripture, He tells us, "I am with you always, even to the end of time" (Matthew 28:20).

Getting Started, Staying Focused

Studying the Bible means we'll be excavating for layers of meaning, stacked one upon the other, like the striated walls of the Grand Canyon. Initially, we may scratch the surface, reading a Bible text in its literal sense, looking for the intention of the author for his audience. Matthew wrote his Gospel, for example, to the Jews of his time, and he therefore included the genealogy of Jesus since, for Jews, heritage is culturally significant. He was establishing that Jesus is King of the Jews, with rightful claim to the throne of David.

Digging deeper, we learn that Scripture has three levels of spiritual meaning. We can drink deeply and even infinitely from Scripture in this sense. First, we examine the text for allegorical meaning. We discover that Abraham's willingness to sacrifice his only son, Isaac, in the Old Testament prefigures God the Father's offering of Jesus Christ.

The second level of spiritual meaning is a moral one. We ask ourselves about this Old Testament story: Is there a lesson to learn from Abraham's unquestioning obedience to God? Is there a promise to claim, perhaps in God's last-minute intervention? Is there an example to be followed? Scripture is chock-full of life lessons, teaching moments, and wisdom for living the moral life.

Finally, there is an anagogical sense to Scripture. In reading, we become conscious of a transcendent quality to the Scripture that helps us to raise our hearts and minds to God, forgetting perhaps, if just momentarily, our earthly troubles, focused instead on the things of Heaven. Consider the benevolence of God who promised to Abraham because of his obedience, "I swear by myself... that because you have done this and have not withheld your son, your only son, I will surely bless you and make your descendants as numerous as the stars in the sky and as the sand on the seashore. Your descendants will take possession of the cities of their enemies, and through your offspring all nations on earth will be blessed, because you have obeyed me." Our hearts are moved to praise God as we learn about His qualities; His power, majesty and superabundant generosity.

It takes some effort to read and reflect this deeply on Scripture, but our Mother Church is always there to offer guidance, as any mother would be. Whether we stumble over basic meaning or seek a more complex interpretation, the Church, empowered by the Holy Spirit, can help to open our minds to understand the Scriptures, just as the risen Christ did for his two disciples on the road to Emmaus. It was the Church, in fact, that established the Canon by confirming that there are 46 books of the Old Testament and 27 in the New Testament. The Old Testament foreshadows the New, and the New Testament fulfills the Old, revealing the unity of God's plan for our salvation. All of it, the Church reminds us, is God's word, given to us to be a "lamp to our feet and a light to our path." With study, these words enlighten our minds and keep us properly focused as can no self-help book written by human hands.

Scripture Especially for Praying College Moms

Melissa encourages every praying college mom to pray the Scriptures for our children. "We become wise when we pray with the Scriptures," says Melissa, "because the mind of Christ is found in His Word. When we get to know God, and we get to know Him through His Word, then we gain wisdom and discernment in all areas of life. We also come to realize that we are not in charge," she says, "so we can relinquish our children to God, knowing that He loves them more than we do."

Melissa shared three of her favorite Scripture verses and how she prays with them below:

I am the Lord your God, who brought you out of the land of Egypt, out of the house of slavery. (Exodus 20:2)

When my children are disobedient, I pray that the Lord will lead them out of "Egypt" into freedom out of whatever captivity they are in.

Psalm 37:3-4: Trust in the Lord and do good that you may dwell in the land and live secure. Find your delight in the Lord who will give you your heart's desire.

I pray that the Lord would shine His light on them and that delight of the Lord would reign in their hearts, that Scripture would be something they read and rely upon for guidance and every other thing.

Proverbs 22:6: Train the young in the way they should go; even when old, they will not swerve from it.

This Scripture says to me that there are going to be journeys in the lives of my children. If children do wander from the faith they will come back to Jesus. I just really rely on that because of this verse.

The next time a delivery from Amazon arrives on your doorstep, will it contain a Bible? That Bible has been delivered by the Holy Spirit, gift-wrapped by our Mother, the Church, and endorsed by a long list of saints who have gone before us. It's number one on life's recommended reading list. Let's hope and pray it becomes everyone's book-of-the-month selection and stays on the a-list permanently.

PRAYER

Dear Lord, I praise you because Your words are spirit and life (John 6:63). Help me to delve deeply into the Scriptures in the coming weeks so that I can draw ever closer to your Divine Heart. As I open my Bible to pray, speak to me Lord in the words on the page, revealing your love for me and for my child _____ so that all fear, worry, guilt and anger are banished from my soul. I want to know You better, love you more, and trust you with my life, my family, most especially, my child _____.

Questions for Reflection:

Thinking about the many kinds of resources at my disposal, what is my honest appraisal of the Bible as a legitimate "go to" when I'm worried, nervous or sad?

How can I best deepen my appreciation of the Bible given my circumstances? A Bible study, small group, online course, daily reading with commentary, other?

Prayer Intentions:

Answered Prayers:

Prayer Practice:

"All Scripture is inspired by God and profitable for teaching, for reproof, for correction, for training in righteousness; so that the man of God may be adequate, equipped for every good work." (2 Tim. 3:16)

Our Lord is waiting to talk with us in the Scriptures. I will open the Bible, read it and reflect. I will ask myself:

What lesson are you teaching me, Lord?

What promise may I claim?

What example shall I follow?

Which mistakes shall I avoid?

As I pray, I will memorize a line or two. They're his love letters to me, after all!

One does not live by bread alone, but by every word that comes forth from the mouth *of God. (Matthew 4:4)*

Lord, how can I love you more today than I did yesterday?

_____

_____

_____

_____

_____

_____

_____

_____

_____

_____

_____

_____

_____

Section II

LOOKING AT COLLEGE CRISES
THROUGH A FAITH-BASED LENS

CHAPTER 9:

———— ⟨⟩ ————

HOMESICKNESS

How ironic…All summer, leading up to the first day of college, the tension in the house mounts. Finally, the shopping is finished, the car is packed, and you leave her on the doorstep of her new college adventure. The aching good-bye is followed by the sadness of those first few weeks when your child is sorely missed at home and seems to be enjoying every last morsel of freedom at college. Then suddenly, about six to eight weeks into freshman year, it hits—she is homesick.[36]

Oftentimes, a new college student has plunged headfirst into the social scene, excited to mingle with so many other young people in close proximity. Realizing that she has time to burn, compared to the academic crush of junior year in high school, this novice of time management finds herself frayed and exhausted just about the time that midterms become a frightening reality. The novelty has worn off. Academic review is over, and new material is being taught at

---

36 This is a typical pattern for homesickness, but a child can feel homesick from the start or can experience periods of homesickness throughout the college experience. It matters not when homesickness occurs but how you manage as a parent of a college-age child.

a rapid-fire pace. Friendships have formed, but the fluidity of these early weeks has caused hurt feelings, confusion, and sadness. The result? Homesickness.

What's a mother to do? In those first weeks, any communication would have been welcome, but now you find yourself fielding daily—sometimes hourly—calls from college. Your heart, perhaps still grieving over the loss of her regular presence in the household, twists and morphs as you now worry about how she will cope. Maybe you even find yourself annoyed at the constant interruptions of her texts and calls.

Should you show up to lend support in person? Fly her home for the weekend? Share your worry and concern over the phone? Most of the time, the answer will be "No, no, and no."

Homesickness is normal...very normal. Nearly all college kids experience at least twinges of homesickness. (If you're one of the few whose child is not homesick, consider yourself blessed. Homesickness is in no way a measure of your child's love for you.) It's usually a temporary phenomenon, most often brought on by adjusting to the more demanding aspects of college, like rigorous academics, competitive sports, or social life. Your child may express feelings of loneliness and may ask to come home...repeatedly. Other symptoms can include irritability, decreased motivation, performance anxiety, pessimism, or isolationism. If homesickness lasts longer than two weeks or the child seems disoriented, seriously depressed, or anxious to the point of suicide, the situation is much more dangerous than a case of homesickness and professional intervention is required.[37]

---

37 Every college manages psychological illness differently, so check with

How can you tell whether your child's homesickness is "normal" or something more serious? To make the most accurate assessment, the cardinal virtue of prudence is helpful.[38] A prudent person seeks advice, makes a sound judgment, and decides a course of action in a timely manner.[39] Lord, please send prudence!

For expert advice, the college itself can be an excellent resource. Often, the school website counsels students at length on the symptoms and remedies for homesickness. It's usually written for students, not parents, so by reading the website you will be able to see things from her perspective and learn what her options are, which can be helpful if action is necessary. Colleges also have counseling centers and medical centers should your child wish to seek professional help. At Catholic schools, campus ministry offers priestly guidance, access to the sacraments, and other faith-based integrative activities, like parties and late-night masses, which can help to ease if not cure homesickness.

Online advice is also plentiful. Wikipedia, for example, suggests "doing something fun to forget about being homesick."[40] That's just what one friend of mine did. Her daughter was so homesick that she begged to attend a college near her home for senior year. She was so close to

---

your child's dorm rector or the medical clinic, or look at the college website to get the help you need.

38 The cardinal virtues are the four principal moral virtues. The English word cardinal comes from the Latin word cardo, which means "hinge." All other virtues hinge on these four: prudence, justice, fortitude, and temperance. Catholicism.about.com.

39 Thomas Aquinas, Summa Theologica, http://www.newadvent.org/summa/3047.htm#article4, Question 47.

40 "Homesickness," Wikipedia, June 10, 2018, accessed March 11, 2016, https://en.wikipedia.org/wiki/Homesickness.

graduation that they wanted to keep her where she was, so they struck a bargain. During the bitter cold winter, they scheduled a monthly visit, meeting her off campus for some downtime. Everyone enjoyed the little getaways, and she graduated with honors.

Another resource not to be overlooked is the Praying College Moms ministry. Moms in the group with children in grades ahead of yours have most likely dealt with homesickness and can help you diagnose the situation. They might suggest a Praying College Mom care package, which is a wonderfully personalized opportunity to show your child you're thinking about her and miss her.

Have you spoken to your husband/your child's father or a trusted family member? What is his assessment of her mood? A father or father figure can offer a very different and necessary perspective on your child's emotional health. Two outlooks, both with intimate knowledge of your child, will be much better than one.

After gathering some sound advice, prudence dictates that you make a judgment and act. How serious is the problem? What is the best recourse? Whatever you decide to do, a prudent mom will pray for her homesick child... daily, even hourly! That's not as tall an order as it sounds. Every time your mind turns to her homesickness, your knee-jerk response can be to lift your heart and mind to our loving Father on her behalf. "With all prayer and supplication, pray at every opportunity in the Spirit" (Ephesians 6:18).

You might pray lines like these from Scripture, perhaps memorizing one or two of them and repeating them every time you find yourself worrying about her.

- Weeping may stay for the night, but rejoicing comes in the morning. (Psalm 30:6, New International Version)
- Take courage, my daughter; the Lord of Heaven grant you joy in place of your sorrow. (Tobit 7:16)
- Blessed are you who are now weeping, for you will laugh… (Luke 6:21)

Customize them, if you like, to help you identify more strongly as the beloved daughter of your Father. Use them as a springboard into your own prayers of petition. For example, in place of the first line, you might pray, "I am sad and worried right now about my daughter. She is really missing us. But I know that it won't last forever, and You, loving Father, accompany me in my tears. Console both of our hearts." For the second verse, you might pray, "*You* are my delight, Father, and I draw courage from Your providential care of things." For the third line of Scripture, pray, "Bless me, Lord, and bless my daughter. We will laugh again! Of that I'm sure."

Praying College Moms has formed a community to support you. If you don't belong to a small group, you can invite these women to pray for your child by name through their website, prayingcollegemoms.org. Grace will flow as they add their voices to yours on behalf of your child.

With the power of prayer buoying you (yours and your friends') the virtue of prudence will surely guide you to make a responsible, measured response to your child's homesickness without overreacting, intruding, or trying to control things from a distance. You'll know just what to say and when to say it. Lord, please send prudence!

PRAYER

Heavenly Father, *Abba*, You are loving and wise. There is no limit to Your understanding (Isaiah 40:28). I need some guidance. My child_____ is sad and lonely and missing me. That makes me sad too, and I want to help her.

Grant me the virtue of prudence to help her so that I can properly assess the situation; then I can get some professional advice and assistance from my godly friends to do exactly what the situation calls for.

I am Your beloved daughter, and I pray that all my actions give You glory. Protect me from overzealousness, from being a "buttinsky," or from doing anything else that will not bring glory to You.

Increase my faith in You, Lord. Help me to trust that You are blessing _____ at college because of my prayers for her and because You love her more than I do. Bring peace to her heart. Hold my hand too! Amen.

Questions for Reflection:

What resources do I have to support me as I assess the needs of my child? Do my husband and I pray together? Do I have a community of prayerful friends? Do I have an intimate relationship with God? Where am I in need?

Where do I recognize prudent thought or action in my child? In myself? Have I thanked God, the giver of every good grace?

Prayer Intentions:

Answered Prayers:

Prayer Practice:

I will listen to my child as often as she calls or texts, silently begging for prudence to say and do the right thing in each moment. Every time I think of her, I will lift her up by praying a short verse from Scripture or a phrase I like from a favorite prayer.

My child, be attentive to my wisdom; incline your ear to my understanding, so that you may hold on to prudence, and your lips may guard knowledge. (Proverbs 5:1-3)

Lord, how can I love you more today than I did yesterday?

_____

_____

_____

_____

_____

_____

_____

_____

_____

_____

_____

_____

_____

_____

CHAPTER 10:

FOSTERING INDEPENDENCE

When he was two years old, my son alternated between tearfully clinging to my legs at the park and racing headlong toward the swing set ahead of me. There was no apparent rhyme or reason, no way to anticipate his mood, and he seemingly felt both ways equally strongly, depending on the day. The only time I could predict with total accuracy what he would do was when I needed to put him in a car seat. Battles always ensued.

When he was away at college those first few weeks, his sporadic communication reminded me of those confusing early days at the park. He would text me three times in an hour, excited about something, and then go radio-silent for the remainder of the week. He would call me one minute elated, and days later, he would be really down in the dumps. He wasn't eating well, stayed up too late some nights, and partied every weekend—perhaps even more often. Despite all this, he assured me he was attending his classes. I wasn't happy. It concerned me that he seemed to be flailing at mature independence, instead relying on me to pick him up or motivate him when he needed it.

I realized after a while that I had to make a choice. I could ride this roller coaster of emotion with him, stop answering the phone (not a real option), or try to help him somehow. I wanted him to be successful and worried that he might be spinning out of control—perhaps a victim of his newfound freedom. It seemed to me he was lacking temperance.

Temperance is a cardinal virtue that, when poured by God's grace into a passionate, erratic soul, empowers him to get a grip on himself, to master his reason, his will, and his heart. When a college student is supposed to be studying but friends are partying two doors down, temperance is what tells him to stay at his desk. (Fortitude is what keeps him there.) Should temperance reach perfection in us, we would lose that ten pounds that we keep talking about, hold our temper 100 percent of the time, and avoid excesses in drinking, shopping or television viewing. It's a valuable asset, isn't it?

Desirable as it is, we know that the virtue of temperance is hard to exercise, especially for young adults. The teens and early twenties are often fueled by unbridled energy and enthusiasm for all kinds of experiences, which can lead to lots of experimentation. They consider themselves invincible and want to live life to its fullest. New scientific evidence suggests that they feel this way because eighteen- to twenty-year-olds have an immature prefrontal cortex (the part of the brain that regulates impulse control). This incomplete development makes them more likely than others to engage in risky behavior, especially if someone is watching them.[41] There's not much room in this young

---

41 Sandra Aamodt, "Brain Maturity Extends Well Beyond the Teen Years,"

psyche for self-control, sobriety, and vigilance...in other words, for temperance.

Nevertheless, as parents, we have more influence in the life of our child than we usually give ourselves credit for. Helping him learn to practice the virtue of temperance now will serve him well in his growth toward independence.

Temperance concerns itself with avoiding overindulgences and restraining impulses. But simply telling a college student that he shouldn't party too late, drink too much, or waste time won't help him develop the virtue. To vent frustration in an authoritative tone or to act out in fear by sounding excessively protective might even inhibit his positive change. A better approach would be to speak and act from a quiet, centered place—an interior heart immersed in the peace that comes from talking first with God the Father. We do well to pray with concentration and focus, asking God for the grace of temperance for our children.

Claire's son Jason learned through experience that late-night parties involving alcohol left him feeling anxious and lethargic. "I'm literally wasting the whole next day," he complained to her. Did he stop partying? No. But he was growing in baby steps. Over time, he learned to stay in the night before an exam or major presentation. When he did party, he still called home the next day because he was anxious, but his tone was different—he knew he was facing the natural consequences of his behavior and had taken emotional responsibility for it. Claire keeps praying for him, and she thanks God wholeheartedly for

interviewed by Brian Candy, NPR, October 10, 2011.

each little "miracle" she has observed in Jason's ability to temper himself.

What Temperance Is NOT

At first glance, it might seem to a college student that people who exemplify temperance are…boring…or at the very least, unbearably stuffy. On the contrary, people who live any virtue are attractive! Temperance helps individuals become well-ordered and essentially free from acting impulsively. These individuals are reliable. Their "yes" means "yes" and their "no" means "no" (Matthew 5:37). They are trustworthy. Temperate people model self-control and achieve what they set out to do, drawing admiration from their peers and acclaim from their teachers and parents. And, in the words of Saint Pope John Paul:

"This does not mean that the virtuous, sober man cannot be "spontaneous," cannot enjoy, cannot weep, cannot express his feelings; that is, it does not mean that he must become insensitive, "indifferent," as if he were made of ice or stone. No, not at all! It is enough to look at Jesus to be convinced of this. Christian morality has never been identified with Stoic morality. On the contrary, considering all the riches of affections and emotivity with which every man is endowed— each in a different way, moreover: man in one way, woman in another owing to her own sensitivity—it must be recognized that man cannot reach this mature spontaneity unless by means of continuous work on himself and special "vigilance" over his whole behavior.

The virtue of "temperance," of "sobriety" consists, in fact in this."[42]

When your child calls to talk, you have another excellent opportunity to help him grow in temperance—your witness. Share with him examples from your own lifestyle, grounded in faith, good works, moderation, and self-control:

Parents need to be courageous in order to personally lead a life of Christian austerity. Precisely because it is a virtue whose acts are directed to detachment, those being educated need to see its good effects. If parents through their temperate lives radiate cheerfulness and peace of soul, their children will have an incentive to imitate them.[43]

We know well from experience that temperance is a difficult virtue to live. It can be nearly impossible to turn off a mind consumed with worry, right? Scripture reinforces this. "The spirit indeed is willing, but the flesh is weak" (Mark 14:38). But it's never truer than for a college-age student with an immature prefrontal cortex. Therefore, in imitation of our Heavenly Father, we watch our son's development with loving mercy, not expecting overnight transformations in him [or in ourselves]. Instead, we share concern, advising when asked, admonishing if necessary, and always...praying...praying...praying.

---

42 Pope John Paul II, "The Virtue of Temperance," General Audience, Vatican City, November 22, 1978. Accessed March 26, 2016.
43 J.M. Martin and J. de la Vega, "Temperance and Self-Mastery," Opus Dei, March 19, 2014. http://www.opusdei.org/en-us/article/temperance-and-self-mastery-i/.

Virtues are formed by prayer. Prayer preserves temperance.
—Saint Ephream of Syria[44]

Never exaggerate but express your feelings with moderation.
—Saint Teresa of Avila[45]

For the grace of God has appeared, saving all and training us to reject godless ways and worldly desires and to live temperately, justly, and devoutly in this age, as we await the blessed hope, the appearance of the glory of the great God and of our savior Jesus Christ, who gave himself for us to deliver us from all lawlessness and to cleanse for himself a people as his own, eager to do what is good (Titus 2:11-14).

---

44 Jacqueline Lindsey, Catholic Prayer Book (Huntington: Our Sunday Visitor, 2003), 9.
45 Teresa of Avila, The Complete Works of St. Theresa of Avila (London: Burns & Oates, 2002), 256.

PRAYER

God, Father of Heaven and earth, You are a true father, full of mercy and goodness. I pray that You give _____ a generous dose of temperance so that he may live in true freedom. Give him temperance over food and drink, over sleep and activity, over study and recreation, and in reliance on me. Help him to grow into a truly independent, mature, and self-possessed adult with a natural spontaneity and a deep joy for life. May his life glorify You.

Lord, Father over all, remove from his life anything that chains him or enslaves him, anything that distracts him from his goals, anything that tempts him beyond his strength.

I ask these graces of You, interceding for _____. I know he needs them! Please, Lord, grant these prayers in the name of Your only Son, Jesus Christ. Mother Mary, watch over him and accompany me as I petition Your Son on my child's behalf. Amen.

Questions for Reflection:

How consistent am I in encouraging my son to become an independent adult? In what ways do I hover? In what ways am I tempted to be too much at arm's length?

What good examples of temperance do I see in his life? In my own? Where in my life can I improve so as to live more virtuously and be a better witness?

Prayer Intentions:

Answered Prayers:

Prayer Practice:

I will examine my life for signs of intemperance and ask the Lord for vigilance to root out and banish these weaknesses, claiming the grace promised to those who "live by the Spirit" (Galatians 5:16). I will offer these renunciations for my son's growth in temperance and, ultimately, for his eternal salvation.

For you were called for freedom, brothers. But do not use this freedom as an opportunity for the flesh; rather, serve one another through love. (Galatians 5:13)

Lord, how can I love you more today than I did yesterday?

_____

_____

_____

_____

_____

_____

_____

_____

_____

_____

_____

_____

_____

_____

_____

_____

CHAPTER 11:

"HOW IS CLASS? ARE YOU GOING TO MASS?"

Driving home with my soon-to-be-freshman son from a pre-college orientation program late one evening, he said something I will never forget. Perhaps encouraged by the excitement of the orientation, the anticipation of heading off to college, or the intimacy of the warm, cozy car shielding us from the frigid night, he took the opportunity to thank me. "I am ready to go to college," he told me confidently. "And I am so grateful to you and Dad." He shared with me how grounded he felt by the support of our family, how appreciative he was for the gift of education, and, most importantly, how grateful he was to have received the faith, which enabled him to trust God with his future. That is a memory I truly cherish.

Ten years later, he still feels the loving support of his family, and, having nearly completed a master's program, he continues to appreciate the value of education. Sadly, however, he no longer practices his Catholic faith. Although the Sacraments were readily available during his four years at a Catholic college, he stopped going to Mass and then left the Church altogether before he graduated.

I became one of so many mothers wondering how their children, who were raised Catholic and went to Mass every Sunday, abandoned the faith during college.

Dwindling Mass attendance is not unique to millennials on college campuses. In today's society, people of all faiths are gradually shifting away from formalized religion to self-professed "nones," according to a Gallup Organization 2016 study.[46] In fact, Gallup's "longest-running religious service attendance question asks, 'Did you, yourself, happen to attend Church, synagogue or mosque in the last seven days, or not?' In 1939, when Gallup first asked this question, 41% said 'yes.' That percentage dropped to 37% in 1940 and rose to 39% in 1950. It continued to climb, reaching as high as 49% at multiple points in the 1950s. Attendance then settled down to figures around 40% for decades, before dropping to 36% for the past three years."[47]

"Everyone is doing it" doesn't assuage a mother's feelings of helplessness as she watches an adult child drift away from the foundational beliefs she worked so hard to teach him as a youth. We know parents are the first educators of their children in the faith, and Saint Pope John Paul II tells us we are well equipped for the job. "For Christian parents the mission to educate, a mission rooted, as we have said, in their participation in God's creating activity, has a new specific source in the sacrament of marriage, which consecrates them for the strictly Christian education of their children: that is to say,

---

46 Frank Newport, "Five Key Findings on Religion in the U.S.," Gallup. com, December 23, 2016, accessed January 10, 2017, http://www.gallup. com/poll/200186/five-key-findings-religion.aspx.
47 Ibid.

it calls upon them to share in the very authority and love of God the Father and Christ the Shepherd, and in the motherly love of the Church, and it enriches them with wisdom, counsel, fortitude and all the other gifts of the Holy Spirit in order to help the children in their growth as human beings and as Christians."[48]

We have our children baptized, they prepare themselves to receive First Holy Communion and Confirmation, we make financial sacrifices to send them to good schools, take them to Mass faithfully, and teach them the faith to the best of our ability…and still they stray. "Did I send him to the wrong college? Was it my parenting? Is secular society just too powerful of an influence?" a concerned mother might wonder.

When children are little, Vacation Bible School, CCD, and Veggie Tales can reinforce the faith lessons we strive to teach them. As they grow into young adults, so does their ability to discern right from wrong. Belief in God is no longer taught as much as it is "caught." At this age, nagging and hand wringing can dangerously erode our most persuasive means of getting teens to Mass: our joyful witness. Buoyed by fidelity to prayer and little hidden sacrifices, our joyful witness is what draws the firepower of the Holy Spirit into the souls of our fallen-away children. And so we ask ourselves: Is our own fervor for the Mass so contagious that those around us can't help but become "infected" with the love of the Eucharist? Do they see us genuflecting reverently, singing along, listening to the

---

48 Pope John Paul, II, Familiaris Consortio (November 22, 1981) #38, accessed January 10, 2017, http://w2.vatican.va/content/john-paul-ii/en/apost_exhortations/documents/hf_jp-ii_exh_19811122_familiaris-consortio.html.

Word proclaimed, and praying with head bowed after Communion? Do we share in natural and loving ways what impact the Mass has on our lives? Do our lives reflect a confidence and dependence on the Lord in the Eucharist? Are we as convinced as the saints are about the spiritual gifts that await us at every celebration of the Mass?

Julie, a young mother from my parish, recently gave a compelling personal testimony about the Mass to her Bible-study group. "Nine months ago," she said, "I prayed a specific prayer asking for the desire to begin going to daily Mass." Shortly thereafter, Julie took the heroic step of bringing her rambunctious two-year-old to Mass. "It was a miserable experience at first" she conceded. "My son was noisy and distracting, and I left feeling defeated more often than not." Within weeks, however, her zeal began to grow. "Do you realize that every Mass brings us divine healing, renewed strength, and transformation?" she asked. "I wish I had known that when my kids were even younger. I could have used those graces!" she laughed. She then shared a concrete example from her life of healing, strengthening, and transformation she said she has received from the Eucharist at Mass.

What young college student wouldn't benefit from a healing of social anxieties so prevalent on campus, or a strengthening to study longer and harder, or a transformation into a more peaceful, balanced, and happy student? Those graces are free for the taking at every Mass. "Healing, strength, and transformation" are the answers to a teen's question, "I don't get anything out of Mass so why should I go?"

Why do you go to Mass? If you're not sure of the answer, or if, like most of us, you find yourself occasionally writing grocery lists, reviewing the day's calendar, or otherwise mentally absent in your pew, reflect on what these great Church leaders and saints have to say about the Mass... Then, like Julie did, humbly ask for the grace of zeal for Our Lord in the Eucharist through the celebration of the Holy Mass.

- The Mass is the most perfect form of prayer. (Pope Pius VI)
- The celebration of the Mass is as valuable as Jesus's death on the cross. (Saint Thomas Aquinas, Doctor of the Church)
- The Heavens open and multitudes of angels come to assist in the Holy Sacrifice of the Mass. (Saint Gregory, Doctor of the Church)
- If we really understood the Mass we would die of joy. (Saint John Vianney)
- Put all the good works in the world against a Holy Mass; they would be as a grain of sand beside a mountain. (Saint John Vianney)
- It would be easier for the world to survive without the sun than to do without Holy Mass. (Saint Padre Pio)
- When Mass is celebrated the sanctuary is filled with countless angels who adore the divine victim immolated on the altar. (Saint John Chrysostom)
- Without doubt, the Lord grants all favors asked of Him in Mass, provided they be fitting for us. (Saint Jerome, Doctor of the Church)

- There is nothing so great as the Eucharist. If God had something more precious, He would have given it to us. (Saint John Vianney)
- What graces, gifts and virtues the Holy Mass calls down. (Saint Leonard of Port Maurice[49])
- It is not to remain in a golden ciborium that He comes down each day from Heaven, but to find another Heaven, the Heaven of our soul in which He takes delight. (Saint Thérèse of Lisieux, Doctor of the Church)
- If angels could be jealous of men, they would be so for one reason: Holy Communion. (Saint Maximilian Kolbe[50])
- Christ is always present in His Church, especially in her liturgical celebrations. He is present in the Sacrifice of the Mass not only in the person of his minister…but especially in the Eucharistic species…He is present in His word since it is He Himself who speaks when the holy Scriptures are read in the Church… He is present when the Church prays and sings, for He has promised "where two or three are gathered together in my name there am I in the midst of them." (Matthew 18:20; CCC 1088)

---

49 RomanCatholic33, "The Catholic Mass," July 13, 2010, accessed January 10, 2017, https://www.youtube.com/watch?v=CJtRXzyWul8&feature=youtu.be.
50 "Quotes on the Most Blessed Sacrament," Real Presence Eucharist Education and Adoration Association, accessed January 10, 2017, http://www.therealpresence.org/eucharst/tes/a7.html.

PRAYER

Heavenly Father, in the words of the second Eucharistic Prayer read at Mass, "It is truly right and just, our duty and our salvation, always and everywhere to give you thanks...and so, with the Angels and all the Saints [I] declare your glory..."

Lift the veil that covers my human eyes and reveal to me the limitless supernatural beauty of the Holy Mass. Empowered by Your grace, enable me to receive Your body and blood in Holy Communion with ever-increasing reverence so that I am healed, strengthened and transformed, according to Your Will.

By my transformation, allow my peace and joy to overflow upon my loved ones, especially _____. When I am provoked by worry and tempted to nag or pester _____ by asking, "Are you going to Mass tonight?" or "How was the homily," or any variation of "Remember, Sunday Mass is not optional..." please "set a guard, Lord, before my mouth, keep watch over the door of my lips" (Psalm 141:3).

Help me, Lord, to depend on You by praying faithfully, offering sacrifices, and living my own very unique version of joyful Christianity, so that _____ cannot help but be attracted to You. I live for Your glory, Lord.

Questions for Reflection:

Which of the quotes about the Mass from saints and/or doctors of the Church most inspire me? Why?

The Church teaches that we have a serious obligation to attend Mass every Sunday and on Holy Days of

Obligation (CCC 2180). Do I attend Mass every Sunday, even on vacations or when there are conflicts with sports or other familial activities?

Prayer Intentions:

Answered Prayers:

Prayer Practice:

I will read and reflect on the Eucharistic Prayer II, which is the most common Eucharistic Prayer used during Mass and is oriented to God our Father. (This prayer can be found in a missal used during the Mass, or in the *Magnificat*.)

While they were eating, he took bread, said the blessing, broke it, and gave it to them, and said, "Take it; this is my body." Then he took a cup, gave thanks, and gave it to them, and they all drank from it. He said to them, "This is my blood of the covenant, which will be shed for many." (Mark 14:22-24)

Lord, how can I love you more today than I did yesterday?

_____

_____

_____

_____

_____

_____

_____

_____

_____

_____

_____

_____

_____

CHAPTER 12:

———— ⌢ ————

STRESSING OUT...IT'S SO...MILLENNIAL

Doctor Smith sees hundreds of students at the large state university where she works, "and many of them are very stressed out," she says. Other than the garden-variety cold, flu, or UTI she sees at the clinic, students come in with non-specific abdominal pains, insomnia, palpitations, and other inexplicable symptoms that boil down to one diagnosis: stress.

"These days I think there is a lot more pressure on students. I don't know whether it's 'getting the right job' pressure or 'succeeding in school' pressure or pressures from comparing themselves to others on social media, but it's ironic...they achieve academically, they try to eat healthfully, and then they go out on the weekends, drink too much, and engage in high-risk behavior that stresses them out," she says. The treatment can vary but usually starts with a conversation opener like, "Tell me what's going on with you," the doctor says. If the student chooses to open up and share, the doctor offers reassurance and counsel. She can also refer the student, as necessary, to the university's counseling center or the mental health clinic.

The doctor's observations are confirmed by studies concluding that millennials are a very stressed-out generation! Stress and/or anxiety are the most highly reported causes of a decline in academic performance among college students, according to the American College Health Association. At some point during a twelve-month period in 2015, nearly 86 percent of students reported feeling overwhelmed, 82 percent felt exhausted (not from physical exercise), 58 percent felt lonely, and 48 percent felt hopeless.[51] For the sixth year in a row, college mental health clinicians across the country are seeing an uptick in the number of students being treated for stress-related issues.[52]

When college students call home complaining of sleepless nights or non-specific aches and pains, parents can find it difficult to know whether medical intervention is required or a little TLC will fix the problem. Four quick assessments can help to determine how stressed she really is.

1. Is she eating well? Many millennials have become rigid about what foods they eat. They consume an average of 20 percent less snack food than their parents.[53] Fueled by opinion sharing and

---

51 "Reference Group Executive Summary Spring 2015," accessed January 26, 2017, http://www.acha-ncha.org/docs/NCHA- II_WEB_SPRING_2015_REFERENCE_GROUP_EXECUTIVE_SUMMARY.pdf.
52 2016 Annual Report, report, (State College, PA: Center for Collegiate Mental Health, Penn State University), 9, accessed January 26, 2017, https://sites.psu.edu/ccmh/files/2017/01/2016-Annual-Report-FINAL_2016_01_09-1gc2hj6.pdf.
53 "Millennials and Food," (College of Tropical Agriculture and Human Resources, University of Hawaii at Mānoa), 2, accessed on January 26, 2017, http://www.ctahr.hawaii.edu/oc/freepubs/pdf/FST-63.pdf.

picture taking via social media, today's youth "have developed values for or against certain food groups."[54] Food is either good or bad. Sugar is "out." Fresh ingredients are "in." They prefer exotic produce when it's available.[55] Have your college students developed a hankering for papaya, dragonfruit, passionfruit, ataulfo mangoes, young coconuts, or Kiwano melons? At the state university where she works, Doctor Smith said many students avail themselves of produce from a weekly farmer's market that comes to the campus. She also said, however, that students tend to make wise food choices during the week and binge on pizza and beer over the weekend.

2. Is she sleeping long enough? A good night's sleep (seven to nine hours) promotes learning, memory retention, emotional balance, problem solving and creativity. Jawbone, the maker of a sleep tracker, monitored 1.4 million nights of sleep on college campuses and found that students get slightly more than seven hours of sleep per night on average.[56] That's good news, right? Their "night" of sleep usually begins after midnight, however. Don't be surprised to find that your college student goes to bed at college between 12:30 a.m. and 1:30 a.m. on weeknights, but much later on weekends,

---

54 Ibid.
55 ibid.
56 Brian Wilt, "How University Students Sleep," The Jawbone Blog, March 20, 2016, accessed on January 30, 2017, https://jawbone.com/blog/university-students-sleep

making it more difficult to get back on track for the next school week.

If she complains she's chronically tired, you might ask about stimulant use or abuse. Adderall, caffeine, and energy drinks are commonly misused on campus to prepare for finals, or to get up for class after a late night of partying. Overuse leads to chronic fatigue. Familiarize yourself with the college website so that you can recommend one or more of the abundant on-campus resources available at most colleges to properly diagnose her fatigue.

3. Is she exercising regularly? Students who exercise score higher GPAs, according to studies by Purdue University and Michigan State University.[57] "[The gym] is a place where students learn to use physical activity to cope with stress," says Tricia Zelaya, assistant director for student development and assessment at Purdue's Division of Recreational Sports.[58] Purdue has a newly renovated 355,000 square foot facility with a twelve-hundred-square-foot cycling center, a recreational pool, climbing and bouldering walls, designated racquetball and wallyball courts, an indoor hockey rink and soccer

---

57 "College students working out at campus gyms get better grades," Purdue University, April 15, 2013, accessed on January 30, 2017, https://www.purdue.edu/newsroom/releases/2013/Q2/college-students-working-out-at-campus-gyms-get-better-grades.html.

"Want a higher GPA in College? Join a Gym," Michigan State University, July 10, 2014, accessed on January 30, 2017, http://msutoday.msu.edu/news/2014/want-a-higher-gpa-in-college-join-a-gym.

58 "College students working out at campus gyms get better grades," Purdue University, April 15, 2013, accessed on January 30, 2017, https://www.purdue.edu/newsroom/releases/2013/Q2/college-students-working-out-at-campus-gyms-get-better-grades.html.

field, and running tracks.[59] Not every school is so well equipped, but colleges have spent more than $1.7 billion since 2010 expanding or updating their recreational facilities.[60] What excuse can there be for *not* exercising, especially since most facilities are just steps from the undergraduate dorms?

4. Is she managing her time appropriately? Doctor Christina Lynch claims that millennials are "over-connected." Sending more than one thousand texts a day, they rely too heavily on social media, which isolates them with thousands of "friends."[61] As a result, their attention span is short, they get easily bored, and they can lack the self-discipline required for a work/life balance, says the psychologist. The way to motivate millennials, she says, is to appeal to their desire for purpose and meaning in what they do. Millennials rise to challenges and long to be inspired. They function better when they see their daily tasks in light of something bigger. As their parents, we can help them by providing a supernatural and practical everyday context for the hard work they do.

A Spiritual Antidote to Stress

At her university clinic, Doctor Smith sees stressed-out students in her office as often as they feel they need to come in. "We try to arrange it so the students consult with

59 Ibid.
60 Ibid.
61 Christina Lynch, Millennials, Professional Resource Guide, (Arlington, VA: Divine Mercy University, 2016), 11.

the same doctor time after time so we get to know their story," she explained. One recent case, however, needed no referral, no prescription, no professional counseling to resolve itself. The young lady experienced a complete relief from stress—a drug-free, intervention-less, 100 percent recovery in twenty-four hours.

The freshman was an international student, her family's only child, from an elite group of the best and brightest sent to this country to study, the doctor explained. "She had been coming in to see me, presenting with gastrointestinal symptoms resulting from anxiety and from restricting her food intake too much," said the doctor, "and we had been trying to work through these issues together." One day, after several visits, the freshman came to the clinic to ask Doctor Smith a surprising question. "Do you believe in Jesus Christ?" she asked. The student told her doctor that she had met Jesus Christ through a friend who had taken her to Church. "Now" she said, "I know that it doesn't matter what my parents think, or what my teachers think, or what anyone else thinks. Jesus loves me for who I am," she exclaimed joyfully. That was her last visit to the health center, Doctor Smith said.

Admittedly, instantaneous conversions like these are rarely reported, but the fact remains that the Great Physician can unburden our children (and us) just as miraculously. When we are faithful to prayer, Christ heals and restores us—sometimes dramatically, sometimes imperceptibly over a longer period of time. The Lord blesses our efforts to draw close, filling us with the freedom and joy this student felt. We can't help but pass it along to our own college students. Joy is contagious!

Saint Paul was mission-driven like many of our modern-day millennials. For his "cause," the Gospel of Jesus Christ, Saint Paul was beaten, shipwrecked, robbed and in "danger from bandits, danger from my own people, danger from Gentiles, danger in the city, danger in the wilderness, danger at sea, danger from false brothers and sisters; in toil and hardship, through many a sleepless night, hungry and thirsty, often without food, cold and naked" (2 Corinthians 11:24-27). He persevered because "Christ Jesus has made me his own" (Philippians 3:12). Saint Paul knew he was loved by Jesus. Are you as confident in the love Jesus has for you?

How often do you reflect on the fact that you are "fearfully and wonderfully made?" (Psalm 139:14)…That you are made in God's image (Genesis 1:27)…That you are "little less than a god," and "crowned with glory and honor" (Psalm 8:6)…That you were adopted by the King of Kings when you were baptized? (CCC 1265). Do these facts bring you joy? "True happiness is not found in riches or well-being, in human fame or power, or in any human achievement—however beneficial it may be—such as science, technology, and art, or indeed in any creature, but in God alone, the source of every good and of all love…" (CCC 1723).

This joy we receive from the Holy Spirit through prayer (Galatians 5:22) is transmitted to our college students when they sense that our confidence is anchored in Christ and can't easily be shaken. Our advice is inspired and wise,[62] grounded in what's best for them, not influenced

---

62 "If any of you is lacking in wisdom, ask God, who gives to all generously and ungrudgingly, and it will be given you" (James 1:5).

by fear or anxiety. Our interactions with our child(ren) are marked by playfulness, laughter, and a spirit of fun. They sense the joy we have in their company because we're not tied up in knots wondering if they're going to Mass or getting good grades. We've removed ourselves from the "driver's seat" of their lives, allowing the Lord, who loves them more than we ever will, to take the steering wheel. And from our new perspective—on our knees, close to Christ—we find life is a lot more en*joy*able. He is in control!

What is this joy? Is it having fun? Having fun is good. But joy is more, it is something else. It is not the product of financial gain, human successes, or fleeting moments of elation; it's something deeper. It is a gift…Joy is a gift from God. It fills us from within. It is like an anointing of the Spirit. And this joy is the certainty that Jesus is with us and with the Father.[63]

---

63 Pope Francis, "Christian Joy Far from Simple Fun," transcript, Vatican Radio, October 5, 2013.

PRAYER

Dear God, Father, Son and Holy Spirit, You are Love incarnate, Giver of all good gifts. Bless my child _____ and protect _____ from being too stressed at college. Help me to discern how to best help _____ if he/she asks.

Bless me with a contagious joy—the fruit of your Spirit within me. I need this supernatural virtue; a joy that overflows to those around me, especially my child _____. By your grace, I want to be wise and loving, living each day with a playful, authentic spirit of joy. I ask for a joy that empowers me to serve my family and accomplish my duties cheerfully.

Finally, Lord, help me to be faithful to my time of prayer, recognizing that the joy I ask for comes from listening to, knowing, loving and serving You as a beloved daughter of the most High King.

Questions for Reflection:

How does the virtue of joy counteract the tendency to become overwhelmed or stressed-out? Read Appendix 4: Ten Weeks to Finding Joy and discuss or journal.

Eutrapelia is a virtue related to joy that directs us to relax and have fun in such a way that our minds, bodies and souls are truly refreshed. How do I relax? Do I know what kinds of activities refresh me? Our Lord gave us Sundays as a day of rest. He gives us "permission" to practice eutrapelia at the very least on that one day a week! Discuss (or journal about) some ways to make Sundays a time of rest and rejuvenation for the whole family.

Prayer Intentions:

Answered Prayers:

Prayer Practice:

Although he endured many hardships for the Gospel, Saint Paul did not complain. In imitation of him, I will strive to replace every complaint with (1) silence, (2) a positive comment, or (3) a prayer of praise as recommended in 1 Thessalonians 5:18.

The Father is the source of joy. The Son is its manifestation, and the Holy Spirit its giver. – Message of Pope Francis for World Mission Day 2014

Lord, how can I love you more today than I did yesterday?

_____

_____

_____

_____

_____

_____

_____

_____

_____

_____

_____

_____

_____

_____

_____

CHAPTER 13:

─────── ⌒ ───────

HOME FOR THE HOLIDAYS ♪

I remember well one Christmas holiday waiting to greet our freshman and sophomore sons after they had driven halfway across the country to make it home from college for the long holiday. Exams were over, and they both had told me how much they were looking forward to coming home, which was music to my ears. In preparation, I had made their favorite cookies, decorated the Christmas tree ahead of time, and put little welcome gifts on their beds to surprise them. Their dad was stringing lights outside (something they had always helped with), and I was inside counting down the minutes until they arrived safely home in the family van.

Finally, they pulled into the driveway. In the front door they came, looking scruffy and carrying assorted bags and luggage, which they unceremoniously dropped in the foyer. After a perfunctory kiss on the cheek, they whizzed past me and headed for the kitchen, ate several cookies, and lumbered upstairs—I supposed, to take showers. I was listening in the kitchen for signs that they had seen their token gifts on the pillows, expecting a "Gee, thanks Mom," or something similar. And what did I hear? Crickets! Nada…

As I wandered upstairs, I saw each of them in their separate rooms, sitting on the edges of their beds furiously texting, trying to set up a social engagement for that night. "You're going out tonight?" I asked incredulously. "You just got home, and it's late." It was as if I hadn't spoken. They smiled, shrugged, and returned to their texting to plan a gathering with their friends for that night.

The boys went out. Later that evening, my husband and I talked it over and decided that we needed to re-communicate boundaries to the boys. What are boundaries? "A boundary is a personal property line that marks those things for which we are responsible."[64] Our freshman didn't know what the boundaries were, and our sophomore needed a little refresher course.

The condensed version of our lunchtime conversation the next day went something like this: "We love you and we are so proud of you. We are glad you are home and look forward to a great holiday together. While you are home, please remember the house rules. Clean out the van and fill up the tank. Do your laundry and make sure you have clothes to wear for Christmas Mass, including polished shoes. Prepare to see lots of family this holiday. Here's our schedule. Communicate your social plans when you know them. And please observe the house curfew while you are home."

Underlying this long list of house rules, our family boundaries were implicit. For example, the boys knew they had to care for the van, because it had been given to them on loan as a privilege. It was *our* property and needed to

---

64 Cloud Townsend Resources, accessed March 11, 2016, http://www.cloudtownsend.com/boundaries.

be maintained according to *our* expectations if they wanted to keep using it. The curfew was to be observed, because my husband and I are early risers and can't be awakened at all hours and still function the next day. Violation of the curfew had consequences, and they knew them.

Everyone sets their own family rules, and the details aren't as important as making sure the conversation happens, often repeatedly. Let's face it, during those first few weeks, college kids take complete responsibility for themselves—for class attendance, bedtime, laundry, assignments, social activity, and extracurriculars. Did your child join a club? Participate in intramurals? Throw a party in his dorm room and stay up all night? He lived by his own rules, right?

Now that the time has come for this newly self-sufficient young man to return home, you're happy because you've missed your son! You can't wait to spend quality time with him. You're anxious for him to reconnect with his siblings. You want to be a whole family again!

He's happy because he's exhausted and wants to sleep in his own bed. He is eager for a home-cooked meal. He missed you too, of course, but he may have plans…lots of plans…and they don't necessarily involve mom.

The need for boundaries is well-established in a book by the same title, *Boundaries*. [65] In their book, Doctors Henry Cloud and John Townsend (psychologists) share Biblical principles for establishing emotional, physical, and spiritual boundaries. By setting boundaries and following through with consequences when your children

---

65 Dr. Henry Cloud and Dr. John Townsend, Boundaries (Michigan: Zondervan, 1992).

cross the line, you're helping them develop the virtue of justice. Justice is a cardinal virtue that propels a person to give God and neighbor their due.

Justice toward God is called the "virtue of religion." Justice toward men disposes one to respect the rights of each and to establish in human relationships the harmony that promotes equity with regard to persons and to the common good (CCC 1807).

What is *due* to the parents of college-age children? We need look no further than the fourth commandment for the answer. "Honor your father and your mother, so that your days may be long in the land that the Lord your God is giving you" (Exodus 20:12). By the fourth commandment, God asks (commands) children to respect and obey parents in all that is not sinful, and to help them when they are in need. The fourth commandment also forbids disrespect, unkindness, and disobedience toward parents and lawful superiors. "Cursed be anyone who dishonors father or mother" (Deuteronomy 27:16).[66]

Respect, obedience, kindness—these are rights as parents because of our inherent dignity as children of God, but also because we provide for the lifelong spiritual and temporal welfare of our children. So we stand on solid footing when we require our children to abide by established house rules and follow up with appropriate consequences when they don't. It's good for us, because it preserves the peace and stability of our home. It's good for them, because it encourages growth in the virtue of justice. The whole family benefits from the peace that results in an atmosphere of mutual understanding and respect.

---

66 Baltimore Catechism 241, 242, 250.

PRAYER

Heavenly Father, I praise You for the blessing of homecomings. The holidays are such a special time for families, and I want ours to be peaceful, joyful, and just plain fun. With Your grace, the tone of our household will be one of mutual love and respect as we welcome our child(ren) home from college and gather with family and friends.

Please give _____ the grace to appreciate the special quality of family life during the holidays. Help him to exchange any feelings of willful independence, entitlement, or myopic self-interest with a genuine desire to be an integral member of the family and a part of our activities this season.

Send Your Holy Spirit in a fresh new way into our family, inspiring each of us to see one another with compassion, love, and a deep sense of gratitude.

May our holiday be a true celebration of Your presence in our lives. May You make Yourself known in new and exciting ways. Amen.

Questions for Reflection:

How do I respond when my child oversteps his bounds? Do I lose my temper? Sulk and retreat? What strategies might be more effective?

How does the virtue of justice empower me to set boundaries with consequences?

Prayer Intentions:

Answered Prayers:

Prayer Practice:

I will remember that by teaching and enforcing boundaries, I am doing myself and my child a service. The whole household benefits.

Be persistent whether the time is favorable or unfavorable; convince, rebuke, and encourage, with the utmost patience in teaching... (2 Timothy 4:2)

Lord, how can I love you more today than I did yesterday?

_____

_____

_____

_____

_____

_____

_____

_____

_____

_____

_____

_____

_____

_____

CHAPTER 14:

HIGH FINANCE

Whether outraged, stupefied, or begrudgingly acquiescent, many parents of young adults write six-figure checks for college tuition, room and board—a financial burden that feels, as my husband says, "like driving a Lexus off a cliff." We all know that the cost of college education rises each year, and much has been written about economical alternatives to four-year institutions, financial aid packages, and availability of unique scholarship opportunities.[67] Regardless of a family's monetary wherewithal, college is a serious investment—for many, the largest investment they'll ever make. To finance this undertaking, a prudent parent exercises stewardship; a virtue that balances foresight and responsible planning with healthy detachment and trust in God.[68]

---

67 Underwater Photography Grant, New Look Laser Tattoo Removal Scholarship, National Cartoonist Scholarship, Vegetarian Resource Group Scholarship courtesy of "The Weirdest College Scholarships website, accessed March 17, 2017, http://www.fastweb.com/college-scholarships/articles/the-weirdest-scholarships.

68 Stewardship is a virtue that helps an individual "spend" their time, talent and treasure for the glory of God. We are applying stewardship to treasure for this chapter about paying for college.

Cathy and her husband began to save for college from the moment their quadruplets were born. "We knew it was going to be a huge expense all at once, so we saved like crazy," she said. Over the years, the family sacrificed by avoiding expensive vacations and home improvements so as to prioritize education. Despite their best efforts, however, when the time came to send all four young adults to college, "we suffered from major sticker shock," Cathy said. The quadruplets were made aware of the family's financial shortfall and each contributed according to his or her ability. Two took part-time jobs during school. One was given an academic scholarship which enabled her to go to school out of state. One did a bridge program, attending a community college for the first year, and then transferring to the four-year university he had set his sights upon. Now within weeks of celebrating their final graduation, Cathy attributes their ability to pay four college tuitions to working together and "praying about it every single solitary day." As good stewards of their financial resources, the family anticipated their expenses well, saved wisely, and left the rest in God's hands.

Stewardship can guide us, not only in how we prepare to pay the *big* college bills, but in how we teach our children to manage finances during college. "Parents are the number one influence on their children's financial behaviors, so it's up to us to raise a generation of mindful consumers, investors, savers, and givers," says Beth Kobliner, who spearheaded the creation of *Money as You Grow*, which offers age-appropriate money lessons for children.[69] Although the council is secular,

---

69 Laura Shin, "The 5 Most Important Money Lessons To Teach Your

Kobliner's advice incorporates many aspects of Christian Stewardship. She advises teaching children to set up "saving," "spending," and "sharing" jars from an early age. She recommends helping them set age-appropriate financial goals for saving and spending as they enter their teens. When deciding on college, Kobliner says parents should be honest about what the family can afford from the very beginning, and calculate the overall costs (tuition, books, and living expenses) thoroughly before making a final decision.[70]

Carolyn and her husband began planning for their oldest child Katie's college years when Katie entered kindergarten. Now nearly sixteen, Katie has saved the money from summer jobs for her own spending needs. "If she goes out with friends, she no longer asks us for money," Carolyn says. This summer, Carolyn plans to help Katie open a bank account and learn to manage credit. Katie will also begin paying for her cellphone and her car insurance, "to get a sense of how much real life can cost," Carolyn says. With this training, Carolyn and her husband hope that Katie will be well prepared to manage college spending as a good steward of the gift of education her parents plan to give her.

Should your college students pay for their books? Should they get an allowance for incidentals? Will they be on the meal plan or buy groceries and cook? Will they

Kids," Forbes, October 15, 2013, accessed March 17, 2017, https://www.forbes.com/sites/laurashin/2013/10/15/the-5-most-important-money-lessons-to-teach-your-kids/#a3517f868269. Beth Kobliner's full title includes author of Get a Financial Life, and a member of the President's Advisory Council on Financial Capability.

70 Ibid.

have a car on campus with the associated costs? Christian parents bring a spiritual dimension to these very practical questions. As stewards of limited financial resources, we embrace with gratitude the means we have, recognizing that every good gift comes from God. We pray for guidance about if and/or how much our young students should contribute to college costs. We allot our resources proportionate to our capability and our discernment. We share the details with them—the what's, whys, and how much—so that they, too, can be good stewards of what they've received whenever they spend on campus. Finally, we require proper accountability, as the Lord teaches in the parable of the Talents (Matthew 25:14-30).

You Spent What?

All money talk—how it's saved, spent, and shared—can be a "hot-button" topic for families, rife with potential for misunderstanding. Holding young adults accountable to their budgets calls for a prayerful and discerning spirit.

"We had the talk and it went well," my friend Tracy says, obviously relieved. "I was really mad about it, but I waited until she was home for the weekend and we could sit down together," she said. Tracy's youngest daughter, Claire, a college junior, had been overspending on the credit card. Claire had been given the card to purchase gas for the car—that was the original plan, anyway. Over time, however, Tracy had correctly surmised that her daughter had been hanging out with friends and joining them in activities with little thought to expense. Ubering while on a trip to New York City was the tipping point, Tracy says. "Claire didn't realize that those costs add up, nor did she consider the cheaper option—the subway. It was a parenting problem to me. I needed to teach her to properly understand the value of a dollar," Tracy explains. A "financial intervention" put an end to the spending in the most productive way, Tracy said, by calmly talking it through. "I told her that, in a short period of time, she'd be on her own making her own financial decisions. Having the credit card was not helping her learn. I took the card and gave her enough cash to make it through the end of the year, so she'd have to budget," Tracy says. "This year," says Tracey, "Claire decided on her own to skip the trip to New York because it was too expensive."

A No-Judgment Zone

The economic disparity among students at college can be startling, especially at large state universities with thousands of enrollees. "There are students who have tuition, room, and board paid for and want to go abroad for a semester, plan spring break trips, and travel all summer…and then there are those kids on campus who live in cheap apartments, work three jobs, and access the university food pantry for their meals," observed one campus administrator. The incongruence is sadly unjust from an objective standpoint. But spiritually speaking, who can say? What's in the heart, not the wallet, matters most to the Lord. "You cannot serve God and mammon," Jesus warns in Matthew 6:26.

Stewardship dictates that, with gratitude we live within our financial means, not striving to "keep up with the Joneses" nor nagging our children over every dime they spend. The criteria for our spending (and our giving) is spiritual detachment. Hoarding, stinginess, selfish "gimmies" are symptoms of attachment to material goods. So are eye-rolling judgment and envy of others. What's our cure? When we approach Our Lord in prayer and ask Him how best to spend our money, He advises us! The Rich Young Man encountered Jesus who told him, "You are lacking one thing. Go, sell what you have, and give to [the] poor and you will have treasure in Heaven; then come, follow me" (Mark 10:21). When Zacchaeus climbed down from the Sycamore tree full of repentance, Jesus permitted him to keep some of his money. "Behold, half of my possessions, Lord, I shall give to the poor, and if I have extorted anything from anyone I shall repay it four times over" (Luke 19:8). Jesus knew what was best for each soul and acted accordingly.

Likewise, Jesus looks deeply into our hearts and offers us freedom from material attachments by living the virtue of stewardship. When we have approached God with our budget, whether meager or grand, and have accounted for tithing (charitable giving) and thoughtful spending, we can be confident that we have become good stewards of our God-given treasures.

PRAYER

God, Father of every good gift, thank You for the financial resources with which You have blessed my family over the years. In good times and in bad, I acknowledge that You are the source of my financial security.

Help our family to be a good steward of Your gifts. Please give us the grace to discern well through prayer how to spend, save, and give according to Your will and for Your glory. I want to spend prudently, save wisely, and give generously.

Since stewardship incorporates time and talent, as well as my "treasure," I humbly ask, Father, that you show me Your will in these areas as well. Amen.

Questions for Reflection:

How do I communicate spending and saving values to my family? Do my actions and words reflect the intentions of my heart or do financial discussions end in chaos or misunderstanding? How can I improve the tone of "money talk" in my home, if necessary?

Do my college-aged young adults abide by the budgets I have set for them at school? If so, why? If not, why?

Prayer Intentions:

Answered Prayers:

Prayer Practice:

In an effort to "Seek first the Kingdom of God" (Matthew 6:33), I will prayerfully reassess my personal generosity towards others with my time, my talent, and my treasure, and make adjustments as necessary.

Tell the rich in the present age not to be proud and not to rely on so uncertain a thing as wealth but rather on God, who richly provides us with all things for our enjoyment. Tell them to do good, to be rich in good works, to be generous, ready to share, thus accumulating as treasure a good foundation for the future, so as to win the life that is true life. (1 Timothy 6:17-19)

Lord, how can I love you more today than I did yesterday?

_____

_____

_____

_____

_____

_____

_____

_____

_____

_____

_____

CHAPTER 15:

HEALTHY INTIMACY

Picture this—the girls are gathered on a Sunday morning in the dining hall on campus. "I did *what*?" One girl nervously giggles. "Yeah, it was just a meaningless hookup," another girl tells her friends. Everyone participates with teasing and laughter as they regale one another with outlandish escapades from the night before. They sit for hours, eating too much and gossiping, apparently enjoying camaraderie among friends.

The young woman who shared this story said that when the girls left the dining hall on Sundays, no one really felt good about their behavior, but they didn't know WHY they didn't feel good. Some promised themselves privately that "it wouldn't happen again," but for many, alcohol, sex, and "morning-after" gossip were habitual *and* deeply unsatisfying.

While our culture screams for *friends with benefits*, the Church whispers, "Live chastely." What is chastity?

The virtue of chastity is what enables a lover to give herself wholly to the beloved—body and soul. Chastity fulfills every person's deepest desire: to be "loved with an undivided heart" (CCC 2520). This grace was poured into us at baptism, and it grows best when watered with a little self-knowledge, a willingness to obey God's commandments, participation in the sacraments, and fidelity to prayer (CCC 2340).

Chaste relationships are self-giving, generous, and kind. They always seek the good of the other and are never utilitarian. Because chastity falls under the cardinal virtue of temperance, the sexual passions, which can be so intense at this age, are brought in check. The young man or woman is truly free to love the other without falling into sexual sin. The temptation is certainly there, but our Lord promises the grace of chaste living to those who ask...or to those for whom it is asked. "No trial has come to you but what is human. God is faithful and will not let you be tried beyond your strength; but with the trial he will also provide a way out, so that you may be able to bear it" (1 Corinthians 10:13).

In other words, chastity is the answer to *why* those girls at the cafeteria table felt unsettled by their behavior and *how* to reframe their choices so that they can find lasting happiness. Unfortunately, the virtue of chastity is almost never viewed as the path to true love by today's teenagers and young adults. In its place are false notions of freedom, personal choice, and tolerance. Furthermore, chastity is not often preached by clergy from the pulpit nor by parents who feel unequipped to make a persuasive argument. This leaves young men and women in the prime of their sexual lives unprepared for nine months of living in close proximity with the opposite sex.

Given the pressure on college kids to experiment with all kinds of intimacy, how is chastity lived out on the average college campus? Differently for men and women…

Although she may not even know it, a young woman with a healthy psychology wants to be loved for nothing less than body and soul. And she deserves to be loved that way, whether or not she acknowledges her body as a temple of the Holy Spirit and that she is made in the image of Christ. She is a treasure, a pearl of great price, a princess, a beloved daughter of God the Father. She wants to be cherished and seeks closeness and commitment in her relationships.[71] Living chastely, she postpones sexual activity until her boyfriend is committed. The Church calls this commitment the Sacrament of Matrimony.

Young men have a different psychological and spiritual bent. They want to provide and protect, serve and lead, work and achieve, and they want to be honored and respected for this.[72] A young beau will subjugate his sexual desires for the greater good of the relationship most readily when he recognizes her human, moral, and spiritual dignity.

Inexperienced, uncatechized, young and in love, college-age couples tend to underestimate the power of sexual temptation and succumb. They seek out and relish the immediate sexual gratification and positive affirmation that can come from a sexually intimate relationship and ignore the disconcerting guilt feelings that follow.

---

71 Emerson Eggerichs, Love & Respect (Nashville: Thomas Nelson Inc., 2004), v.
72 Eggerichs, vi.

These same couples validate their level of commitment by the intensity of their feelings, confusing raw passion for enduring, self-giving love. She mistakes his sexual appetite for dedication, and he assumes her emotional and physical attachment means she wants sexual intimacy.

To complicate matters further, coed dorms and bathrooms at some universities promote an uncomfortable familiarity between the sexes. A junior from an Ivy League school complained vehemently about the coed bathrooms in her dorm. "It's OK to have guys in the next apartment," she said, "but it's stupid to share the bathrooms with them. How come you can ask for 'quiet' dorms, or substance-free dorms, but you can't have single-sex bathrooms?" she asked rhetorically. This kind of environment crosses boundaries that are meant to facilitate and encourage mutual respect between the sexes.

And what of the "walk of shame"[73] so commonly alluded to by college coeds? It's appropriately named. Saint John Paul II says shame is a response to the realization that someone has been used, not loved.[74] Friends laugh it off and offer false hope, saying, "You're too good for him anyway." But interiorly, maybe even subconsciously, they acknowledge that it's never right to treat another person as a means to an end. In fact, "not even God can treat man as a mere means or redeem him against his will, since he has created him with an intelligent and free nature."[75]

---

73 The "walk of shame" is a term used by some college students to refer to women who come back to their dorm after a night out wearing the same clothes they left in the night before.

74 Karol Wojtyla, Love and Responsibility (London: William Collins Sons & Co. Ltd.,1981), 182.

75 Mary Shivanandan, Crossing the Threshold of Love (Washington, DC:

Where can college coeds turn for advice and examples of lasting marital love? Hopefully, they turn to their parents. Fathers can be especially influential in fortifying chastity. When a father loves his wife selflessly (Ephesians 5:25-29), he shows his son that girlfriends are "pearls of great price." He also strengthens his daughter's femininity and "bolsters her self-esteem and self-confidence. He gives her a solid foundation for life-long self-respect."[76]

You can support your sons and daughters in romantic relationships by reminding them often of their truest identity and by helping them feel loved unconditionally, as our Father loves each of us. What we want for our sons and daughters—chaste relationships and lasting happiness—our Lord wants even more. And so we pray for their purity and chastity and for their future spouses. By prayer, we accomplish more on their behalf than any other words we speak.

Catholic University Press, 1999), 33.

76 "Dads and the Influence They Have on Their Daughters," Focus on the Family, July 31, 2015, , accessed March 15, 2016, https://www.focusonthefamily.com/family-q-and-a/parenting/dads-and-the-influence-they-have-on-their-daughters. http://family.custhelp.com/app/answers/detail/a_id/26403/~/dads-and-the-influence-they-have-on-their-daughters.

PRAYER

Heavenly Father, You are Pure Goodness. By the power of Your Holy Spirit, You purify our minds, hearts, and souls when we ask for Your grace. Father, in the area of sexuality, the beautiful gift You made of man to woman (and woman to man) has been twisted and confused almost beyond recognition. Many men, women, and children are damaged by the destructive sexual lies propagated in our time. Rid our society of these ills and send, instead, an outpouring of mercy and love that will purify sexual desires and redirect them toward the spiritual good of every individual, for Your glory.

I ask also, Lord, that You inspire my child, _____, to love everyone with an authentic, chaste love. Keep her pure in heart, mind, and soul. Grant _____ the grace to live chastely—to see herself as a unique gift preserved for the one whom You have chosen as her life partner.

I pray for the life partners of all of my children. Please help them to grow into the men and women You want them to be. Send them into our lives in Your perfect timing and help us to welcome and include them in our family so that as our family grows, our unity, mutual love, and respect is preserved.

Bless all of my child's friends and the other kids on campus. Keep them pure and good and send Your Spirit upon them to live chastely and, by their example, to transform the college campus environment. Thank You for hearing my prayers. Amen.

Questions for Reflection:

How and when do I talk to my child about chastity?

How do I live chastity in my own life?

Prayer Intentions:

Answered Prayers:

Prayer Practice:

What do I see, hear, watch, or read that keeps me from purity of heart or from living chastely? I will assess my television habits, my novel reading, and my conversations with friends and choose something to abstain from this month as a sacrifice, asking for the grace to grow in purity so that I can better witness to others—especially my child.

I urge you therefore, brothers, by the mercies of God, to offer your bodies as a living sacrifice, holy and pleasing to God, your spiritual worship. Do not conform yourselves to this age but be transformed by the renewal of your mind, that you may discern what is the will of God, what is good and pleasing and perfect. (Romans 12:1-2)

Lord, how can I love you more today than I did yesterday?

_____

_____

_____

_____

_____

_____

_____

_____

_____

_____

_____

_____

CHAPTER 16:

SHALT THOU NOT DRINK?

Emma's parents raised her with a strong faith in a loving, stable family. Her faith was nurtured as she attended CCD and later taught side by side with her mother. Although her father was Jewish, he unwaveringly endorsed the raising of their children in the Catholic faith, and Emma felt his strong support. When the time came, Emma enrolled in a state university in the South to study elementary education, inspired by her experience teaching CCD. She left home with the confidence that her parents and God loved her very much. Apparently, this foundation wasn't sufficient enough to protect her from the dangers of binge-drinking when she became immersed in the social environment at school.

Within days of her arrival at college, Emma said she had made the following "shocking observations":

- Everyone called themselves Christians, but it seemed that no one went to Church. No one was active in their faith.
- The college atmosphere seemed very liberal.
- Everyone drank alcohol, and many smoked marijuana.

- Casual sex seemed to be the norm.

By the second semester of her freshman year, Emma had succumbed to her surroundings. Drinking heavily one night, she slept with a young man she had just met. "I knew sex was sacred and to be kept for marriage. It was not supposed to happen," she said. "But, I had seen my friends…some of them had told me to 'just get it over with.' So I threw away everything I had learned about my faith for a one-night thing."

Drinking, dating, and partying every weekend, Emma still went to Church once in a while and volunteered for a Christian group on campus. "I was going through the motions of faith—doing what I'd always done—while I tried to figure out who I was," she said.

Emma came close to despair one night when she saw "the guy" at a party. "I felt a wave of guilt that sent me into a tailspin," she said. "That night, I came back to my dorm and lay on the floor and cried. I tried to pray, telling God I was done…tired of searching for happiness in all the wrong places. No more boys…no more drinking…I was a mess. I knew that if I kept it all up, things would end poorly, and I needed to turn my life around." Despite her frenetic emotional state, Emma says she realized God was present. "He was there, and I felt He would forgive me," she said. "I still need to forgive myself."

Emma didn't have to wait long for goodness to enter her life. The next day, an upperclassman named Pete, whom Emma had met briefly weeks before, sent her a text asking to meet for coffee. Pete was a junior and an officer in the Christian fraternity on campus. Under the rules of his fraternity, members do not drink or engage in premarital sex. "I feel lucky he is Catholic, because there are so few Catholics in the South," said Emma. "We're both young and have things we're working out, but we're doing it together," she said. "He's my first real boyfriend, and I respect Pete. I didn't respect the other guys I dated."

Meeting Pete helped Emma make up her mind to return to her faith, but he's not the only reason she's living differently. "It's tough to see everyone partying and know that that's not something I need to be doing. My freshman roommate is still drinking and being crazy, and she's right next door in the dorm. But I'm on a different path now. I know who I am when I'm drunk, and it's not someone I want to be."

"Drinking at college has become a ritual that students often see as an integral part of their higher education experience," according to the National Institute on Alcohol Abuse and Alcoholism.[77] The majority of college students drink, and the vast majority of those who drink binge, NIAAA reported a national study in 2014.[78] The consequences for students who abuse alcohol can be deadly.

- Researchers estimate that each year:
- **Death:** About 1,825 college students between the ages of eighteen and twenty-four die from alcohol-related unintentional injuries, including motor-vehicle crashes.

---

77 "NIH Fact Sheets - Underage Drinking," National Institutes of Health, accessed March 15, 2016, https://report.nih.gov/NIHfactsheets/ViewFact-Sheet.aspx?csid=21.
78 Ibid.

- **Assault:** About 696,000 students between the ages of eighteen and twenty-four are assaulted by another student who has been drinking.
- **Sexual Assault:** About 97,000 students between the ages of eighteen and twenty-four report experiencing alcohol-related sexual assault or date rape.
- **Academic Problems:** About one in four college students report academic consequences from drinking, including missing class, falling behind in class, doing poorly on exams or papers, and receiving lower grades overall.[79]

Few of us doubt that alcohol abuse on campuses poses a significant public health risk, but we parent on the issue in vastly different ways. Aware that their children likely drank in high school, some parents give their tacit blessing to college-aged kids who drink. "Hey, these kids are old enough to go to war. They can certainly have a drink or two, or three." Other parents "cross their fingers" and hope for the best because they don't know how to prepare their children to face these pressures on campus. And a third group of parents forbids their children to drink (reminding them that drinking is illegal at their age), and those results are mixed.

Understanding what motivates college students to abuse alcohol can be an important first step in persuading under-aged adults not to drink. When they arrive on campus, college students mix with hundreds or thousands of strangers, resulting in a uniquely complex situation fraught with social anxiety. More than 75 percent of college

---

79 Ibid.

students admit that they drink to quell this anxiety.[80] Alcohol is also an integral part of many long-standing collegiate sports traditions, like pre-gaming in dorms and tailgating at sports arena parking lots. Administrations, alumni, and students can be reluctant to abandon these rituals. Greek life can also promote heavy drinking, although, as Pete's choice illustrates, not all sororities or fraternities do.[81]

One Parent's College Orientation Program

Shopping "back to school" specials, loading the car, or setting up the dorm room does not adequately prepare your freshman for his/her first weeks of school in the alcohol-laden environment on most college campuses. These young adults need praying parents, a strong moral foundation, and some well-timed words of advice to resist these ever-present temptations.

Mike and his wife equip their college-aged students with what Mike calls a coherent philosophy of life years before they go to school. "They know that we think they are unique and special, that they have an irreplaceable mission from God, that God loves them, and they can trust God with anything. When they screw up, and they're

80 Robert Yagoda,"College Students and Binge Drinking: When a Rite of Passage Becomes a Path to Destruction," US News and World Report, November 9, 2016, accessed November 14, 2016, http://health.usnews.com/health-care/for-better/articles/2016-11-09/college-students-and-binge-drinking-when-a-rite-of-passage-becomes-a-path-to-destruction. Accessed November 14, 2016.
81 National Institute on Alcohol Abuse and Alcoholism College Fact Sheet. http://pubs.niaaa.nih.gov/publications/CollegeFactSheet/CollegeFactSheet.pdf

going to screw up, God is there for them and so are we," Mike says.

Mike, his wife, and their extended family drink socially in their home where alcohol is not treated as the "forbidden fruit." The children are sometimes poured a thimble full of wine during the family meal, and as they grow up, they are invited to join the adults drinking wine around the dinner table.

Mike wants to help his children develop a mature relationship with alcohol that will serve them through their adult lives. He believes that they must learn to avoid situations where alcohol can lead to trouble, especially during those heady early days of college.

Mike recognizes, as do many parents, that college drinking on college campuses is dangerous, and often illegal, and that during the first six weeks of freshman year students are particularly vulnerable to peer pressure. Before his children leave for school, Mike sits down with each one for an "orientation" of his own design. The topic of alcohol is addressed in the context of the personal responsibility each has to make the most of school. First, he reminds them that college is a privilege others have worked hard to give them. He reminds them that studying is their job for the next four years, and if they do well, it can set them up for the rest of their lives. Mike then paints a visual picture of what they are likely to encounter. "You're going to see really outrageous things, and I want you to see them sober," he says. "I want you to have a good time, but I am asking, as your father, that you do not have a drop of alcohol for the first six weeks."

"You don't trust me?"

"Of course I don't," Mike responds. He reminds them that everyone is "deeply flawed" and that self-sufficiency "is a myth." One beer can easily lead to two, "and we don't know what we're really capable of when we're 'half in the bag,'" he says. With a mixture of humor and candid illustrations, Mike then goes through practical scenarios with them, and together they work out strategies for keeping the six-week pledge and remaining sober thereafter.

Have Mike's kids kept their pledge? Yes. Much later, they have acknowledged that they did indeed see "outrageous things"—enough to convince them that getting drunk isn't cool at all.

Is Drunkenness a Sin?

Mike's approach to college drinking is practical, and more importantly, persuasive. He gets results without dwelling directly on the sinful nature of drunkenness. However, it's important to note that drunkenness is a sin—one that separates us from God permanently if not repented of, according to Saint Paul. "Now the works of the flesh are obvious: immorality, impurity, licentiousness, idolatry, sorcery, hatreds, rivalry, jealousy, outbursts of fury, acts of selfishness, dissensions, factions, occasions of envy, *drinking bouts*, orgies, and the like. I warn you, as I warned you before, that those who do such things will not inherit the kingdom of God" (Galatians 5:19-21) [emphasis added].

In fact, Scripture has a lot to say about drunkenness. A quick search reveals nearly forty verses of Scripture warning against the "evils of drunkenness." Proverbs

23:29-35 reads as if it was written by an observer at a college frat party:

> Who scream? Who shout?
> Who have strife? Who have anxiety?
> Who have wounds for nothing?
> Who have bleary eyes?
> Whoever linger long over wine,
> whoever go around quaffing wine.
>
> Do not look on the wine when it is red,
> when it sparkles in the cup.
> It goes down smoothly,
> but in the end it bites like a serpent,
> and stings like an adder.
>
> Your eyes behold strange sights,
> and your heart utters incoherent things;
> You are like one sleeping on the high seas,
> sprawled at the top of the mast.
>
> "They struck me, but it did not pain me;
> they beat me, but I did not feel it.
> When can I get up,
> when can I go out and get more?"

Drunkenness falls under the capital sin of gluttony; a disordered appetite for food or drink. Saint Paul defines the glutton as someone whose god is their belly (Philippians 3:19). "Their end is destruction," he says. "Their glory is in their shame…Their minds are occupied with earthly things" (Philippians 3:18-19).

Binge drinking at college is an obvious sin of gluttony, but children who never take a sip might also be culpable, according to the Catechism 1868:

Sin is a personal act. Moreover, we have a responsibility for the sins committed by others when *we cooperate in them*:

—by participating directly and voluntarily in them;

—by ordering, advising, praising, or approving them;

—by not disclosing or not hindering them when we have an obligation to do so;

—by protecting evil-doers.

Cheering at the beer pong table? Egging on the guys taking shots to celebrate a football win? Standing by while a girlfriend gets drunk, or worse…leaving her behind at a party? Covering up a friend's drunken indiscretions? Comforting the hung-over friend with comments like, "Whatever" and "It's OK; everyone does it."

Not many college students are blessed with the moral integrity to abstain from alcohol or refrain from encouraging it, much less proactively oppose it. Our college-aged children need our help, whether they vocalize it or not. "Research shows that students who choose not to drink often do so because their parents discussed alcohol use and its adverse consequences with them."[82] Additionally, drinking is least probable among students who live at home and commute to school,[83] presumably because of ongoing direct accountability to their parents.

---

82 Ibid.
83 Ibid.

Parenting with Prudence

Fighting a temptation to gluttony (in our example, overdrinking) requires the exercise of temperance. A perfectly temperate college student overcomes peer pressure by simply and self-assuredly explaining that he doesn't drink. He moderates his food and alcohol intake in the football stands, at late-night dorm parties, off and on campus—in every circumstance. His exceptional self-mastery shines as he stands apart from his peers, restraining every appetite for the glory of God. Does that sound like any college student you know?

Desirable as it is, we know that the virtue of temperance is hard to exercise, especially for young adults. As I mentioned earlier, "scientific evidence suggests that temperance is difficult because eighteen to twenty-year-olds lack a fully developed pre-frontal cortex, the part of the brain that regulates impulse control. This makes them more likely than others to engage in risky behavior, especially if someone is watching them.[84] There's not much room in this young psyche for self-control, sobriety, and vigilance…in other words, for temperance.

Temperance defeats the sin of gluttony head-on, but the sister virtue of Prudence might more effectively inspire college students to win the cultural battle against alcohol abuse. Temperance draws on emotional and mental willpower in a moment of temptation, but the prudent person uses reason to conquer vice. The Catechism tells us that "Prudence is 'right reason in action,'" as defined by Saint Thomas Aquinas, following Aristotle (CCC

---

84 Sandra Aamodt, "Brain Maturity Extends Well Beyond the Teen Years," interviewed by Brian Candy, NPR, October 10, 2011.

1806). To evoke prudent decision-making, children are given a thorough understanding of moral principles—not just the "what" but the "why." This "remote preparation" then kicks in when college students face a dilemma. They exercise prudence, acknowledging its obvious merits by weighing the pros and cons of getting drunk, and concluding rightly to stay sober. In other words, they "apply these moral principles to particular cases without error and overcome doubts about the good to achieve and the evil to avoid" (CCC 1806).

Mike hopes that, by telling his children about the dangers of drunkenness—possible arrest, unplanned sexual encounters, hangovers, etc.—and by making his expectations very clear, they will see enough evidence in the first six weeks to convince them not to put themselves at risk in that way. In effect, he hopes that they are empowered by his moral teachings and their own observations to exercise prudence when the time comes: to discern how to drink responsibly. It has worked for them. How do you talk to your college students about alcohol? Do you discuss the destructive consequences of drunkenness? What about its sinfulness? You know the best way to approach your child, and prudence dictates that you must. Since college students fare better if their parents discuss alcohol use with them, how much better prepared are those whose parents have prayed to God for prudence, and in that same Spirit, offer their loving support and guidance?

PRAYER

Dear Father, Creator of every good thing, Your Son made wine from water. Alcohol is a gift and blessing—one that requires virtue to enjoy. I ask you as a praying college mom to bless _____ and help her resist the temptation to drink alcohol at school. Bless her with the gift of Prudence so that she can make wise decisions in every circumstance. Give her courage and strength to stand apart from those who live the status quo in social situations on campus. May she be a sober, light-filled, genuine friend to others. Allow her to radiate your love, so that she is a good example of virtue and brings glory to You. And if she falls, Lord, forgive her! And bless me with the grace to help reorient her in a spirit of love, not judgment, so that she can learn to lean on You the way I do, knowing that You are trustworthy and good.

Questions for Reflection:

What is my family's attitude about drinking alcohol? How do I feel about college-aged drinking in general? How does my outlook contribute to my child's inclination to drink on campus, or strengthen her to resist?

Saint Paul says that drunkenness is a sin—one that separates us from God. Is getting tipsy sinful? What about "accidental" drunkenness? Alcoholism? What are the criteria for mortal sin? For a thorough explanation from the Catechism about mortal sin, see Appendix 5.

Prayer Intentions:

Answered Prayers:

Prayer Practice:

I will pray for the gift of prudence for myself, my husband, and my college student(s) every morning during this next month, listening for inspiration about when to talk to him/her about alcohol and what to say.

So whether you eat or drink, or whatever you do, do everything for the glory of God. (1Corinthians 10:31)

Lord, how can I love you more today than I did yesterday?

_____

_____

_____

_____

_____

_____

_____

_____

_____

_____

_____

_____

_____

_____

_____

CHAPTER 17:

NOT HAPPY AND GAY

For Ryan, the four years at his Catholic college were fraught with anxiety, teasing, foiled heterosexual experimentation, and uneasy bonding with the guys in his all-male dorm. He coped by calling home to "talk things out." He also drank alcohol and smoked marijuana. Periodically, he attended group therapy provided by the university to allay his anxiety. He excelled academically and socially. No one suspected he was gay, or if they did, they didn't say so.

Sally told her parents in a letter when she was thirteen years old that she felt differently than other girls, according to her mother. "I am either gay or bi or do not know what. I hope you will accept this," she wrote. Sally's mom was surprised by the letter, felt that Sally was too young to know for sure about these things, and decided to wait and see. "I didn't know what to make of it," Sally's mom said. In high school, Sally had very few close friends. During sophomore year she wore contacts, makeup and mascara. That summer, she shaved her head. By her junior prom, Sally had become vegan, lost weight, and looked beautiful, "like Audrey Hepburn," her mother said. She attended that prom with a gay girlfriend. Just before college started, Sally had a brief summer romance with a young man who thought he was a girl. None of these iterations of personality seemed to work for Sally, according to her mom. Sally finished college and now lives miles away with some "very accepting" friends and her mom is "happy Sally is happy."

Jason experimented with same-sex relationships as a young teen and was "found out" by his mother. Dangerously depressed, Jason visited doctors and psychologists trying to sort things out during those years. He took medication but continued to suffer under the watchful and concerned eye of his doctors and his mother. He withdrew emotionally, sharing very little with his mother, and nothing with his father. The family moved often, and Jason ended up at a college half a continent away from his parents. They didn't hear much from him for a while. After his father's posting concluded, however, Jason's parents were able to move close to his school. "I was so happy to be near Jason again," his mom said, "and he brought some friends over for dinner a couple of times. They were effeminate, although Jason is not." Then, one night, Jason was rushed to the hospital by his friends. He called his mom the next morning to fill her in and let her know he was OK. She raced to see him and found his friends there also. "I was really hurt he didn't think to call me first, especially since we were only fifteen minutes away," she said. "He told me the problem was a stomach ulcer, but I worry that wasn't the truth," she added with concern.

Dave's parents discovered he was gay late one night when he came home in a drunken stupor as a high school junior. Awakened by the dog barking, Dave's mother Julie was surprised to find him crying on the stoop in the freezing cold. Seeing that he was also drunk, she lost her temper and ushered him into the house, waking Dave's father in the process. "What were you doing, and what do you have to say for yourself?" she asked.

"If you really want to know, I just hung up from the suicide prevention hotline because…I am gay," he sobbed. His father immediately engulfed him in a gigantic bear hug and the three of them talked well into the next morning. Slowly he told his siblings, other family members, and close friends.

When the time for college arrived, Dave chose a Catholic school and entered as an openly gay freshman. He pledged a fraternity and the men acknowledged and welcomed their only gay pledge. Dave has graduated from college and lives at home. For now, his mother's chief concern is not his sexuality but his drinking. When he drinks, he often overdoes it, she says. Dave is now a bit of a homebody, and his mother is grateful for the relative peace in the house.

All of these young people share similar backgrounds: They were born into loving Catholic families, educated at prominent institutions, and are gifted with intelligence and talent. They also share a monumental cross—same-sex attraction and an inability to reconcile it with their faith and their perceived expectations of their parents. Several of them sought relief through Catholicism; one went to daily Mass for a period, another said novenas.

Their parents, all practicing Catholics, mourn the loss of a "white picket fence" future for their children and pray for those who have left to return to the faith. Outside this microcosm of suffering, how does the rest of the world, in particular this college-aged generation, feel about same-sex attraction?

The Ways of the World

When Ryan came out shortly after graduating, his parents were devastated but most of his college friends didn't react negatively. Same-sex attraction elicits a "yawn" from millennials on college campuses. The latest studies indicate a similar attitude in the nation at large. According to the Barna Group, between 50 and 79 percent of Americans consider it "very or somewhat extreme" to believe that sexual relationships between people of the same sex are morally wrong.[85] With the Supreme Court's legalization of same-sex marriage in 2016, it seems that those who uphold the Catholic Church teaching on homosexuality are now a minority in this country. Even the word "homosexuality" has been replaced by the culturally applauded all-inclusive term "LGBTQ."[86]

By contrast, the Church teaches that a homosexual act is intrinsically wrong. According to the Catechism, "[homosexual acts] are contrary to the natural law. They close the sexual act to the gift of life. They do not proceed from a genuine affective and sexual complementarity"

---

85 "Five Ways Christianity Is Increasingly Viewed as Extremist - Barna Group," February 23, 2016, accessed November 21, 2016, https://www.barna.com/research/five-ways-christianity-is-increasingly-viewed-as-extremist/.
86 Lesbian, gay, bisexual, transgender, and questioning or queer.

(CCC 2357). Homosexuals are called, like all children of God, to live chastely—a lifestyle that resonates with few college-aged hetero- or homosexuals, so steeped are they in modern culture, which aggressively promotes infidelity and fornication through the likes of reality television and online pornography.

Anticipating the need for a cohesive and compelling restatement of Church teaching about sex, Saint John Paul II left us *Theology of the Body*, a series of 129 lectures given from 1979 to 1984, which communicate the transcendent beauty of human sexuality. This pontificate also bequeathed to us a newly revised Catechism of the Catholic Church, published in 1992. Together, Catholics of all ages have the tools we need to comprehend the Church's teaching on sexuality, and, with the help of grace from the Sacraments, to embrace these natural and supernatural truths, and live them.

Additionally, the Church has provided pastoral support for more than thirty years to those with same-sex attraction and their loved ones through two ministries: EnCourage for families and Courage for the individual. These ministries "promote close Christian friendships as an antidote to the kind of sexual activities that same-sex attracted are urged to adopt as part of the gay scene. Here, they can share their heavy cross with other like-minded Catholics and find the strength to live chastely," says Burman Skrable, a co-coordinator for EnCourage.

An Uphill Battle

A gay person's desire for intimacy, for a lifelong committed relationship, or for a feeling of belonging is natural to every human, man or woman. Catholicism teaches that the homosexual act is wrong, but that same-sex attraction is *not* a sin. For those with same-sex attraction who want to partake in the Sacraments—to say "Amen" and receive the Eucharist, or be absolved of sin and strengthened through Reconciliation—the desire to want to live chastely is required; as it is of all of us. What would motivate college-aged homosexuals to want to live chastely when the rest of society says they don't have to?

- •   ...a profound personal relationship with Jesus
- •   ...a deep reverence for the beauty of human sexuality
- •   ...an understanding of the nature of true sacrificial love
- •   ...an uncommon self-mastery
- •   ...a willingness to forgo marriage and children for a higher ideal
- •   ...an ability to see this life with the perspective of eternity; that "this slight momentary affliction is preparing us for an eternal weight of glory beyond all measure" (2 Corinthians 4:17)

All of the young people profiled once embraced the Catholicism they now shun, claiming that those principles are irreconcilable with a homosexual's nature. The Church acknowledges their difficulty: "The number of men and women who have deep-seated homosexual tendencies is not negligible...These persons are called to fulfill God's will in their lives and, if they are Christians, to unite to the sacrifice of the Lord's Cross the difficulties they may encounter from their condition" (CCC 2358).

A psychologist,[87] who has seen same-sex attracted young adults postulates that society does not provide these emerging adults with a language or conceptualization of love that is not sexual. "Many of the students I see are looking for connection and relationship but the only example of connection they see is sexual." Ryan, Jason, and Dave have, in fact, claimed at different times that emotional intimacy, not the act itself, drives them to seek the company of other gay men. "Much of my therapy focuses on what it means to be human and seen as a subject not an object, what embedded meaning their bodies have (as explained in *Theology of the Body*) and how they can connect to others in a deep, significant, and nonsexual way. Regardless of gender, sex, and sexuality, we have a very confused generation," the therapist concluded.

Mothers of Sorrow

Second only to the emotional turmoil felt by these same-sex attracted young people is the sorrow of their families…more specifically, their mothers. Ironically, their mothers draw strength from the very faith their children have forsaken. Yet, by the way that these mothers courageously share their stories we can see that their cross, too, is very heavy.

The Early Years:

Ryan's mom: Ryan was very different from his brothers—much more talkative and social. All through grade school and high school he struggled with anxiety

---

87 This psychologist declined to be identified so as to protect her professional relationships with clients.

and I think the anxiety was caused by the slow realization that he was gay. I remember crying myself to sleep on occasion worrying about it from the time he was ten years old.

Sally's mom: I was older when I had Sally and she was a little miracle. We dressed her in pink gingham and raised her as a little girl, but she struggled from the beginning. Was it environmental pollutants? A chromosomal disorder? My late age? Chemicals in the food supply...I don't know...she grew up chubby too. Maybe that had something to do with it? Urgh...I don't know...I don't think I realized how much influence I could have had.

Jason's mom: Jason has never told us he is gay, but...he was really depressed one night when he was young, sitting in his bedroom looking at his computer and I went in and knelt next to him. He said, "Mom, I am just not going to be the kind of boy you want me to be." We both cried. I understood what we were dealing with.

Dave's mom: I would have told you when Dave was about three or four that there was something different about him. A couple of times over the years I asked him if he thought he might be gay and he denied it and got very defensive. Neither his siblings nor my husband and I were surprised when he came to terms with it.

For their physical health:

Ryan's mom: I've read about what it can be like among gay men and I worry that Ryan will get caught up in drugs, or in a bad social scene, or in a hookup gone wrong and could literally die. He had one really scary experience which he told us about. I know he is smarter than he used to be, but I still worry...

Dave's mom: Dave's psychiatrist pointed out that he's not doing what other men like him are doing: drugs, pornography, self-harm, trolling the bars, promiscuity... Dave chose to go to a Catholic college and now he is living at home, surrounded by people with family values. These are safety nets he has set up for himself, whether he recognizes it or not. I have talked to him about being safe, safe, safe. I've been really open with him about his drinking and his overall health. He scared us with talk of suicide twice, but I think he's outgrown that and now he seems to be in a good place. Dave talks to a psychiatrist every six weeks, and that schedule works for him. The older he gets the more comfortable he is.

Sally's mom: In college, she went on antidepressants, became suicidal and checked herself into the psychiatric ward. Her friends were there for her and visited. She rallied, but when her LGBTQ friends graduated, Sally followed them without finishing school.

For their future:

Ryan's mom: When Ryan finally told us, my overwhelming thought was, "Whew, now maybe some emotional healing can begin." But it's still very difficult for everyone. He really wants a long-term committed relationship—a life companion—and I want that for him too. When he comes home, he sees the grandkids running around, and his married siblings go off to their rooms two-by-two. I wonder if it's hard for Ryan...But I believe that his way would not make him happy in the long run. He disagrees with me, of course.

Jason's mom: Jason just loves kids and I want that for him...children, his own progeny. What a great source of joy and satisfaction children are, especially as you age. I worry about loneliness...He may be very lonely one day...

Sally's mom: Sally is happy with her friends, still studying...she has many piercings and tattoos and she thinks they make her look beautiful! I just don't get it... but we're friends now. I keep in touch through Facebook and text her a couple times a week. I pray about it, and I think she will be fine, really just fine.

Dave's mom: Life is just easier when you're heterosexual. I know Dave asks, "why me?" because his other siblings are straight. For now, he has no interest in getting married. But I would like him to be in a relationship because I think the alternative is very lonely and pretty miserable.

For their faith:

Ryan's mom: I knew he had suffered emotionally for years, and that he was mad at God but it all became very clear when Ryan told us he was gay. We have talked very honestly about the faith and he told me one time, "I tried Catholicism. I prayed so hard when I was younger, and it didn't work out." He really did try to pray it all away. He says now, fifteen years later, that he finally feels free of the constraints Catholicism has put on him all these years and he is happy with his life.

Jason's mom: My husband is in complete denial, but I know...and it's the biggest sword in my side. Jason is at the top of my prayer list...I say every novena for him. I don't pray for anything else as fervently as for this. I have hope he will change. I don't know what I would have done differently...I just don't know...We are told it does not bring you salvation, so how can I accept it when I know it's not good for him? My other kids know, I think.

But my husband would never accept it, and so I just keep praying.

Sally's mom: When I talk to my daughter about religion and the Church she tells me, "I love Jesus, but His Church does not like me." In a book she read by Scott Hahn in high school, she crossed out "Marriage was made by God," and wrote in, "Marriage is a man-made construct." She does not practice her faith, yet when I told her about one of my troubles the other day, she said, "Oh Mom, I'm going to light a candle for you." I thought that was sweet. She is a good person.

Dave's mom: In high school, Dave became very religious, going to daily Mass and weekly confession. He told me later that he had been praying that he wouldn't be gay. When God didn't make Dave straight, he gave up on God. I pray every day that he comes back and I think it might be years…and not to the Catholic Church. He just feels that the Catholic Church doesn't have a place for him. I have given up on the idea that he'll ever become Catholic, but I hope he finds a Christian Church community so that he can have Christ in his life.

Making Burdens Light

As fellow Christians and imitators of Jesus Christ, we are called to welcome same-sex attracted people of good will into our lives and our pews. According to the Catechism, "They must be accepted with respect, compassion, and sensitivity. Every sign of unjust discrimination in their regard should be avoided" (CCC 2358). Yet, a 2013 Pew Research Center survey found that 79 percent of LGBTQ adults who practice a faith see the Catholic Church as unfriendly. Three in ten LGBTQ said they personally were made to feel unwelcome in a religious organization.[88]

Eve Tushnet, a Catholic gay author, describes the benefits of a Church with doors wide open to same-sex attracted individuals:

> One of the parish communities in which I've served a lot of time is my Church's ministry to gay and lesbian Catholics and our families and friends. This ministry is not the easiest one to work with. We try to "meet people where they are." We don't require you to have a position on the Church's teachings before you attend. That means meetings can sometimes feel like trying to herd not just cats, but cats plus dogs plus ferrets plus that one person who's gotta be a badger. But it also means that people who always thought celibacy destroyed the soul can get to know people whose souls are nurtured by fidelity to Church teachings. It means that people who might be antagonists if the subject were gay marriage can come together to reassure a mother whose son just came out to her—who is choking back tears as she asks what she did wrong and mourning because she believes her son is doomed to misery in both this life and the next. I've seen this solidarity and it's one of the most powerful things you can imagine.[89]

---

88 Caryle Murphy, "Lesbian Gay and Bisexual Americans Differ from General Public in their Religious Affiliations," Pew Research Center, May 26, 2015, accessed March 10, 2017, http://www.pewresearch.org/fact-tank/2015/05/26/lesbian-gay-and-bisexual-americans-differ-from-general-public-in-their-religious-affiliations.
89 Eve Tushnet, Gay and Catholic: Accepting My Sexuality, Finding Community, Living My Faith (Notre Dame, IN: Ave Maria Press, 2014), 141-142.

By drawing strength from Christ, same-sex attracted men and women may find the courage to live celibate, fruitful Christian lives. Where better to meet Christ than in our Churches, among our families, in our Catholic communities? Does this make you uncomfortable? Do you wonder how parish life would change? What kinds of conversations would happen at the dinner table? "You can't be talking about those radical agenda-driven gays, can you? Invite *them* to my house?" Ryan's mom thought that way...

Ryan asked one summer day if he could have a big party to celebrate his graduation and new job. He wanted to invite the extended family, his grade school and high school friends and his new gay friends, some of whom he warned were nontraditional. "I was conflicted," said Ryan's mom, "because I didn't want to seem to be normalizing the gay lifestyle, and, honestly, I worried about what my family would say." She and her husband prayed about it and decided to go ahead with the party. "I wasn't comfortable when a group of colorfully dressed men rounded the corner to mingle with the family but everyone handled it better than I seemed to," said Ryan's mom. "Under my breath, I quietly asked the Lord to be present, and then I gave it all over to Him. Thinking back on it, I've come to understand that Christ is the one who does the heavy lifting when it comes to conversion," she said. "All we had to do that day was offer hospitality and love the people Christ put in front of us."

Speaking in *The Joy of Love* about the family's obligation to evangelize, Pope Francis invites us to reach out to others without compromising our convictions in imitation of Jesus Christ.

We know that Jesus himself ate and drank with sinners (cf. Mark 2:16; Matthew 11:19), conversed with a Samaritan woman (cf. John 4:7-26), received Nicodemus by night (cf. John 3:1-21), allowed his feet to be anointed by a prostitute (cf. Luke 7:36-50) and did not hesitate to lay his hands on those who were sick (cf. Mark 1:40-45; 7:33). The same was true of his apostles, who did not look down on others, or cluster together in small and elite groups, cut off from the life of their people. Although the authorities harassed them, they nonetheless enjoyed the favor "of all the people" (Acts 2:47; cf. 4:21, 33; 5:13).[90]

College-aged men and women with same-sex attraction are at the peak of their physical sexual development, pummeled like everyone else by pornography, and affirmed in their same-sex attraction by most of their peers. They need our unconditional love—a love that doesn't compromise truth, but reaches out, invites, welcomes, and invests in the lives of our Christian brothers and sisters. "If one member suffers, all suffer together with it…" (1 Corinthians 12:26).

For whom are you called to be the face of Christ?

---

90 Pope Francis, The Joy of Love: On Love in the Family (Erlanger, KY: Beacon Publishing, 2015), 217.

PRAYER

Heavenly Father, you are a wise and loving Father of *all* of us. Your care and concern for each soul You've created is profound and unchanging. You weep with those emotionally, physically, or spiritually hurt by same-sex attraction and you accompany those suffering the consequences.

Help us comprehend the beauty of chastity. Raise up heroes in our culture to testify to the sanctity of chaste marriage, chaste celibacy and chaste single living. Show us, Lord, how to please you with our sexuality.

Please bless my child _____ and all those in college with him/her. Protect all those on college campuses from sexual sin.

We ask for all these graces through the intercession of your Blessed Mother, Virgin and Queen, Mary most Pure.

Questions for Reflection:

What is my immediate emotional response to homosexuality? Anger? Fear? Curiosity? Numbness? Never thought about it? I will write down at least three of my reactions. I will discuss my thoughts with the small group, or write a prayer asking for a deeper enlightenment.

Considering the relationships I have with those who are gay in my community, at work, or in another circle of influence, how well do I radiate the love of Christ to them?

Prayer Intentions:

Answered Prayers:

Prayer Practice:

The next time I am in a crowd of any size, I will scan the faces and make eye contact with someone I might not have otherwise noticed. I will offer him/her the smile of Christ, following the advice of Saint John of the Cross, "Where there is no love, put love, and there will be love."[91]

---

91 Letter from Saint John of the Cross to Madre María de la Encarnación, discalced Carmelite, July 6, 1591, Segovia, Spain.

Jesus replied, "Who is my mother, and who are my brothers?" (Matthew 12:48)

Lord, how can I love you more today than I did yesterday?

_____

_____

_____

_____

_____

_____

_____

_____

_____

_____

_____

_____

_____

_____

_____

_____

_____

CHAPTER 18:

PORNOGRAPHY: A MODERN PLAGUE

Jane noticed a change in her son midway through his sophomore year. She knew that his pre-med major at an Ivy League school was stressful, but until recently he had been able to juggle academics and a vibrant social life. But now his grades were slipping, his girlfriend was no longer, and he seemed unusually melancholy, even lonely, for the first time since leaving home. She grew particularly concerned when she learned that he was spending weekends alone in his dorm room instead of socializing with friends.

In recent decades, the relentless assault of our increasingly secular culture, spurred by information technology and social media, has plagued the emotional, spiritual and psychological development of our children in ways that parents never dreamed were possible. Sadly, pornography is wreaking havoc on college campuses, especially since the internet proffers cheap, fast, and anonymous around-the-clock access. Moreover, many parents of young adults have no idea how much pornography has changed since their childhood days when exposure was limited to magazine centerfolds or late-night movies. Today's internet pornography, by its very nature, can be shockingly graphic, violent, and dehumanizing—all one click away.

The last thing Jane would have suspected was a pornography addiction. Her son was raised in a strong Catholic home, was respectful of women, and had never been "caught" viewing pornography at home. Parents aren't the only ones who miss problems linked to pornography. Mental health professionals—the very ones who are treating college kids for depression and anxiety—often fail to connect pornography with a host of mental and physical health issues. And despite the growing cultural acceptance of pornography, users rarely discuss its hold on them, and instead withdraw from the world in shame, isolation and hopelessness.

Statistics tell the story: In a survey on pornography acceptance on college campuses across the United States, 87% of college-aged men and 31% of college-aged women reported viewing pornography.[92] The same survey also reports that 67% of college-aged men and 49% of college-aged women believe that consuming porn is acceptable. Porn has become ubiquitous and mainstream.

Parents often feel hurt, confused or somehow responsible for their child's porn exposure, but there is little to shield young adults at college. Internet pornography is free, and the supply is virtually as endless as the variety. Peer pressure coupled with unmonitored and unfiltered screen time can tempt the most well-intentioned student.

---

92 Carroll, J. S., Padilla-Walker, L. M., Nelson, L. J., Olson, C. D., Barry, C. M., & Madsen, S. D. (2008). Generation XXX: Pornography Acceptance and Use Among Emerging Adults. Journal of Adolescent Research, 23(1), 6-30. doi:10.1177/0743558407306348

A friend's daughter, Candace, corroborated the ease with which porn can be accessed at school. "Oh sure, it's, like, no big deal," she said without hesitation. "It's not unusual to see people watching porn on their computers. Some people are more into it than others. But really, nobody cares, it's just background noise sometimes."

Like any addictive behavior, some people are more prone to it than others. But even at the most basic level—call it background noise—pornographic images distort our basic understanding of human sexuality, and the integrity of the whole person, body and soul. Saint John Paul II's Theology of the Body calls the flesh good and valuable, first because God created it, and more so because God united Himself to it in the Incarnation.[93] In his pastoral letter, *Bought With a Price*, the Most Reverend Bishop Paul Loeverde put it this way: "God gave us the earthly gifts of sight and sex and ordered them towards a Heavenly end: everlasting life with Him. When we subvert use of those gifts, we lose interest in their true end. Our perspective gets stuck on earth and its low pleasures. Thus, we endanger not just our temporal relationships but our eternal destiny."[94]

Inoculation Against the Plague?

As Catholics, we have some powerful therapy to fight the enticement of pornography, (or any other plague): the Sacraments. Seeking forgiveness through Reconciliation

---

93 John Paul II (2006). A Theology of the Body: Man and Woman He Created Them. (Boston, MA: Pauline Books & Media).
94 Loeverde, Paul. (2014, March 19). Bought With a Price [Letter]. Catholic Diocese of Arlington, Arlington, VA.

is an essential step toward healing. While some people convince themselves that pornography is harmless, the human heart knows deep down how it distorts the way relationships were meant to be. As with any grave sin, guilt or shame may be keeping your child away from the confessional.

Luanne Griffin, a Catholic-trained psychology professional, recommends these tips for talking to a child who watches pornography:

- Open the conversation with a compassionate and understanding tone. You may find your child is relieved to talk about it. Remind him that God's love and mercy are infinite, and that grace received through Reconciliation will give him strength to overcome any challenge, but especially this one.

- Encourage him to receive the Holy Eucharist often, and spend time in Eucharistic Adoration, if possible.

- This may sound surprising, but sometimes it's best to tell your child that he can't trust himself to win this fight alone. The temptation and easy availability of pornography can overwhelm him. Ask him to install the filters to block porn on his computers and mobile devices.

- Seek the support of the college rector, or campus ministry. They can help to provide accountability on campus. They can also refer you to a variety of completely anonymous Catholic-based programs that provide help for recovery and healing.

- Entrust them to Our Lady. Pray the rosary daily and suggest that your child take the small step of praying three Hail Mary's each day for chastity and purity.

Pornography erodes chastity and purity, two virtues for which we have few contemporary, high-profile role models. Because so few young people live chastely in our hyper-sexualized society, many people believe that it's not possible for our youth to control their natural desires for sexual intimacy. We know this is a lie, a contradiction of the teachings of the Church, and a serious barrier to future happiness in marriage, family, or religious life. Freedom from pornography is essential for the flourishing of a Catholic Christian person made in the image of God.

The virtuous living of chastity or purity can powerfully impact others—even those not well-intentioned. Carla ran a very popular yoga class on campus. Three college lacrosse players joined the class one day, intending to ogle their spandex clad classmates and to mock Carla as she taught. Carla, it should be noted, was a toned, cherub-faced coed who, in addition to teaching yoga, sang "like an angel" for weekend liturgies and volunteered for campus ministry. As the yoga class began, the three men began cat-calling under their breath and causing other rude disruptions. Carla ignored their antics and, instead, treated them as serious students of yoga. She smiled at them sweetly, calmly corrected their form, and showed them the respect they had withheld from her. In short order, they were stunned to silence. In fact, they were so impressed with Carla that they became regulars in her class and advocates of yoga to their teammates. "Carla really has something special," her girlfriend told me. "Those boys knew it and they reacted to it," she says. Charisma? Maybe. Charity? Certainly. But, perhaps, the most potent of Carla's virtues was purity. The lacrosse players and many in her yoga class perceived it, although they couldn't put a name to it, and they reacted accordingly by giving her the respect she is due.

As mothers, we can fight pornography at large by taking the simple but effective step of eliminating it in all forms from our family life. We send a strong example to others when we are able to sincerely, humbly and cheerfully admit, "Nope, I didn't see that show," or "I don't listen to that band," or "I don't watch those kinds of movies. They make me too uncomfortable."

And as praying mothers, we can continue to rely on the aid of Our Lady, Most Pure, who specializes in helping and protecting her children from plagues like this of every kind.

PRAYER

Lord, few things demonstrate to me the power of evil in this world than the plague of pornography. Protect me, my child _____ and my whole family from exposure to pornography in any form. I am grateful that you "arm me with strength and keep my way secure" (2 Samuel 22:33). I love that You are Almighty and rely on your power to safeguard my family.

Questions for Reflection:

Knowing that my witness as a parent is powerful, I ask myself, how prevalent is pornography in our family life? Do we watch sexualized television shows? Do I know what apps my children use on their phones or ipads? Do I age-appropriately monitor/limit screen time in the home? Do we have an understanding, as a family, of what is and is not acceptable to watch/read/listen to? Journal and/or discuss.

How well prepared am I to broach the subject of pornography with my college-aged young adult? Am I confident in what the Church teaches? Do I know the psychological effects of exposure or addiction? Am I ready to be calm, loving and compassionate? Journal and/or discuss.

Prayer Intentions:

Answered Prayers:

Prayer Practice:

I will pay special attention this week to examples of chastity and purity in my life: in the media or modeled by others around me.

How can the young keep his way without fault? Only by observing your words. (Psalm 119:9)

Lord, how can I love you more today than I did yesterday?

_____

_____

_____

_____

_____

_____

_____

_____

_____

_____

_____

_____

_____

_____

_____

CHAPTER 19:

APPRECIATING THEIR GIFTS

Every spring, as I write congratulatory notes to the graduates in my life, I am reminded what a milestone graduation is and how universal the expectation is that they use their talents to better themselves and the world! Here's a sampling from this year's card selection:

Your graduation marks a new beginning with new opportunities waiting for you. You have all you need to make your dreams come true. Aim high and have fun doing what you love to do.

Like shining stars, every one of us has the potential to light up the darkness with our own particular brilliance.

And just for fun:

Respect your elders. We graduated without Wikipedia!
May your great college memories last longer than your
student loan payments.

The tassel was worth the hassle.

What will you say when it comes time to write out your child's graduation card? Of what will you be most proud? Do you ever wonder what our Lord will say? He is, after all, the giver of all good things, including college degrees. God has a plan for your child, as He says through the prophet Jeremiah: "For I know the plans I have for you, declares the Lord, plans for welfare and not for evil, to give you a future and a hope" (Jeremiah 29:11, English Standard Version, ESV). Of what will God be most proud at graduation?

How has God showered His gifts on your child? Does your child recognize them? Do you know what God has in mind for the use of his talents? Now's the time to assess. With a plethora of opportunities for academic, personal, and spiritual growth, the four years of college are ideal for identifying, unwrapping, examining, exploring, and using all of the gifts that God gives.

Natural gifts

Did your son inherit his father's athletic prowess? Does your daughter have your mathematical, left-sided brain? Natural talents come to us from God through our parents. God metes out to some great beauty, to others creativity, and to still others, a winning personality. He distributes these gifts according to His perfect will for our personal delight, for the good of others, and for His glory.

Many students enter college with an awareness of their natural giftedness, because they were recognized for their success in high school and marketed their skills during the application process. In some cases, their talent was rewarded with scholarship money or priority placement. But there are also plenty of students whose natural talents will develop in college or afterward. We were surprised, for example, when my freshman son turned down an invitation to sing with the *a capella* club—something he enjoyed in high school and said he wanted to continue. He chose, instead, to use his musical ear to learn languages in college. He is now pursuing a career in international food manufacturing and distribution.

Because our world so highly values natural talent, we can get lost in the accolades that come with our child's temporal success. It's easy to forget that God is the originator of every talent and that He has a plan for their use. It's our job to help our children discover and hone their talents and listen closely to hear what God's plans are. If they get derailed (or we do), God will graciously reorient us every time we glance in His direction. We need only stop…reflect…and thank Him for His gift using our own words or by praying a line of Scripture like, "I praise you, because I am wonderfully made; wonderful are your works" (Psalm 139:14).

Spiritual Gifts

In addition to natural gifts, God gives other more desirable but less obvious gifts, or charisms, to those who are open to the Holy Spirit. These "talents" would look out of place on a resume, but the recipient could change the world more readily than with a PhD. Scripture identifies supernatural gifts in four places (with some overlap): Romans 12:6-8, 1 Corinthians 12:8-10, 1 Corinthians 12:28, and Ephesians 4:11.

- To each individual the manifestation of the Spirit is given for some benefit. To one is given through the Spirit the expression of *wisdom*; to another the expression of *knowledge* according to the same Spirit; to another *faith* by the same Spirit; to another gifts of *healing* by the one Spirit; to another *mighty deeds*; to another *prophecy*; to another *discernment of spirits*; to another varieties of *tongues*; to another *interpretation of tongues*. (1 Corinthians 12:7-10) [emphasis added]

- Some people God has designated in the Church to be, first, apostles; second, prophets; third, teachers; then, mighty deeds; then, gifts of healing, assistance, administration, and varieties of tongues. (1 Corinthians 12:28)

- Since we have gifts that differ according to the grace given to us, let us exercise them: if prophecy, in proportion to the faith; if ministry, in ministering; if one is a teacher, in teaching; if one exhorts, in exhortation; if one contributes, in generosity; if one is over others, with diligence; if one does acts of mercy, with cheerfulness. (Romans 12:6-8)

- And he gave some as apostles, others as prophets, others as evangelists, others as pastors and teachers… (Ephesians 4:11)

As noted in chapter 7, we don't actually know exactly how many spiritual gifts there are, but God gives them to us for the benefit of others, according to Sherry Weddell, developer of the Spiritual Gifts Inventory and cofounder of the Catherine of Siena Institute.[95] In addition to the list from Saint Paul, Ms. Weddell has identified craftsmanship, hospitality, music, writing, encouragement, leadership and many others.

Spiritual gifts differ from natural talents in two important ways, according to Ms. Weddell. "Spiritual gifts are not inherited from our parents, but are given to us by the Holy Spirit," she says. These charisms are "supernaturally empowered" to help us "bear results for the Kingdom of God above and beyond our normal human abilities."[96]

Like natural talent, exercising spiritual gifts can be very gratifying, and that feeling can be a good way to recognize the gift in yourself or your child. A young friend with the spiritual gift of music says when she cantors at Mass, she is "in the zone." Music is her spiritual sweet spot. "I feel close to God and confident that He is giving to others through my singing," she says.

Perhaps less observable, Joey, a newly graduated senior, related how he feels college helped him grow in

95 The Catherine of Siena Institute equips parishes to form lay Catholics for their mission in the world. Sherry created the first gifts-discernment program designed especially for Catholics.
96 Eryn Huntington and Sherry Anne Weddell, Discerning Charisms (Colorado Springs: The Siena Institute Press, 2002), 6.

mercy toward others. "When I went to high school, I got great formation, but everything was black and white. In college, my faith grew a lot, because I was confronted with exponentially more situations, and even world issues, that caused me to pray and reflect," he says. "It got personal," he says, "when a guy—he was an interesting kid—wanted to hang out with us all the time. He always got into intense conversations that didn't make a lot of sense, and he suffered from depression. He was sad and lonely, so I tried to do little things to make his life better." When pressed to explain further, Joey says, "One weekend night he was texting me. He was having trouble with his roommates, and they had left for the night. He was alone and sad, so I went over there and just hung out with him. It was the right thing to do, even though I didn't want to go."

People who know you well can also identify spiritual gifts of which you might not be aware. For example, in my young friend Mary, I see a supernatural dose of fortitude. Entering college this fall, Mary wants to study communications because of her interest in social media. She says her strength lies in her determination to succeed. At age nineteen, she will leave her parent's home, wheelchair-bound by cerebral palsy, to go to college two states away. "I think it's my motivation that's my gift," she says. "I will not quit until I have to," she adds.

Acknowledging and nurturing natural and spiritual gifts is vital for reaching full human maturity, since our Lord intends for us to use them to benefit our neighbors. Each of us is an essential, irreplaceable part of His greater plan, and He's given us everything we need to accomplish His will.

So…is your child an apostle? An evangelist? A leader? Maybe a healer? Or an administrator or a poet/musician? Affirm him when you see these manifestations. He's cooperating with the Holy Spirit for God's glory! If there's no sign of gifts like these in his life yet, that's not unusual. Everyone has them. His have yet to be discovered. The first prerequisite is a strong relationship with God, which we have established is difficult to sustain on the average college campus. A parent's attentiveness, positivity, and fidelity to prayer are enough.

PRAYER

Heavenly Father, like all good fathers, You have given my family and me the perfect gifts to accompany us through this life. In Your fatherly love, You have distributed them according to Your perfect will. As a result, each of us shines as a unique reflection of You, bearing Your family resemblance. "Wonderful are Your works"! (Psalm 139:14)

Today, I want to thank You most especially for the natural and supernatural gifts You have given _____. (Spend a few minutes quietly recalling his gifts, thanking God after each one.)

Allow me, Lord, to recognize the giftedness in everyone as a glimmer of Your life within them. Help me to remain positive and peaceful as I watch while Your grace continues to manifest itself in my child and my family.

"I give thanks to You Lord, for You are *good*. Your love is eternal" (Psalm 107:1). [emphasis added] Amen.

Questions for Reflection:

What natural and spiritual gifts does my child have? How is he using them? Do I see giftedness where he does not? If so, how can I encourage him to explore this area of giftedness?

Prayer Intentions:

Answered Prayers:

Prayer Practice:

I will acknowledge my natural and supernatural gifts, and those of my family, with graciousness and humility. To compliments, I will respond with a sincere thank you and praise the True Giver of all good things in my heart.

And all differ according to the grace given us. (Romans 12:6)

Lord, how can I love you more today than I did yesterday?

_____

_____

_____

_____

_____

_____

_____

_____

_____

_____

_____

_____

_____

_____

_____

CHAPTER 20:

———— ⟨⟶⟩ ————

CAREER AND VOCATION

Imagine that God leads us through life by a strong two-ply rope. Intertwined are God's desires for our vocations and our careers. If we stay safe and secure tethered to this rope by following God's will, our rope draws many others to Christ, according to His divine plan.

Do you know what calling[s] God has given your child[ren]? Since college is such a unique time of discovery, we can be certain that our Lord is trying to get their attention. God's desire for their ultimate happiness is tied to their discernment of His will in these two areas. You can help by affirming their giftedness (see the previous chapter), by understanding the meaning of "call," by listening as they discern, and by praying.

Career

From the moment of creation, God intended for men and women to work (Exodus 20:9). Work "is an indispensable means which God has entrusted to us... to fill our days and make us sharers in God's creative power,"[97] according to Saint Jose María Escrivá. Knowing that honorable work can bring glory to God adds an important dimension to something generally considered a means to an end—financial stability, support of a family, personal development, or societal good.

Some college students consider their careers an extension of the long, laborious application process that began with the selection of AP courses in high school and ends in some kind of money-making venture. Others take a circuitous route, changing majors, transferring, taking time off, etc. Meg is the mother of three sons, and her oldest, John, hasn't graduated yet. "He's twenty-five, so it would be so nice for him to get the degree and have a career," she says, "but you can't take someone to a place he is not ready to go." Meg and her husband try to "let go" and lovingly accept John's prolonged college experience.

Whether your child makes a beeline to a fulfilling career or gets there in fits and starts, every parent needs divine perspective to properly support and encourage them. Knowing God is in control, you parent with grace in the power of the Holy Spirit. Without that understanding, you may transmit an anxiety that can zap the joy out of what could have been a glorious period of college exploration for your child.

In the end, it's not so much *what* they do with their talent, but *how* they do it. "To me," says Saint JoseMaría Escrivá, "every job that is not opposed to the divine law is good and noble, and capable of being raised to the

---

97 Saint JoseMaría Escrivá, Friends of God (Manila: Sinag-Tala Publishers, 1981), 85.

supernatural plane, that is, inserted into the constant flow of Love which defines the life of a child of God."[98]

Vocation

Every man, woman, and child is called to a vocation of holiness and to evangelize the world, the Catechism tells us (CCC 1533). But God pierces the deepest part of an individual with a more specific invitation to religious life, marriage, or single life. This vocational call becomes the practical means by which we bear fruit and find happiness in this world.

How does one discern such a significant call? God steers a moving ship, I told my daughter long ago. During retreats in her late teens, she wondered if she might have a "higher calling," a religious vocation, even though she really, really wanted to be married one day. She mistakenly assumed that religious life trumped a call to marriage and that God would ask "the more difficult thing" of her, rather than the vocation that made her heart sing.

Vocational discernment can be lengthy, confusing, and even painful, and my daughter spent years praying about it. At the same time, however, since she knew that God steers a moving ship, she moved! She followed up on a vocational pamphlet that was dropped by her door. The dates didn't work for her. She went to the dances at college and dated as much as college kids do. She sought regular spiritual direction from a lay consecrated woman. She made good friends of both sexes. Last year, after a two-year courtship, she married a wonderful man: handsome, kind, prayerful, and Catholic. Her vocation to marriage—

---

98 Escrivá, 90.

the one she always felt called to—was fulfilled by God, whose generosity is boundless.

Fr. Justin Huber[99] was studying investment strategies in college when his call began to reveal itself. "I was trying to answer the question, 'How ought I live to be happy?' looking at ways to make money," he explained. "During my research, I read that a significant number of American millionaires are very religious, and that got me thinking about religion," he said. So he asked to accompany a friend to Mass. "Doing something spiritually healthy felt good, like exercising or eating well, but I quickly realized that Catholicism had the ability to answer the most fundamental questions that had been with me my whole life, and bring me peace and joy," he said. A pivotal confession with a dynamic priestly mentor set the twenty-year-old firmly on the path to the priesthood. "That priest suggested the vocation to me, and it stuck," says Fr. Justin. "I began to see my identity not as a college student, but as a potential seminarian," he explained. "There were parties I didn't go to, more secular, superficial friendships dropped away, and I stopped dating," he said. "I began hanging around the Catholic Student Center, and it helped that one of my roommates was also discerning the priesthood," he said. As a junior and senior, he attended daily Mass, went to Confession twice a month, and sought spiritual direction to help him discern. But Fr. Justin also finished his engineering degree and worked, in the eventuality that he discerned the single or married life. After college, two years in the seminary, and four years studying in Rome, Fr. Justin Huber was ordained. An exceptional homilist

---

99 Fr. Justin Huber is a priest of the diocese of Washington D.C.

with an impressive intellect, he serves his diocese well with the gifts God has given him. "I became a priest because I want to hand on the faith the way it was given to me," he says. "And I learned that faith has everything you need in life," he adds.

Talented students don't always perceive their own gifts, according to Fr. James B. King, a rector in an all-male dorm at the University of Notre Dame. "One of our more important roles is to get them thinking about how to discern a vocation, not just a career—to think and pray about possibilities they had never imagined and realize that how one lives is at least as important as what one does. There are many people teaching in classrooms, operating in hospitals, and sitting on benches in courtrooms because someone said, 'I think you'd make a good (fill in the blank)' when it was the farthest thing from their own mind," he says. [100]

As parents watching our children mature and discern a vocational call, our own "two cents" can sometimes be less persuasive than wisely placed advice from another trusted adult. Augustine wasn't much older than our college-aged young adults when he met Saint Ambrose in 386 AD. At the time, Augustine, a brilliant orator and teacher, had rejected Catholicism, the faith of his childhood, despite the pleas of his mother, Monica. Saint Ambrose was able to sway his protégé back to the Church and baptize Augustine in 387 AD.

I like to think Ambrose's influence over Augustine was advanced by Monica's prayers. Augustine wouldn't listen

---

[100] James B. King, CSC, Known by Name, (Notre Dame: Corby Books, 2008), 111.

to his mother, (doesn't that sound familiar?) but Ambrose caught his attention so that the Lord could convert his soul. To that end, I regularly ask the Lord to send an "Ambrose" into the life of my children when they won't listen to me. I recommend the same to you!

PRAYER

Heavenly Father, I praise You for the glory of Your gifts of career and vocation. You have allowed us to cooperate in Your ongoing creation by sharing with each of us the life of the Trinity so that we can, in turn, share this love with others.

Lord, You have a beautiful life plan for my child _____. Inspire him to work for Your glory, to follow a career path that will bring him personal fulfilment and contribute to the greater good. Allow the vocation You have given him to take root in his soul and flourish so that Your every desire for him is fulfilled. Give him zeal for his mission to share the Gospel, the fruits of which only You know.

I ask for the intercession of Saint Ambrose, Bishop and Doctor of the Church. Please send advocates to my child _____ to help him faithfully fulfil the mandate to work for the glory of God and the good of mankind. Amen.

Questions for Reflection:

Am I open and supportive of the vocation to which God calls my child? If so, how? If not, why?

Prayer Intentions:

Answered Prayers:

Prayer Practice:

Does my child feel called to a particular career or vocation? If not, what help does he need? Career counseling? Spiritual direction? Mentorship? I will prayerfully discern how I can help, or if I know an "Ambrose" with influence.

But let our people, too, learn to devote themselves to good works to supply urgent needs, so that they may not be unproductive. (Titus 3:14)

Lord, how can I love you more today than I did yesterday?

_____

_____

_____

_____

_____

_____

_____

_____

_____

_____

_____

_____

_____

_____

_____

CHAPTER 21:

―――――――――――――――――◦―――――――――――――――――

OUR HIGHEST CALLING—MISSION

"Christ has no body now, but yours.
No hands, no feet on earth, but yours.
Yours are the eyes through which
Christ looks compassion into the world.
Yours are the feet
with which Christ walks to do good.
Yours are the hands
with which Christ blesses the world."
--St. Teresa of Avila

As the oldest daughter in a large family, Cate grew up thinking of and caring for others. The summer after her first year of college, she announced that she wanted to engage in some type of service project. Her mother, Louisa, expressed no surprise. The next logical inquiry, though, was what would Cate do and where? Based on the emailed requests Louisa frequently received for funding from college students embarking on various mission trips, she says that "it seems in vogue to do mission work abroad that involved digging a well, bringing much needed medical supplies, or spreading the faith in third world countries." Cate, though, desired to remain in the States and work with children in some capacity. She found a summer camp for autistic children and teens in her home state on the Atlantic seaboard.

For this generation of college-aged young adults, humanitarian mission work is indeed "in vogue." And these young adults often carry their desire to serve beyond college and into the workplace, according to a 2016 Gallup study. "Millennials want to understand how they fit in with their jobs, teams, and companies. They look for work that fuels their sense of purpose and makes them feel important."[101]

To be united in mission and career is ideal, as long as there's a proper understanding of *mission*. Read what our Lord's representatives, three recent popes, explain as the Catholic meaning of mission.

- To all people you bring the peace of Christ, and if they do not welcome it, you go ahead just the same…To you, young people, to you boys and girls I ask: you, are you brave enough for this, do you have the courage to hear the voice of Jesus?… Everyone must be a missionary, everyone can hear that call of Jesus and go forth and proclaim the Kingdom! (Pope Francis, July 7, 2013, Angelus)

- Today, as never before, the Church has the opportunity of bringing the Gospel, by witness and word, to all people and nations. I see the dawning of a new missionary age, which will become a

---

101 Amy Adkins, "What Millennials Want from Work and Life," Gallup, May 11, 2016, http://www.gallup.com/businessjournal/191435/millennials-work-life.aspx?utm_source=genericbutton&utm_medium=organic&utm_campaign=sharing.

radiant day bearing an abundant harvest, if all Christians, and missionaries and young Churches in particular, respond with generosity and holiness to the calls and challenges of our time. (Saint John Paul II, Redemptoris Missio #92)

- The Church is missionary by her very nature. We cannot keep to ourselves the words of eternal life given to us in our encounter with Jesus Christ: they are meant for everyone. (Pope Emeritus Benedict XIV, Verbum Domini, 2010)

The Church equates mission with evangelization. However, Catholics, in general, are not known for their willingness to evangelize. Scott Hahn, author, speaker and professor at Franciscan University of Steubenville attributes our reluctance to several factors: a breakdown in catechesis—we don't know our faith, so we don't share it; unfortunate experiences with evangelical proselytizers who attack our faith while trying to convert us; an "American attitude" that faith is a private matter; and a false notion that tolerance of others is the highest virtue.[102]

The concept of *evangelization* does not resonate with most college students either. "When I hear that word, I think of going door-to-door," says college sophomore Amy. "My faith is one of the most important things to me, but I don't like that approach, although there's merit to it," she adds. "At my school, people aren't in your face about their faith, but then you walk by the chapel and there they are, praying. That's encouraging and inspiring

---

102 Scott Hahn, Evangelizing Catholics: A Mission Manual for the New Evangelization (Huntington, IN: Our Sunday Visitor Publishing Division, 2014), pp.28-36.

to me," Amy says. "Living life in a Christian way speaks for itself," she adds.

Perhaps we misunderstand the meaning of the word, "evangelization." According to Christian author Gabe Lyons, this generation of Christians wants "to infuse the world with beauty, grace, justice and love," he says.[103]

The next Christians, Lyons says, are:

- Provoked, not offended
- Creators, not critics
- Called, not employed
- Grounded, not distracted
- In community, not alone
- Civil, not divisive
- Countercultural, not "relevant"

It's an appealingly modern take on evangelization—one that our college students can embrace, because, as the Gallup study reported, they are "a largely optimistic group, and they believe that life and work should be worthwhile and have meaning. They want to learn and grow."[104] That attitude is good for everyone!

Bella chose to forgo college and serve the poor in a faraway country for two years as a missionary affiliated with a religious organization. She was accompanied by consecrated women and they worked as a team to provide prayer support and faith-based youth activities for the needy population there. Bella subscribed to the prayer

---

103 Gabe Lyons, The Next Christians (Colorado Springs: Multnomah Books, 2010), 47.
104 Gallup, Inc. "What Millennials Want from Work and Life." Gallup. com. May 11, 2016. Accessed May 28, 2018. http://www.gallup.com/businessjournal/191435/millennials-work-life.aspx?utm_source=alert&utm_medium=email&utm_content=morelink&utm_campaign=syndication.

regime of the order and worked day after day to evangelize the youth. It was an intensely spiritual experience, she says. When the time came for college, Bella easily won a service scholarship at a small Catholic college. Her transition to college life was difficult because of the intense cultural shift she experienced, but she roomed with a companion from the mission, so they assimilated into college together, which made it easier for both of them.

Discerning one's mission requires looking with a compassionate heart upon those hurting in the world and desiring positive change. Mission-based organizations strive to solve the world's problems in an orchestrated way. But mission also happens person-to-person, one soul at a time, according to the promptings of the Holy Spirit in a missionary soul. Mission is never imposed on us by God, nor do we take it up out of fear or duty. In the words of Pope Francis, a missionary simply says, "I am giving you what gives me joy."[105] We are all called to serve God and others in this way.

A prayerful person evangelizes for at least three reasons. First, she knows that every soul has incomparable value because Christ shed his blood for each one. Secondly, she realizes that we are all called to know, love and serve the Lord and that every soul has a part to play in the coming of the kingdom of God. Finally, she knows that by doing good to a soul, we do good to Christ in his Mystical Body.[106]

105 Pope Francis, Papal audience, January 30, 2016.
106 Raoul Plus, Radiating Christ: An Appeal to Roman Catholics (Oak Lawn, IL: CMJ Associates, 1998), 13.

Models of Service

Bella, Cate and thousands of other young adults have chosen to serve the poor or disadvantaged in answer to a call from God. Often, however, these young adults were disposed to serve because they learned it first at home. Cate's father had greatly influenced her by stories he told from his own experience working summers during college with mentally and physically disabled adults. As Cate recalled, "He told me that people challenged him to show through service that he truly believed in the inherent value of these souls." Cate sought out a similar experience— genuine interaction with individuals with whom it was difficult to work or to communicate.

Jesus teaches us *all* how to serve in Mark 6:30-44. The story unfolds as Jesus invites his companions to leave the crowds and rest with him in a quiet place. They have been so busy ministering that they haven't even had the chance to eat, the Scripture says. When they arrive at their destination, however, throngs of people greet them, eager to be with Jesus. His heart is so moved that he heals and teaches them. Here's our first lesson. To imitate Jesus, our hearts must be expansive enough to occasionally lay aside our own legitimate needs for those who do not know Christ. Servants of Christ sacrifice for others—even when they're ravenous and dog-tired. Good works spring from souls enkindled with this kind of love.

The gospel tells us that Jesus' disciples spent countless more hours tending to the crowd while he taught. As evening approached, they said to Jesus, "Dismiss [the crowd] so that they can go to the surrounding farms and villages and buy themselves something to eat." Jesus knew it was a lonely place and that his friends were tired and hungry, but he replied, "You give them something to eat" (Mark 6:37).

At certain moments in our lives, Jesus looks at each of us and says: *You* work at the soup kitchen tomorrow and smile at each soul with My eyes. *You* host a prayer group in your home and welcome the eccentric neighbor with open arms. *You* organize meals for the family who is grieving and invite the larger community to participate. We might panic and answer, "I can't. There's no time. I don't know how..." The apostles expressed it this way: "Are we to buy two hundred days' wages worth of food and give it to them to eat?"

In the Gospel account, the apostles are not asked to perform miracles. They are told to do some very simple things. "Go and see" how many loaves there are among the people, Jesus says. They find five loaves and two fishes. Next, he asks them to seat the crowd into groups. They look on as Jesus multiplies the loaves and fishes. They collect leftovers. Jesus invites us to step out in faith and share in large or small ways our love with others! Then He gives us every means to accomplish what He asks. He does all the heavy-lifting. He'll do the same for us. He does the same for our children.

The Need Is Great

Who can doubt that our world needs ambassadors of Christ's love? Our culture wears battle scars imposed by modernity: secular humanism, abortion, divorce, rampant pornography, disintegration of the family. Conflicts rage on every front: shootings in our high schools, murder stemming from internet chat rooms—we feel almost palpably an undercurrent of rage and anger. We know, beyond doubt, that evil is at work. St. Paul tells us that "the time will come when people will not tolerate sound doctrine, but following their own desires and insatiable curiosity, will accumulate teachers and will stop listening to the truth in all circumstances." His advice? "…Be self-possessed in all circumstances; put up with hardship; perform the work of an evangelist; fulfill your ministry" (2 Timothy 4:2-6).

Every person possesses human life that is uniquely her own. She also expresses the hope of her Maker that she will lovingly correspond to grace and place her humanity at the service of others, in imitation of him. A woman who says, "I love you. Send me," is pleasing her Lord, no matter how many times she trembles, hesitates or fails. With God's grace, her life will reflect a uniquely creative fruitfulness. One day, after a valiant fight, she will take her last breath, forever surrender her weapons, and receive a long-awaited hero's welcome. "Well done, good and faithful servant…Come share in your master's happiness" (Matt. 25:21). For now, however, she remains engaged in the battle, striving to radiate Christ in everything she says and does. She is a valiant soldier: an apostle for Christ.

PRAYER

Dear Lord, I admire the people you have called to change the world, but Mother Teresa I am not! Please instill in my heart a deep sense of sacrificial love for my family, and for the larger community in which you have placed me. Give me a desire to serve others, and a zeal to spread Your Gospel message. With these graces, I hope to be a witness and inspiration to my child _____ of a humble servant fulfilling her God-given mission.

Help me also, Lord, to be supportive to my child when she discerns her calling to serve you with her life in whatever way You call her. I pray she hears Your call clearly and generously complies with all You ask of her. Lord, make her holy and bring her, with our whole family, to Heaven one day.

Questions for Reflection:

How have I modeled for my college-aged young adult an evangelizing spirit in my home? At work? When I volunteer?

What are my obstacles, if any, to fulfilling the mission to evangelize the Lord calls me to? How do I support and encourage my child in her mission as well?

Prayer Intentions:

Answered Prayers:

Prayer Practice:

Jesus tells us to assess our resources before we build a tower (Luke 14:27-29). I will spend this week in prayer evaluating my strengths and weaknesses, and read it over repeatedly, giving thanks to God. I will prayerfully consider how to put these gifts at the Lord's service at home, at work, in his Church, or for the community and how to model, encourage and support my children in their own missions.

But how can they call on him in whom they have not believed? And how can they believe in him of whom they have not heard? And how can they hear without someone to preach? And how can people preach unless they are sent? As it is written, "How beautiful are the feet of those who bring [the] good news!" (Romans 10:14-15)

Lord, how can I love you more today than I did yesterday?

_____

_____

_____

_____

_____

_____

_____

_____

_____

_____

_____

_____

_____

Section III

WHEN WE DOUBT

CHAPTER 22:

FINDING PEACE WHEN COLLEGE ISN'T AN OPTION

Living in a suburb where nearly every child goes to college, Ellen navigated the typical conversation starters with some trepidation: "How are your kids doing? How old are they now? Oh, wonderful…where do they go to school?" It was challenging to offer a response that did not reveal too much personal information about her daughter Anna's life, yet addressed the question head-on. The simple truth: the twenty-year-old had withdrawn from community college—for the second time—and her future college enrollment was uncertain. Ellen, who counsels students preparing for college, knows very well that not everyone graduates in four years, and that some don't graduate at all, "but it feels so different, when it's your own child," she said. Is Ellen despondent? Angry? Frustrated? Or even embarrassed? Surprisingly not. "Last Tuesday, I came out of the chapel with the most remarkable peace," said Ellen. "I was almost levitating," she joked.

Ellen's peace is of the supernatural variety—a peace "surpassing all understanding" (Philippians 4:7), borne of her fidelity to prayer. Jesus first gave this peace to his disciples immediately after His resurrection. "Peace I leave with you; my peace I give to you. Not as the world gives do I give it to you. Do not let your hearts be troubled or afraid" (John 14:27). His peace is a gift given to souls who draw close to receive it. Yet, when we're anxious or afraid, the last person we tend to trust is the one who can fix everything: Jesus.

Seventeen years ago, Ellen's faith was shaken when doctors confirmed that Anna had juvenile diabetes. A later diagnosis of celiac disease complicated Anna's dietary regimen and probably contributed to the deterioration of her mental and physical health. When Anna went from a happy eighth grader to a depressed high schooler and eventually dropped out altogether, "life became torturous," Ellen said. "I even questioned the use of praying," Ellen said. "We saw doctors, we worked with the school, we would try to be with our other two younger kids, but it was one disappointing, discouraging thing after another," she said. "I subconsciously took the attitude with God that, since He didn't seem to be responding to my prayers, He must be off doing His own thing."

Meanwhile, Anna spent difficult days that turned into months getting a GED[107] and taking the SAT to prepare for college while working part-time. She was not managing her illnesses well, which caused a tremendous strain on the family. At wit's end, Ellen eventually drew inspiration from her husband who attended daily Mass and visited Jesus in the Blessed Sacrament at the parish Adoration chapel. "I wasn't very good at getting there, but one Sunday at Mass, as I was thinking about it, the

---

107 General Education Development, a high-school certification.

pastor invited people to sign up for specific hours before the Blessed Sacrament," Ellen said. She signed up for one hour weekly.

The time Ellen spent with Jesus in Adoration didn't bring her peace instantaneously. "I was so distracted at Adoration that I was becoming discouraged. I started feeling that I haven't been as good a person as I could have been, and I felt a little like what was going on with Anna was my fault," she explained. The Catechism teaches that distraction is a "habitual difficulty in prayer. To set about hunting down distractions would be to fall into their trap, when all that is necessary is to turn back to our heart..." (CCC 2729).

Our Lord intervened, sending Ellen a spiritual companion for her holy hours in the person of Father Jacque Philippe. "I've read all his books," Ellen said, "but the most helpful has been *Searching for and Maintaining Peace.*" Father Philippe's writings "hold you to account but don't beat you down," she said. "Through Saint Thèrése of Lisieux and Saint Teresa of Avila, who are often quoted, I began to understand that I was making myself too big in all of this. In a beautiful way, I started to realize my littleness and to trust...fully trust...in God's love for me and for my children. I slowly began to become more peaceful even though our outward circumstances had not markedly changed," she said.

At Adoration, Ellen says she often feels as if God is talking directly to her. Last Tuesday, she was especially consoled when she read from a chapter on confronting the sufferings of those close to us. "One thing is certain: God loves our dear ones infinitely more than we do, and infinitely better. He wants us to believe in this love, and also to know how to entrust those who are dear to us into His hands. And this will often be a much more efficacious way of helping them."[108]

The peace that Ellen now feels has positively impacted her home life and her relationship with Anna. "I approach Anna differently these days. She is much more inclined to hear what I have to say if I'm not agitated. And, I'm not as frustrated, thinking that I can change things by myself. This is good for both of us," said Ellen.

Anna's life is still not unfolding the way Ellen would choose for her, but Ellen draws spiritual consolation from two recent developments. Anna agreed to enroll in a trial which requires wearing a continuous glucose monitor. Ellen hopes it will help Anna manage her blood sugar levels more efficiently. While she was at the office, Anna met a nurse who convinced her to follow a gluten-free diet to address her celiac disease, finally. "I had told her all of this before, but this time she listened," Ellen said. "These little glimmers of hope for her physical well-being have been so uplifting to us! I consider them tangible answers to prayer."

Ellen acknowledges that prayer has also helped her appreciate God's perfect timing in her life. "I'm growing in my faith—maybe later than I would have liked—but I believe I am reading these books at a time when I really need them. They really set me straight, reminding me that I need to let go." Ellen now knows that God is not, "off doing His own thing." Instead, God is helping her to trust

108 Jacques Philippe, Searching for and Maintaining Peace: A Small Treatise on Peace of Heart (New York: Alba House, 2002), 48.

in His plan for Anna and for the whole family. "I don't have the same sadness about Anna's future. Whatever happens, God is with us. He has always been with us."

PRAYER

God my Father, You are the source of all peace. Your Son, our Lord Jesus Christ, is the Prince of peace. Our Blessed Mother, Mary, is the Queen of Peace. You mention "peace" in the Scriptures more than four hundred times. Through the Holy Spirit, I receive the fruit of peace. As Jesus brought the gift of peace to His disciples on the eve of His resurrection, I ask you Father for this same gift. Shower me, my child _____ and my whole family with Your peace.

When I am distracted in prayer, be my peace, Lord.

Help me to be faithful to my time of prayer.

When I am worried about my child _____, be my peace, Lord.

When I dwell on past circumstances, be my peace, Lord.

When I fret about the future, be my peace, Lord.

When I resist surrendering to You and try to control things, be my peace, Lord.

When I worry about what others think, be my peace, Lord.

Lord, you know better than I do how I need Your peace. I trust in You and praise Your name. Amen.

Questions for Reflection:

Peace is a fruit of the Holy Spirit. What spiritual dispositions, thoughts, or attitudes promote peace in a soul? Conversely, identify some dispositions that wreak havoc with peace in the soul. What is their origin?

Prayer Intentions:

Answered Prayers:

Prayer Practice:

What has caused me to worry in the last twenty-four to forty-eight hours? (Make a list of each circumstance—big or small.) Read over the list, adding each "worry" to the prayer above, followed by, be my peace, Lord. Pray the prayer and repeat as necessary.

"When we are powerless, let us be quiet and let God act. How many people lose their peace because they want, at any price, to change those around them!" Searching for and Maintaining Peace, p. 55.

Lord, how can I love you more today than I did yesterday?

_____

_____

_____

_____

_____

_____

_____

_____

_____

_____

_____

_____

_____

_____

CHAPTER 23:

ARE PRAYERS ALWAYS ANSWERED?

When Nancy said good-bye to her daughter at college, she felt the predictable tug at her heartstrings, but immense relief was the prevailing emotion. Gail had given her parents some trouble in high school and continued to push back all summer leading up to her departure for college. Nancy always worried about Gail, and (by her own admission) hovered too much, straining their relationship. She had hoped the distance between them now would do Gail some good.

It was not to be. After several weeks, Nancy could see Gail was doing well academically, but she had many visits from high school friends—the very friends Nancy worried were a dangerous influence. Gail related stories that fueled Nancy's fears.

Nevertheless, Nancy began to realize that Gail would build strong bonds elsewhere if Nancy couldn't stop herself from nagging. She tried valiantly not to be such a prickly presence in Gail's life, striving instead to radiate cheerfulness. Still she found herself being confrontational, strangled by anxiety, frustrated by Gail's ongoing misbehavior.

As Gail's second semester began, Nancy had had enough of her own emotional ups and downs. She desperately wanted peace of mind, so she decided to go on a retreat to pray for herself and for Gail.

Nancy had been on retreats before, and once she arrived, she quickly settled into the silence, reflecting deeply on her relationship with Gail and God's love for both of them. The first evening's talk focused on trusting God. The retreat master offered a simple prayer: "There's nothing to worry about. It's not important. And if it is important, why worry?"

The Holy Spirit convicted Nancy when she heard that prayer. "Why do I worry?" she thought. "God is all-powerful. The worry is only hurting Gail and others I love."

Nancy said that she began praying those lines over and over and felt God's peace entering her heart in a new way. In fact, she lulled herself to sleep that night repeating the phrase, praying for Gail.

At 4:30 a.m., Nancy awoke to her cellphone buzzing. Gail had texted a crude, disjointed message—words no mother wants to read—implying that Gail was out carousing and who knew what else? Nancy was devastated. "It was night" (John 13:30).

Unable to reach Gail or her husband, Nancy feverishly prayed the phrases she had heard, counting on God to be in control of this situation she was too far away to manage. Was this a test? she asked herself. Could she trust in God when her inner voice was screaming, "Get to that campus *now*, bring Gail home, and lock her up!"

Nancy tossed and turned for the rest of the night, drowning in turmoil. But the little prayer stayed in the forefront of her mind, and she says she even had a certain vague peace that things would *eventually* be all right. Later that morning, Nancy's husband called. He had received a similar text from Gail, and it now looked as if Gail's phone was turned off. No one could reach her. Together they decided that he would drive over to the school to check on Gail right away. But first, Nancy shared with him what she had been praying about and asked him, unlikely as it seemed, to presume Gail was innocent until proven otherwise. If the worst were proven to be true, only then would he take appropriate action.

Gail's father arrived at the dorm just as Gail and some friends were happily bounding down the front steps. Gail greeted him with clear eyes, a wide smile, and a happy disposition. She shared that she had lost her phone at a party the previous night. She knew nothing of the texts her parents had received. Gail and her relieved father spent the rest of that day together. Trust had been built between them instead of eroded by hasty and wrongful accusation.

Gail continued to try her parents' patience during college, but Nancy persevered in prayer. Very recently, the Lord rewarded her faithfulness with a little miracle, she says. Gail uncharacteristically invited her mom to "go for a walk and say the rosary together." Astounded and grateful, Nancy prayed that rosary with gratitude for the care God and His Blessed Mother had shown her and Gail over those five difficult years.

When, Where, and How

Everyone who prays has some experience of petitions that seem to go unanswered. The waiting is painful. We begin to wonder, to doubt, to wring our hands. Sometimes, no matter how serious our concerns or how much we plead, nothing seems to change. Or, as in Nancy's case, the very opposite of what we prayed for actually happens. How we respond in times like these depends on how we think about God.

Seeing the Big Picture

Our five senses put us in touch with the world around us, but wonderful as they are, they can lead us astray when it comes to knowing what's really going on from God's perspective. The Lord reminds us through Scripture, "My thoughts are not your thoughts, nor are your ways my ways...For as the Heavens are higher than the earth, so are my ways higher than your ways, my thoughts higher than your thoughts" (Isaiah 55:8-9).

By relying solely on our human understanding of God's ways, we almost certainly jump to the wrong conclusions. This never happened more tragically than to the Pharisees of Jesus' time. They heard the Son of God preach in their temples. They witnessed His miracles. Jesus was so close they could have hugged Him had they wanted to. But the Pharisees remained deaf, dumb, and blind to Jesus' true identity, because they clung to a false notion and their human pride.

Some in the crowd who heard these words said, "This is truly the Prophet." Others said, "This is the Messiah." But others said, "The Messiah will not come from

Galilee, will he? Does not scripture say that the Messiah will be of David's family and come from Bethlehem, the village where David lived?" (John 7:42)

How could it be that the Pharisees did not know where Jesus had been born? They interrogated Him on multiple occasions. Perhaps they were so wrapped up in the threat this Prophet posed to their authority, or so preoccupied keeping the political peace, that they neglected to ask Jesus the simple question that might have confirmed His messianic mission to them.

That's exactly what can happen to us! When we really want something from God—especially where our children are concerned—fear, anxiety, or impatience can blind us to God's miraculous workings in our lives. Churning with emotion, we validate our prayer by how we feel, and we lose our humble disposition before Him. We're so sure we're seeing clearly—that God is not answering and doesn't care—that we challenge Him with emotional fist-shaking or worse. Full of angst, we forget that God is a loving Father and has our best interest at heart.

Anna felt this frustration. Her daughter, Joy, was a sophomore at a prestigious conservatory-based college for the performing arts. A contemporary dance major, Joy was almost six feet tall, had endured two operations on her ankles, and said her shoulder was freezing up. She also wasn't getting cast into major dance roles but still loved dancing. Afraid for Joy's health, Anna was convinced her daughter needed to transfer to a state school to widen her career options. "There was also a financial pull," she adds. Joy reluctantly agreed to move, but she was anxious about the academics, didn't want to leave her friends, and was angry with Anna. One week before Joy had to accept, a relative came forward to help with tuition at the conservatory. Joy finished college and now dances in New York City. Anna, a prayerful woman, says that this experience was a wake-up call. "I was certain I understood what was best for Joy, but God knew exactly what she (and I) needed and made it possible. I was humbled and have a new reverence for the power God has to work all things for our good, even when we're clouded by egotism or anxiety," she concluded.

The Catechism tells us that all of our petitions should be "founded on the prayer of the Spirit in us and on the faithful love of the Father who has given us his only Son" (CCC 2739). When we pray that way, the first fruits of our prayer are hearts made more like Jesus', which enable us to wait on His answers to prayer, acquiesce to His timetable, and accept the unexpected with grace.

Bold, Yet Childlike

Little children don't know the meaning of impossible, right? The Catechism teaches us to pray in trust and boldness as children, to "obtain all that we ask in his name, even more than any particular thing: the Holy Spirit himself, who contains all gifts" (CCC 2741). How willing are we to put aside our preconceived notions—whatever they are—and invite the Holy Spirit into our hearts to convince us our loving Father is acting in our best interest? God abundantly rewards this kind of filial trust, as the life of Elisabeth Leseur illustrates.

The French laywoman Elisabeth Leseur, who lived from 1866 to 1914, married an atheist husband, Felix, who cruelly persecuted her for her faith. She offered everything up for his conversion—the teasing, the public humiliation (they were wealthy members of high society), and her subsequent battle with breast cancer. She saw no change in Felix but persevered in prayer for him to her death. When her husband read her diary after she died, in which she recorded her prayers and sufferings, he converted to Catholicism, became a priest, and spearheaded her cause for canonization.[109]

Perseverance

Elisabeth embodied perseverance by praying until her death for her husband's conversion. Our persistence in prayer may not always get us what we want when we want it (God is not a genie, after all), but we can trust that we will receive something better: God will be actively drawing us closer to Himself. He is always faithful. When we pray, we are to be patient and hope! "Faith asks, knowing the Father hears us. Hope waits for His reply. Love accepts that reply with joy," said Mother Angelica[110], founder of EWTN.

---

109 Elisabeth Leseur, My Spirit Rejoices (Manchester: Sophia Institute Press, 1996).
110 Mother M. Angelica, Healing Your Faith vs Faith Healing, Electronic Copyright © 1999 EWTN. (Accessed April 16, 2016).

PRAYER

Dearest Father, You are all-powerful and perfectly loving. You know how my heart aches as I pray for my child _____. It is painful to watch her make mistakes and live out the consequences. And it is very difficult to wait on Your action in her life. So I beg You once again, Father, to protect her. Teach her. Guide her. Wrap Your loving arms around her and keep her from harm.

And while I wait for You to act, Father, send me peace—superabundant, all-consuming, otherworldly peace. Help me also to radiate Your peace to her in all of our conversations. Fill me with Your Holy Spirit so that I can't help but reflect Your love for her and share it with my family.

I trust in Your fatherly love, and whether I see an answer to my prayer or not, I know You are acting in our lives for our greater good and Your glory. I will persevere in prayer and, by my effort, express my trust and confidence in Your holy will. Amen.

Questions for Reflection:

What is my disposition before God when I am earnestly praying for my child? Anxious and fearful? Determined and forceful? Or simple and childlike? Trusting? Believing that the Holy Spirit is all I really need in any situation?

What resources are available to me to help me persevere in prayer?

Prayer Intentions:

Answered Prayers:

Prayer Practice:

Relying on the power of the Holy Spirit, I will persevere in praying for my child's needs and the needs of my family…by praying _____ [what prayer you will say] at _____ [time] for _____ [how many days].

Wait for the Lord; be strong, and let your heart take courage; yea, wait for the Lord! (Psalm 27:14, RSV)

Lord, how can I love you more today than I did yesterday?

_____

_____

_____

_____

_____

_____

_____

_____

_____

_____

_____

_____

_____

_____

_____

_____

CHAPTER 24:

PRACTICING...GULP...FORGIVENESS

Marsha had never been so angry at her son, Dave, as she was at his college graduation. The whole family had looked forward to this first familial milestone for weeks. The siblings were excited to travel, to see their oldest brother again, and to celebrate for a whole weekend together. Marsha says that trouble began before they even arrived to campus. Distracted by all-that-is-college, Dave failed to transmit the ceremony details to Marsha before the deadline had passed. Tickets to the Saturday event had become scarce. Additionally, the family was scheduled to arrive *after* a special awards ceremony to be held on Friday night. "How could he have been so careless?" Marsha thought.

Once the family arrived, events swirled downward until Marsha was beside herself with disappointment and frustration. Dave seemed to have no time for the family, choosing to celebrate instead for the "last time" with his roommates. The morning of graduation, he missed his cue in line because he had been up all night partying with friends. He and his two friends were the only ones in the class who wore no miter caps. When questioned about it,

Dave replied, "We were late, and I couldn't find mine at the last minute."

"His blasé attitude hurt my feelings beyond telling," Marsha said. On Sunday, as the family prepared to return home, they stopped by Dave's off-campus house to pick up some items to bring home in the car. "The house was filthy. Obvious signs of partying were strewn everywhere. From the look of things, he and his roommates were in danger of losing their security deposit and being fined for the condition of their home," Marsha said.

Weeks after the graduation, Marsha still fumed at the memories and wondered how to broach her disappointment with Dave, or if she should at all. "I really prayed about it," she said. "I just wanted him to say he was sorry, but I realized that I had to find a way to forgive Dave first, and really mean it from my heart. Only from that place of forgiveness could any kind of productive conversation happen between us," she said.

We've all heard the old adage: "To err is human, to forgive is divine." It is by God's grace that we are able to forgive, in spite of the hurt we feel, which can sometimes run very deep. Since forgiveness is an act of the will, not a feeling, we often have to pray the words "I forgive you" over and over until the peace of God catches up with our willingness to forgive. According to the Catechism, "It is not in our power not to feel or to forget an offense; but the heart that offers itself to the Holy Spirit turns injury into compassion and purifies the memory in transforming the hurt into intercession" (CCC 2843).

As strange as it may sound, when I struggle to forgive someone, I find it helpful to think back on my own behavior (especially those times for which I am really, really sorry) and gratefully remember how generous Our Lord has been to forgive me through the Sacrament of Reconciliation. C.S. Lewis says, "To be a Christian means to forgive the inexcusable, because God has forgiven the inexcusable in you."[111] The Lord forgives...and forgets... over and over again. A charming story involving an exchange between St. Claude de la Colombiere and St. Margaret Mary Alacoque proves this point. Saint Margaret Mary was told by the Lord who visited her to seek out Fr. Claude as her spiritual director. When she approached him, he was taken aback by this nun who said she talks to Jesus. He tested her by asking her to go back and ask Jesus what sin he last confessed. Saint Margaret Mary returned to Fr. Claude with a three-word answer, "Jesus said, 'I don't remember.'" Fr. Claude became her spiritual director.[112] If Jesus can forgive and forget my sins, can I do any less, knowing that He provides all the grace I need?

A rather persuasive reason for striving to forgive each other comes as an admonition from the mouth of Jesus Himself: "If you forgive others their transgressions, your Heavenly Father will forgive you. But if you do not forgive others, neither will your Father forgive your transgressions (Matthew 6:14-15). Every time we pray the Our Father, "Forgive us our trespasses as we forgive those who trespass against us," we condemn ourselves if we hold a grudge against another. The Catechism explains why this is so:

---

111 C.S. Lewis, The Weight of Glory (New York: Harper Collins, 2001; Originally published 1949), 181.
112 Sewell, Matthew. St. Claude and the Lord's Radical Forgiveness. National Catholic Register, 15 Feb. 2017, www.ncregister.com/blog/msewell/st.-claude-and-the-lords-radical-forgiveness.

"…this outpouring of (God's) mercy cannot penetrate our hearts as long as we have not forgiven those who have trespassed against us. Love, like the Body of Christ, is indivisible; we cannot love the God we cannot see if we do not love the brother or sister we do see. In refusing to forgive our brothers and sisters, our hearts are closed and their hardness makes them impervious to the Father's merciful love; but in confessing our sins, our hearts are opened to his grace" (CCC 2840).

Forgiving someone does not mean that no harm has been done. We don't clench our fists to try to forget or deny what has happened to us. Rather, we mouth the words of forgiveness in spite of the hurt by surrendering our aching hearts to the open arms of our Father so that His healing touch can empower us—even if the other party never apologizes. And if our hurt persists, our complete healing might require what I call "chemotherapy for the soul,"—a program of prayer and fasting for the person who has hurt us so deeply. We might not *feel* like doing so, but we heed and obey Our Lord who says, "love your enemies, and pray for those who persecute you," (Matthew 5:44). And just like chemotherapy, the resulting purification may be painful, and seem a bit drawn out. Healing may require professional therapy. But we can trust that the Lord, who cannot be outdone in generosity, will use everything to heal and restore our heart and soul, all the while building up a treasure-trove of blessings for us in Heaven! "For this momentary light affliction is producing for us an eternal weight of glory beyond all comparison, as we look not to what is seen but to what is unseen; for what is seen is transitory, but what is unseen is eternal" (2 Corinthians 4:17).

Marsha said she eventually decided not to talk to Dave directly about graduation. "Praying for him in a focused way changed me," she laughed. "I felt like his poor behavior meant I had failed," she admitted. "But I try to remember that Dave is God's son, that God knows I'm doing my best, and I can relax a little bit, be more patient with Dave, and enjoy every little bit of progress he makes toward maturity."

PRAYER

Loving Lord and Divine Physician, may I always remember to bring my hurting heart to You. I know that You recognize my hurts, large and small, and that You want give me the grace to forgive. Come, Lord Jesus. Through your Spirit, strengthen my will and heal my hurt so that I can forgive from the very depths of my soul and begin a true restoration of the relationship(s) I value so much.

Questions for Reflection:

How readily do I forgive the driver who cut me off in traffic? The stranger who stole my purse? Do I hold grudges against my children? My spouse? If so, why? Do I also struggle to forgive God? What kinds of recourses do I find most helpful to move my heart toward forgiveness rather than bitterness?

Prayer Intentions:

Answered Prayers:

Prayer Practice:

I will ask God for the grace to examine one area of unforgiveness in my life in order to see more clearly the causes of hurt and willingly turn them over to Him, as a first step toward complete forgiveness in this relationship.

Then Peter approaching asked him, "Lord, if my brother sins against me, how often must I forgive him? As many as seven times?" Jesus answered, "I say to you, not seven times but seventy-seven times." (Matthew 18: 21-22)

Lord, how can I love you more today than I did yesterday?

_____

_____

_____

_____

_____

_____

_____

_____

_____

_____

_____

_____

_____

CHAPTER 25:

LORD, WHY DO WE SUFFER?

Suzi excelled in her arts program at college but developed an eating disorder requiring therapy and medication, a torturous situation her mother vainly tried to manage long-distance. Daniel showed no sign of mental illness until his Sophomore year. After many dark and frightening days, his diagnoses—schizophrenia—shocked the whole family. They watched as he spiraled downward and out of control, eventually leaving college altogether.[113] The stories are heartbreaking...families grieve...where is God in all of this suffering?

Suffering is a deeply profound mystery that Woody Allen, Hollywood screenwriter, author, actor, and atheist, elucidates this way: "To love is to suffer. To avoid suffering, one must not love. But then, one suffers from not loving. Therefore, to love is to suffer; not to love is to suffer; to suffer is to suffer. To be happy is to love. To be happy, then, is to suffer, but suffering makes one unhappy. Therefore, to be happy, one must love or love to suffer or suffer from too much happiness."[114] Allen, and other self-proclaimed

---

113 As always, these stories are true but the names have been changed.
114 "Woody Allen Quotes," ThinkExist.com, accessed May 03, 2018,

sceptics, will find little meaningful context for suffering. Suffering is, in fact, a foreign language to those who do not know God. Those of us who do know God must still learn His language.

Ted, a college sophomore studying romance languages, carefully planned out his coursework to capitalize on what he calls the three phases of learning a language. The first phase, he says, consists of memorization and vocabulary tests. In the intermediate phase, the subject matter becomes more difficult and the goal is to speak coherently and read with comprehension. The last phase, fluency, is achieved by immersion in the culture.

Ted's approach can be a helpful way of understanding the very mysterious and profound other-worldly language—the love language of suffering. Our Lord wrote the rubric and encouraged us to learn it when he recommended that we take up our cross and follow him. Then he showed us the meaning behind these words when he died on his cross for love of each of us.

We are students of Suffering 101, so to speak, when we find ourselves impatient in traffic, short-tempered with the kids, or sick with the common cold. We pass these elementary tests by calling on God for extra patience. With his grace, we slowly grow in virtue. As the subject matter becomes more difficult—disease, addiction, anxiety, soured relationships—we pray with fervent constancy for his help, so as to dialog with God, and He rewards us with His peaceful presence. In the third phase, immersion, it can be dark and lonely. God seems to have abandoned us.

http://thinkexist.com/quotation/to_love_is_to_suffer-to_avoid_suffer-ing-one_must/9546.html.

Our sufferings are acute. Yet, the famous *Footprints in the Sand* poem reminds us that the Lord is actually carrying us. Because of his nearness, we are becoming fluent in his love language, speaking as he teaches us, loving as he desires our love, not as we thought to give it. With mastery, we speak a rare and worthy poetry to God who perfectly comprehends, because he has been the language's originator.

Before we explore tough questions like, "Why do good people suffer?" let's examine some of the faulty assumptions humankind has made regarding the nature and meaning of suffering.

Suffering is *not...*

As far back as the Old Testament, people mistook suffering for chastisement at the hand of a merciless God. "Our fathers sinned and are no more, and we bear their punishment," cried the prophet Jeremiah (Lamentations 5:7). Our Lord corrected this false notion when He explained to His followers that a tower, which had fallen on 18 people in Siloam, had nothing to do with the state of their souls. "Do you think they were guiltier than all the others living in Jerusalem? I tell you no" (Luke 13:3-5).

A large swath of modern society, especially the younger generation of "nones",[115] look at suffering as an

---

115 Young people who are not particularly religious seem to be much more comfortable identifying as "nones" than are older people who display a similar level of religious observance. Nearly eight in ten Millennials with low levels of religious commitment describe themselves as atheists, agnostics or "nothing in particular." Gregory A. Smith and Alan Cooperman, "The Factors Driving the Growth of Religious 'nones' in the U.S.," Pew Research Center, September 14, 2016, accessed May 03, 2018, http://www.pewresearch.org/fact-tank/2016/09/14/the-factors-driving-the-growth-of-

inconvenience or an obstacle to living the "good life," ignoring any potential for transcendent meaning. Theirs is a Band-Aid approach to suffering. "Just fix it," they say as they medicate with drugs, sex, thrill-seeking, work or alcohol. Inevitably they bury themselves under their fix, not curing their pain, but piling it on. When the cures don't work, they sink into despair.

Horizontal remedies, those of our world, cannot explain or eradicate suffering. Only folded hands pointed vertically tap into the real cure. The great saints of the Church modeled this for us. Through ardent and steadfast prayer, they not only endured great pain, sorrow and suffering, but found exquisite joy in the midst of their trials. Mysterious, to be sure, but also very hopeful!

Why do people suffer?

We know that everyone suffers sometimes. Yet, when it's our turn, we can ask, "Why me?" What a perfectly normal and acceptable question. God knows our hearts and expects the question. His answer, however, is so supernatural that our hurting humanity can misinterpret or fail to hear it at all. We must have "ears to hear" (Matthew 11:15).

Bridget and her husband heard the Word of God very clearly and, as a result, received His divine consolation when the hospital called to say that their son, John, had been involved in a drunk driving accident while coming home from a party at college. The driver of a car in which he was riding hit a tree. They drove four hours that night to the hospital, saying the rosary the whole way, and arrived

religious-nones-in-the-u-s/.

to hear their son tell them, "It's all going to be OK. Don't worry." His spinal cord had been severed and the doctors did not expect him to walk again.

Bridget and her husband briefly left John's bedside the next morning to take some of their son's friends to Sunday Mass. Our Lord spoke clearly to them during Mass. It was the Feast of Our Lady of Guadalupe and here's what they heard:

"Then the eyes of the blind shall see, and the ears of the deaf be opened; Then the lame shall leap like a stag, and the mute tongue sing for joy." (Isaiah 35:5-6)

"That's nice," Bridget thought.

"The Lord sets prisoners free; the Lord gives sight to the blind. The Lord raises up those who are bowed down." (Psalm 146 :7-8)

"Hmmm...well, that's nice too," she thought.

"Be patient, therefore, brothers, until the coming of the Lord. See how the farmer waits for the precious fruit of the earth, being patient with it until it receives the early and the late rains. You too must be patient." (James 5:7-8)

"Wow, is God speaking to us?" she wondered.

Finally, in the gospel of Matthew, John the Baptist asked from prison if the Messiah was the promised one. Jesus told those who inquired, *"Go and tell John what you hear and see: the blind regain their sight, the lame walk, lepers are cleansed, the deaf hear, the dead are raised, and the poor have the good news proclaimed to them. And blessed is the one who takes no offense at me." (Matthew 11:4-6)*

"Our mouths just flew open and my husband held my hand very tightly and said, 'Our son is going to walk again.' I said, 'I know.' These Scriptures were my comfort," Marianna said.

We begin to understand God's ways when we dispose ourselves to believe what St. John tells us: "God is love" (1 John 4:8). Our Father, Abba, always has our best interest in mind.[116] To be otherwise would contradict His perfect nature. Because He loves us infinitely, God has managed to imbue our suffering with His merit to accomplish profound spiritual good in our souls and those we love. "God is always doing something greater than we can see," Bridget said.

Power in Suffering

God actually intended for us to live in original justice (CCC 400), in complete harmony with the world and each other. Original sin thwarted that plan and, as a result, we are vulnerable to weakness, suffering and death. Two thousand years ago, Jesus permanently bridged the gap between the perfect love of the Father and our fallen state. By His passion, Jesus infused meaning to suffering and He extends an invitation to us, mysterious as it is, to join Him in the act of redemption. Saint Paul understood this: "Now I rejoice in my sufferings for your sake, and in my flesh I am filling up what is lacking in the afflictions of Christ on behalf of his body, which is the Church," (Colossians 1:24). In other words, all of our little or big

---

116 St. Paul reminds us, "He who did not spare His own Son, but delivered Him over for us all, how will He not also with Him freely give us all things?" Romans 8:32

sufferings, if offered, are co-joined with Christ's sufferings and are infused with the power to save souls. What a privilege suffering has become! By our pain, we are made a gift to others.

Our beneficent God works other miracles through suffering as well. He uses our sufferings to repair the damage caused by our sin. Every sin has two sad components. Sin distances us from God and corrupts our humanity. A sincere reception of the sacrament of Reconciliation always restores our filial relationship with God, but attachments to unhealthy earthly things sometimes remain. This is known as temporal punishment (CCC 1742). By turning our pain into a love offering, some or all of the temporal punishment we owe for our sins can be removed. This "time off in Purgatory," as Catholics are wont to say, shows that our Lord is "always at work for the good of everyone who loves him" (Romans 8:28).

Very often, says the Catechism, suffering in the form of unexpected trials "provokes a search for God and a return to him" (CCC 1501). St. Ignatius of Loyola owes his salvation to a war injury that required a lengthy hospitalization. In 1521, Ignatius' salacious life as a Spanish soldier was interrupted by a cannonball that tore between his knees, forcing him to endure months of recuperation. To cure his sedentary boredom, Ignatius requested books on knighthood and chivalry. The only books on hand at the castle were about Christ and the saints, so Ignatius resorted to reading those. He was so moved by the spiritual courage and the religious devotion he discovered in those books that, within the year, he repented, left his former life and set out to spend time praying, studying and counseling those who came to him. Much later, the fruits of Ignatius' continual sufferings, study and prayer were born. He founded the Society of Jesus, known today as the Jesuits, and wrote the famous *Spiritual Exercises,* which has been used by thousands as a means for coming close to Christ.

Sometimes God allows his good friends to suffer so that they get to know Him even better—and they're not always happy about it! One rainy afternoon, the story goes, St. Teresa of Avila fell out of a carriage into some mud and protested, "If this is how you treat your friends, no wonder you have so few," she exclaimed.[117]

Bridget believes that friendship with Christ is the greatest solace for a suffering soul. "Right after the accident, I was trying to control things by getting the whole family together, saying all these novenas, and thinking for sure John would walk, and he didn't. Now I am sure that God has a plan and He will do the best thing in His time. As those readings suggested, we are waiting patiently on God," she said.

I'm Not Brave Enough

Our human response to suffering is often very far from the perfection we read about in the lives of great saints. Fortunately, God is most pleased with our *effort* to love him and not *success* defined by someone else's standard. In this love relationship, Our Lord acknowledges whatever we are able to offer, and showers us with all the graces we need, according to His divine prescription. We need not

---

117 William A. Barry and Cecilia Tan, A Friendship like No Other: Experiencing Gods Amazing Embrace (Chicago: Loyola Press, 2011), 127.

worry that we aren't able to "suffer well." Our Father loves us anyway.

Let's take a moment to acknowledge that all suffering is relative. A hangnail is as painful to one person as a root canal can be to another. Doctors measure degrees of pain in medical diagnostics, but to attempt to quantify an individual's pain in emotional or spiritual terms can lead to folly and even sin. Our hurting selves can be sorely tempted to compare our sufferings to another's. "Misery loves company," the saying goes. Or we might even presume that one kind of suffering is more valuable than another. Almighty God is the great arbitrator. He showers on us the spiritual benefits of suffering in his own mysterious but infinitely trustworthy way. Our little child-like minds cannot comprehend his ways—so unfathomable are they—most especially where suffering is concerned.

Life usually provides suffering in one way or another. When the "opportunity" arises, God understands and blesses our prayer for relief. If we become discouraged—unable to pray because of the pain—our Christian community intercedes for us. Praying College Moms, for example, unites as community to pray monthly by name for over 500 college students. We help each other carry the burden when we feel incapable.

Doubt can plague us if our prayers for reprieve seem to go unanswered. Saint Paul encourages us with this beautiful promise: "Do not lose heart. Though outwardly we are wasting away, yet inwardly we are being renewed day by day. For this slight momentary affliction is preparing for us an eternal weight of glory beyond all comparison, because we look not to the things that are seen but to things that are unseen. For what is seen is temporary, but what is unseen is eternal" (2 Corinthians 4:16-18, NIV).

A Word from Saint Thérèse

In the midst of suffering, especially the macro kind, nothing is as consoling as having faith in the meaning of suffering, hope in eternity, and love for others and for Jesus. In letters to her sisters Celine and Pauline, St. Thérèse of Lisieux revealed a deep spiritual wellspring of faith, hope and charity, resulting in sound advice for us as well.

Thérèse tells us to *have faith* in the power of suffering to transform us.

- I find that trials are a great help towards detachment from the things of earth: they make one look higher than this world.[118]
- I know that by humiliation alone can saints be made, and I also know that our trial is a mine of gold for us to turn into account.[119]

She urges us to *hope* in Heaven!

- Life is passing, and eternity is drawing near. Soon we shall live the very life of God…soon we shall see new skies—a more radiant sun will light with its splendor crystal seas and infinite horizons.[120]

---

118 Letters to Mother Agness of Jesus, by Thérèse of Lisieux. Letter #1, 1887.
119 Letters of Saint Thérèse to her Sister Celine, Letter #4, Feb. 28, 1889.
120 Ibid, Letter #5, March 12, 1889

- "Yes, it is very hard to live upon this earth, but tomorrow, in a brief hour, we shall be at rest…and all of this will come soon, very soon, if we love Jesus ardently."[121]
- Time is but a mirage, a dream. Already God sees us in glory, and rejoiced in our everlasting bliss. How much good I derive from this thought![122]

Focus on Jesus instead of ourselves, Thérèse says. *Love* him.

- Do not let your weakness make you unhappy. When, in the morning, we feel no courage or strength for the practice of virtue, it is really a grace: it is the time to 'lay the axe to the root of the tree' relying upon Jesus alone…Our Lord does not look so much at the greatness of our actions, nor even at their difficulty, as at the love with which we do them. What, then, do we have to fear?[123]
- Jesus offers you the cross, a very heavy cross, and you are afraid of not being able to carry it without giving way. Why? Our beloved Himself fell three times on the way to Calvary, and why should we not imitate our Spouse?[124]

Thérèse helps us realize that, when we unite our suffering with the Lord, we gain much more than we lose. Pain can incline us to want to close our eyes and isolate ourselves as our suffering intensifies. Souls who

121 Ibid, Letter # 6, July 14, 1889
122 Ibid, Letter # 8, July 18, 1890
123 Ibid. Letter #2, Oct. 20, 1888
124 Ibid. Letter # 3, January 1889

open themselves to faith, hope and charity find they can resist this human tendency. Their serenity and joy attracts others to them and they become beacons of hope. As the others come close, they discover not the patient or the victim, but the very person of Christ within.

Such little children we are! And such an awesome and almighty God is He! No matter how imperfectly endured, whether we fail daily or even hourly, Christ accepts our suffering offered with love and he rewards us with grace. Our personal Way of the Cross can lead us quite efficaciously to a taste of Heaven while we're here on Earth and to the glory of the Resurrection for all eternity.

PRAYER

Lord, as your beloved daughter I want to ask, "Why must there be suffering in our lives?" But I know that the answer is deep and mysterious. You tell me so in Isaiah 55: 8-9: "For as the heavens are higher than the earth, so are my ways higher than your ways, my thoughts higher than your thoughts." Nevertheless, I pray that when I suffer You will give me glimmers of Your Truth to encourage and enlighten me so that I may endure it joyfully as did all of the saints, and thereby bring glory to You and blessings upon my family.

Questions for Reflection:

Imagine for a minute a world without suffering—no aging, no disease, no hurt feelings, not even a stubbed toe. God knows how difficult suffering is to our human nature, so He has raised up messengers over the years to embolden us. Do you have a favorite line of Scripture or a quote from a saint that you cling to when you're angry, sad, sick or worried about your college kids? Below is a sampling of wisdom from saints and spiritual writers. Which of these inspires you most?

- It is You Jesus, stretched out on the cross, who gives me strength and are always close to the suffering soul. Creatures will abandon a person in his suffering, but You, O Lord, are faithful... -Sister Faustina[125]

---

125 Faustina and Faustina, Diary of Blessed Sister M. Faustina Kowalska (Stockbridge, MA: Marians of the Immaculate Conception, 1998), #1508.

- The condition for intimacy with Christ is to open one's arms wide to suffering, but when we realize that suffering as His suffering, it does not crush us, but on the contrary we discover that love makes it light. -Caryll Houselander [126]

- Never look at the cross without Jesus. If I must bear the cross all alone, I renounce it in advance. I do not want to touch the onerous burden with the end of my finger: I am too weak, too cowardly, too sensitive. It is too hard to suffer. -Saint Thérèse of Lisieux [127]

- Do not despair. Do not give up; but with perseverance offer body and soul for the glory of God. Your reward will be abundant and I will be with you in all your tribulations. -Imitation of Christ [128]

---

126 Frances Caryll. Houselander and Maisie Ward, The Letters of Caryll Houselander; Her Spiritual Legacy (London: Sheed and Ward, 1973), 40.
127 Elbée, Jean Du Coeur De Jésus D, I Believe in Love: Retreat Conferences on the Interior Life (Still River, MA: St. Bedes Publications, 1982), 195-196.
128 Thomas and R. M. C. Jeffery, The Imitation of Christ (London: Penguin Books, 2013) #35.

Prayer Intentions:

Answered Prayers:

Prayer Practice:

During this next week, I will be more attentive to what causes me any kind of suffering (large or small) and strive, in that moment, to unite my pain with Christ in prayer through a simple movement of my heart.

But we even boast of our afflictions, knowing that affliction produces endurance, and endurance, proven character, and proven character, hope, and hope does not disappoint, because the love of God has been poured out into our hearts through the Holy Spirit that has been given to us. (Romans 5:3-5)

Lord, how can I love you more today than I did yesterday?

_____

_____

_____

_____

_____

_____

_____

_____

_____

_____

_____

_____

_____

CHAPTER 26:

———⟨ ⟩———

SUFFERING…BY CHOICE

Marianna's daughter, Ellen, had an accident in high school that left her absent-minded, forgetful, unable to concentrate, and seriously depressed. Ellen soon began to self-medicate by drinking. She was angry with God and refused to attend Mass. The family sought out doctors for medication and a trusted priest for guidance. "During that time, I felt like I was fighting for Ellen's soul and it was a huge battle that left me feeling depleted," Marianna said. "It was some of the worst suffering I've ever had because I didn't know if her life would be taken. I really felt the weight of the spiritual battle," she explained.

Marianna learned to fight this battle with the weapons of prayer and sacrifice.

She decided to give up two of her favorite foods, hoping that her little deprivations would hasten Ellen's cure. She also went to daily Mass and began to visit Jesus in Adoration daily. "I would go there and talk to Him, say the rosary, pray with the Gospel, and see how He is leading me," Marianna says. "I also prayed for others who asked for my prayer." She persevered with her prayer and sacrifice for two years.

Ellen recovered well enough to go to college but Marianna said that, in retrospect, sending her away to college had been the wrong decision. "Ellen wasn't healthy enough. She was still drinking," Marianna explained. A family crisis brought Ellen home during her sophomore year and she didn't return, deciding instead to finish college nearby. All the while, Marianna kept praying and sacrificing.

One summer's eve several months later, Ellen had what her mother described as a "spiritual Pentecost." An overwhelming experience of Christ had apparently left Ellen completely cured. Four years later, Ellen is still free from alcohol and depression. She is happy, employed and thriving. "I just believe that prayer and sacrifice together are so extremely powerful! Even so, God really surprised me with this one," Marianna said joyfully.

Must I Fast?

People in all walks of life regularly endure self-inflicted pain in pursuit of love. Women diet for love of being thin. Athletes train intensively for love of winning. Men and women spend thousands of dollars on cosmetic surgery for love of a youthful appearance. Workers put in long hours for weeks on end for love of success. We're all accustomed to these kinds of hardships. So, why do we resist mortification for love of God and others, especially when it's so good for us? According to Thomas Aquinas, a doctor of the Church, practicing mortification out of love for God has wonderful spiritual benefits. He says that "offering it up" frees our mind to pray better, makes reparation for our sin, expands our freedom as we exercise our self-discipline, and opens us to even more grace. God is good to shower us with such spiritual superabundance in response to our simple sacrifices!

My kids used to roll their eyes when I responded to their complaints with, "offer it up!" After a while, I realized that they didn't understand *how* to offer up their sacrifices. I shared with my daughter one day how to visualize the act of offering up a sacrifice—an idea that I had heard from a priest friend. I suggested that she envision wrapping up her suffering as a gift with a beautiful bow and handing it over to Christ, who then delivers it to the person she's praying for as a special grace. This visual really helped her to understand how God transforms our daily offerings into treasures for others.

Voluntary sufferings are meant to hurt, just a little. After all, we are carving away at the raw material of ourselves to expose the masterpiece God has always intended for us to be. In the meantime, however, we might uncover some rather humiliating weaknesses in our character. "Last March," says Sally, "I gave up sweets for Lent and offered it for my two college kids. I was doing pretty well until my co-worker brought Angel Food cake to the office one day. With the best intentions, I took five generous slices home for my family—one for each person there, excluding myself, of course," she says. "On the way home, the plate was sitting on the front seat screaming my name. By the third stoplight, just two miles from home, I had eaten every single slice. I acted like a starving maniac. How embarrassing was that? I ended up laughing at myself and apologizing to God for being so pathetic," she joked. "I literally can't do anything without God's help," she added.

Sometimes we grow to love our mortifications as they become a new and rewarding part of our lives. Marianna says daily Adoration has become a habit. "It is never drudgery. I know it's a gift God gave me. He wants me there. I don't have a lot of other gifts but that's one I have," she says.

How Much Is Too Much?

If giving up coffee for the intention of my son is a good thing, should I also give up wine? If I am trying to get to Mass more often for his sake, shouldn't I make it a point to go every day? Not necessarily. Seeking out and imposing penances on ourselves requires prudence. By adhering to our daily prayer, we have a better chance of hearing the voice of Our Father who will guide us in these pursuits. However, for long-term fasts, or especially arduous ones, the advice of a spiritual director is recommended to help us keep our intentions pure and our efforts balanced.

Opportunities Abound

Jesus confirmed the eternal value of our little offerings of love and explained how to "offer it up" when He told Sister Faustina, "My daughter, I want to instruct you on how you are to rescue souls through sacrifice and prayer. You will save more souls through prayer and suffering than will a missionary through his teachings and sermons alone. I want to see you as a sacrifice of living love, which only then carries weight before Me...And great will be your power for whomever you intercede. Outwardly, your sacrifice must look like this: silent, hidden, permeated with love, imbued with prayer."[129]

Our ordinary lives present many more occasions for sacrifice than we often feel like making. A *ll of it* can become a powerful prayer for our loved ones—even the routine chores we dislike, the neighbor who chats endlessly, and the self-induced pain of an exercise class or a long run. God blesses it all, if we offer it to Him with love.

---

129 Faustina and Faustina, Diary of Blessed Sister M. Faustina Kowalska (Stockbridge, MA: Marians of the Immaculate Conception, 1998), 1767.

PRAYER

Loving Lord, my human weakness is never more evident than when I try to offer to You a little inconvenience with a smile on my face. Sometimes these hidden sacrifices can cost me so much that I throw my hands up in despair of doing anything well. In your Divine Economy, these pinpricks of life, offered to you with love merit graces for me and for my child _____. Help me to see with the eyes of faith how much You love my humble effort to "offer it up," whatever trifling thing comes my way.

Questions for Reflection:

How often do I remember to offer little sacrifices to God when I find myself annoyed or in any kind of pain during the day? What good have I seen in my life or the lives of others by the practice of "offering it up?" Journal and/or discuss.

Prayer Intentions:

Answered Prayers:

Prayer Practice:

A priest once told me that every friend of Christ receives at least a dozen roses each day from Him. All we have to do is look for them. I will strive to find my roses and give my Lord 12 little offerings each day in return, knowing in faith that He does great good for others by my efforts.

Offer fitting sacrifices and trust in the Lord. (Psalm 4:6)

Lord, how can I love you more today than I did yesterday?

_____

_____

_____

_____

_____

_____

_____

_____

_____

_____

_____

_____

_____

_____

_____

_____

CHAPTER 27:

A MOTHER'S FORTITUDE

The day that Brian's father unexpectedly died, his mother returned to prescription drug use and alcohol. The fourteen-year-old was headed for foster care on the small tropical island he called home, which seemed like anything but paradise to Brian. The Lord, however, had a marvelously different plan.

Two thousand miles away, Brian's aunt Marypat and her husband John were in the throes of college decision making for their daughter, a senior in high school. Their older son was a junior in college at the time. Hefty college bills kept John and Marypat at work for long hours, but they were proud of their children's accomplishments and felt blessed to have been able to provide them with a quality education—something the couple set as a high priority for the family.

Hearing of her brother's unexpected death, Marypat was devastated and felt compelled to intervene. With John's wholehearted support, she decided to try to bring Brian home to their Washington, DC suburb, acknowledging that it would be a tough transition for him. They hadn't spent time with Brian since he was two years old. Marypat and John would face major familial shift, make a radical commitment to parenting a virtual stranger, and take on an unanticipated financial burden, including another four years of college tuition one day. To hear Marypat tell it, three of them arrived that day in 2008 to meet Brian, plead his case in court, and bring him home: Marypat, John, and Saint Thérèse of Lisieux.

"Thérèse of Lisieux was the saint I chose for Confirmation," Marypat explained, "and I have always prayed to her. My good friend, Judy, knew this, and during those difficult days preparing to meet Brian and hopefully bring him home with us, Judy encouraged me to ask Thérèse for a rose as a sign that things would work out according to God's plan. I had never asked for a sign, nor did I know that Thérèse of Lisieux was famous for showering her spiritual friends with roses! But on the plane to meet Brian, I prayed for the sign, because Judy told me to, and for peace and reassurance that we were doing the right thing."

Marypat said her heart was pounding as she heard Brian's footsteps bound up the stairs to the office in which they were to meet. He rounded the corner carrying a single artificial red rose, which he presented to her as a greeting. When she asked, Brian explained that he had found the rose on the floor in the jewelry store below the office and thought to bring it as a gift. Marypat further investigated and found no explainable source for the rose—her beloved Thérèse had been accompanying her. "The peace was surreal, and I felt a renewed confidence that Brian would be moving in with us," Marypat said.

With legal custody sealed, the family welcomed Brian in January 2009 to his new home in a neighborhood steps from the local Catholic grade school and Church. However, troubles continued. Marypat was hoping Brian would repeat eighth grade, but the principal refused to accept him at all because of his prior poor academic performance. "Since I live across the street from the school, it was clearly the best option to help Brian integrate into the community, so I was devastated at the news," Marypat said. Next, Brian's grandmother, (Marypat's mom) became seriously ill with cancer. Brian's mom, they realized, was also dying. "It was more than any human being could have dealt with, but I just kept praying," said Marypat. She also kept advocating. Marypat visited the pastor who overturned the principals' decision and opened the doors to Brian as the winter break ended. Whew!

No sooner had they started to feel their land legs than preparations for high school had to be made. Grades could not be leveraged, but Brian excelled at baseball, just as his father had in college. Those hopes were dashed as Brian was rejected from the high school his stepbrother had attended. Undaunted, Marypat armed herself with eight pages of handwritten notes and the power of Thérèse of Lisieux. She requested a meeting with the headmaster. "I was sure it was the place for him and felt pushed by some supernatural force to get him in there," she said. Brian was admitted in June.

The troubles did not cease. Brian's mother died in 2010 of liver cancer. Marypat's mother's health grew worse. "There were so many funerals, and so much sadness, I really don't know how Brian managed," Marypat said.

Evidently, God was using these circumstances to bring Brian, who had been completely uncatechized, to the Catholic faith. At age sixteen, he added RCIA[130] to his already challenging academic load. "He was like a sponge," said Marypat. "I think the faith really helped him process all of his losses in a healthy way," she added. One year later, on Good Friday, 2012, Marypat's mother died. The next day, Brian was baptized and received his First Holy Communion and Confirmation. Buoyed by those graces, Brian and his family in June faced the sudden death of Brian's uncle, age fifty-six (Marypat's brother who died of a massive heart attack while taking a shower). "I think we all grew in faith even though it was a really painful period," said Marypat.

Marypat called Saint Thérèse back into action that fall when it came time to look for a college for Brian. Marypat and John had vowed Brian would receive every advantage their two children had, which included debt-free college education. Marypat was insistent that the education be top-notch, and Brian wanted to play baseball but knew little else about the American college application process. Many of the schools interested in Brian were too expensive. Marypat prayed. In late March, on their way to a baseball game, their coach invited them to look at a nearby school. The school's president was originally from the D.C. area and knew Brian's coach. They looked at the school as one among several options, but they had a "good feeling" about it.

Marypat pursued financial aid and set up a few meetings one spring day with the school. She knew it wasn't going

---

130 Rite of Catholic Initiation for Adults

to work if they couldn't obtain some financial assistance. Praying while driving there, Marypat stopped at a hotel to check in and prepare for her meetings. She was greeted at the door of her room with a fresh red rose hanging from the knob with a sign welcoming her as a new customer. Apparently, that's how they welcomed every new guest, but Marypat's was the only door that morning so adorned. Marypat knew Saint Thérèse was interceding again. Two weeks later, the day she finished a novena, a letter from the school arrived with the scholarship offer they needed to make things work.

Brian is now a senior in college, a regular at Sunday Mass on campus, playing baseball, and looking forward to a career in lobbying or government. Marypat and John are ready to take a deep breath.

In retrospect, Marypat says that the "avalanche of crises" her family faced forced her to get real with God. "It wasn't like I would do something like vacuuming and say six Hail Marys. I would vacuum and say, 'OK, Lord, I need serious help here! How are we going to get through… (name the crisis of the moment).'" Our Lord, it seemed, sent Saint Thérèse armed with a strong dose of fortitude. According to the Catechism of the Catholic Church, "the virtue of fortitude enables one to conquer fear, even fear of death, and to face trials and persecutions. It disposes one even to renounce and sacrifice his life in defense of a just cause" (CCC 1808).

This virtue, full of strength and perseverance, is available to everyone. All we have to do is surrender and ask for it. Fortitude empowered Marypat and her family to embrace Brian wholeheartedly in the midst of grief and sorrow.

Fortitude prompted Marypat to plead with the pastor for Brian's acceptance to the neighborhood school. Fortitude energized Marypat as she insisted on an audience with the high school headmaster, knowing full well her case was shaky. And Saint Thérèse brought Marypat fortitude with the sign of a red rose on a door knob, encouraging her to pursue the college that ended up being very well suited for Brian.

Souls with fortitude have conquered their fears out of love. For that reason, fortitude is not a comfortable virtue. Marypat, for example, was anxious and worried about decisions regarding Brian's assimilation into the family, his education, and the accompanying financial challenge. She could have hidden from her fears, settling for less than the best for Brian because of timidity. On the other hand, she might have reacted rashly, alienating school administrators with foolhardy pushiness, for example. However, by surrendering to God in prayer out of love for Brian, Marypat opened her heart to grace in the form of supernatural courage, or fortitude, and the Lord's mission for Brian was accomplished.

Because the college years can be a time of painful transition for mothers, reliance on God, especially through regular daily prayer, avails us of fortitude in the face of our grief or fear. We also build the virtue of fortitude every time we master a new skill, exercise patience (behind the wheel of a car, in line at the grocery store, bearing with a colleague at work), or postpone gratification (amazon. com can make this difficult). We need not wait for a major crisis to ask for this grace. Pope Francis has this advice: "For most of us, the gift of fortitude is exercised in our patient pursuit of holiness in the circumstances of our daily lives. Whenever we feel weary or discouraged along the journey of faith, let us ask the Holy Spirit to grant us the gift of fortitude, to refresh us and to guide our steps with renewed enthusiasm."[131]

131 General Audience, by Pope Francis, Vatican City, Italy, May 14, 2014.

PRAYER

Almighty Father, I praise you for your strength and might! Raising adult children, especially through the college years, calls for more power and might than I have. I am grateful to have such a strong and loving Father watching over me and my child _____. Please grant me, and all Praying College Moms, the gift of Fortitude. Help me to fight my fears, not with cowardice, but with supernatural courage. I will not run from my troubles but will face them with grace-infused fortitude. Protect me also, Lord, from the other extreme, which is overreacting, rash behavior, or rudeness, stemming from my fears. I surrender to Your strength and count on the grace to live Fortitude whenever life's circumstances require it.

Questions for Reflection:

Pope Francis says fortitude is often exercised in the ordinary circumstances of daily life. What kinds of ordinary situations in my daily life tempt me to rashness or timidity? What can I do about it?

Prayer Intentions:

Answered Prayers:

Prayer Practice:

When the ordinary things in life feel overwhelming, I will take a deep breath and say a prayer for fortitude, surrendering to God control over everything.

Living is the spirit of those who fear the Lord, for their hope is in their savior. Whoever fear the Lord are afraid of nothing and are never discouraged, for he is their hope. (Sirach 34:14-16)

Lord, how can I love you more today than I did yesterday?

_____

_____

_____

_____

_____

_____

_____

_____

_____

_____

_____

_____

_____

_____

CHAPTER 28:

━━━━━ ⟨━⟩ ━━━━━

WORRY...OR NOT!

Margaret worries a lot—understandably! Her four young adult children are making their way through the college years. Margaret worries that her oldest son is sleeping with his long-time girlfriend, that her only daughter will be roofied and taken advantage of at a college party, that her son, "Mr. Fun," will drink too much or be tempted to sell his ADHD medication as a freshman next year (which can be a lucrative proposition on college campuses) and that her youngest son, now a high school junior who hopes to pursue football at an ivy league school, will be clobbered on the playing field by bigger stronger guys in college and party with his new buddies. He has a heart condition, Margaret says, that can make drinking alcohol dangerous and "he knows better, but..." And if sex, drugs and alcohol weren't enough to distress Margaret, she shares with so many other praying college moms the concern that her children will lose their faith while away at school.

What does Margaret do with all of her pent-up anxiety? It's *not* pent-up at all because Margaret takes everything to Jesus in prayer. "Jesus brings me peace," she says, "enough to assure me that God is in control." One night, for example, Margaret's son, Mark, made a bad decision. "He was supposed to be in by 11:00 p.m. As the hours ticked past midnight, I really fretted," Margaret said, "so I got on my knees in the living room under an image of the Blessed Mother and said the rosary, and the most wonderful peace overcame me. 'He's going to be OK,' was what I felt in that rosary," she said. Margaret and her husband went to bed and managed to sleep for a few hours.

The next morning, through a series of texts, Margaret was able to identify her son's whereabouts. When he reported in, Margaret greeted him, not with an emotional outburst of anger or fear, but with tears of relief and joy that he was home and alive and well. "Punishment would come later but for the moment I was just happy to be able to embrace my son with sincere gratitude, which turned out to be a very effective way of dealing with the situation! I couldn't have done that without prayer."

When we're worried, Jesus Christ does not force His way into our consciousness. Instead, He meets when we're ready, of our own free will. If we're serious about living with a lot less worry, then let's move beyond infatuation to a place of deep prayer with Christ. What do I mean?

Erin's 21-year-old daughter, Kate, rushed through her college experience, graduating in three years because she was so eager to marry a young man from home. Their wedding was a joyful occasion, celebrated by friends and family who recognized their young love as something special for which they thanked God. When we first make the commitment to pray, we bring our inexperience and hopeful anticipation to the moment. We feel wooed by

God because He is always courting us, even when we're not aware of it. And, we enter into our prayer with a healthy naiveté, an eager enthusiasm, and an expectation that this new relationship will last a lifetime and beyond! Our "I do" to prayer means we are ready to abandon ourselves to God, to live happily ever after, wedded in a permanent and eternal relationship with Him.

As women in love, we ardently commit the best time of the day to give our attention to God. We ask not, "When can I find 15 minutes to pray?" but rather, "When am I most alert? When am I most likely to follow through? How can I separate out this time from my household and office duties?" These are tough questions and making that 15-minute commitment is truly heroic—but not for a woman in love!

Some women ask, "Who's got that kind of time? Can I pray while I'm exercising? During breakfast? I think I can focus on the metro to work. I'll cut my lunch short by 15 minutes..." It doesn't work to *squeeze* God into our overscheduled lives. We ask instead, "Lord, how can I give you top priority?"

God, who devised time and the means for measuring time, knows every hair on our head and all of the circumstances of our life down to the detail. He is *waiting for us* to "make the date" by getting to our prayer corner each morning. Jesus tells us in the Gospel of Matthew, "For everyone who asks receives; he who seeks finds; and to him who knocks, the door will be opened" (Matthew 7:8). As the Catechism of the Catholic Church teaches, "One does not undertake contemplative prayer only when one has the time: one makes time for the Lord, with the firm determination not to give up..." CCC 2710.

Prayer is difficult for everyone sometimes. Like Margaret, worries about our children can steal our focus during prayer. When our prayer time is dry or distracted, praying with a few lines of Scripture can re-set the stage for our sacred dialog with Jesus.

When we say, "It's impossible—he'll never get into his first college choice!" God says, "What is impossible for human beings is possible for God" (Luke 18:27).

When we say, "I'm too tired and can't edit her essay one more time," God says, "Come to me, all you who labor and are burdened, and I will give you rest...I am meek and humble of heart; and you will find rest for yourselves" (Matthew 11:28-30).

When we say, "I can't face the empty nest after he goes," God says, "My grace is sufficient *for you, for power* is *made perfect in weakness"* (2 Corinthians 12:9).

When we say, "I'm so worried about her so far away at school," Saint Paul encourages us to, "cast all your worries upon Him because He cares for you" (1 Peter 5:7).

When we say, "I am afraid to let him go," the prophet tells us, "Cast all your worries upon Him because he cares for you" (Isaiah 41:10).

When we say, "I can't manage without her companionship," Saint Paul promises us, "My God will fully supply whatever you need, in accord with his glorious riches in Christ Jesus" (Philippians 4:19).

By bringing our "concerns of the moment" to the Lord in prayer, we open ourselves to a deeper understanding of His power and might, *and* His tender love for us. We bring our worry to Him and leave it there, as many times as it takes us to mentally lay it at the foot of His cross. The Lord can then shower us with peace and wisdom to be the very best parent that we can be. He desires more than anything to bless us during prayer so that all we do will be for His greater glory, for our spiritual and temporal welfare, and for our child's well-being.

"I admit that I worry," Margaret says, "but I work on entrusting everything to Christ, especially my children. It's a spiritual journey that is made easier when I pray every morning. I have found that the Lord consistently works little miracles in my life, and that experience in answered prayer really helps me to trust Him when the stakes are much higher."

PRAYER

Dear Lord Jesus, help me to trust you with my concerns for
_____. I want her to be safe, successful, and
happy! When circumstances seem to thwart my desires for
her, You are the cure for my anxiety. By spending some
moments each morning talking with you, sharing my
worries with You, and asking Your grace and blessing, I
receive what I need to parent well.

Bless me with the grace to talk with you daily so that
I may grow in my love for You and learn to "cast my
anxieties upon you" (1 Peter 5:7).

Questions for Reflection:

As a college mom, what do I worry about most
often? (Make a short list below.) How often do I bring
these concerns to the Lord in prayer? Daily? Weekly?
Periodically? Never? What one or two concrete changes
can I make so as to be more faithful to prayer?

What experiences have I had in prayer, past and present?
What have they taught me about Jesus? I will share with
the group and/or journal about times God has answered
my prayers and what He revealed about Himself.

Prayer Intentions:

Answered Prayers:

Prayer Practice:

I will place my worry at the foot of the cross every single time the thoughts intrude in my consciousness, and silently pray "Jesus, I trust in You."

And we have this confidence in him, that if we ask anything according to his will, he hears us. (1 John 5:14)

Lord, how can I love you more today than I did yesterday?

_____

_____

_____

_____

_____

_____

_____

_____

_____

_____

_____

_____

_____

_____

_____

_____

CHAPTER 29:

GOD WRITES STRAIGHT WITH CROOKED LINES

If you had a smidgen of pixie dust or a magic wand, what kind of academic future would you conjure up for your college student? Perhaps he would be accepted to Harvard or Stanford, with a full merit-based scholarship. Or, she would win the high school science award and earn a place of honor at MIT? Or the twins would dance so well that the Juilliard School would plead to admit them. Regardless of the specifics, most parents would imagine a no-cost, four-year degree, concluding with a summa cum laude award ceremony, featuring a happy graduate, well prepared for the future. Waving a magic wand can satiate the imagination but a future plotted out in our own reality can twist, turn, zig, and zag until we are so disoriented that we make a fatal mistake…We rely on our own strength! God Our Father is a creative genius, and only He can write straight with crooked lines.

Katie chose a college with a lot of familial connections that wasn't too far from home, which made her mother happy. The school had name recognition, a solid reputation, and a Catholic identity. As the oldest, she was determined to make her family proud over the next four years. Everything changed when she arrived on campus.

"I don't understand why people put a bunch of eighteen-year-olds in one place and expect them to behave," Katie says of her freshman year experience. "I was very cognizant going into college that there would not be as much support for my morals as I was used to, but I thought that nothing would challenge me so much that I would break. I was way overconfident. I started to see awful things right away," she said.

The campus, which was located in the center of a large metropolis, shielded the students from urban dangers like nearby gang activity, but Katie felt that "...it was always kind of a dangerous environment." The school reported three times as many sexual assaults than at other similar institutions during her years there, Katie said. There were bar fights and altercations between students of different ethnicities, she said. "I was on edge a lot of the time," she added.

Katie began to date midway through her freshman year, but the relationship was short lived. "After three months, he said he was breaking up with me because I wouldn't sleep with him and he began dating the girl the next dorm over," she said. The rejection hurt less than the attitude of her girlfriends, Katie said. "Instead of supporting me, some of them encouraged me to compromise or give in to him," she said. "And then, one by one by one, they all gave in saying 'Whatever' or 'It's fine,'" Katie said. "It was totally demoralizing to watch."

Katie says she could have stayed, but, by sophomore year she was asking herself, "Why am I spending every day fighting against all of this?" If she transferred, Katie would be swapping the prestige of a nationally ranked institution for a lesser-known school. When she talked to her parents, they supported her wholeheartedly and the transfer happened quickly over Christmas break of her sophomore year.

The new environment was safe, the curriculum was solidly Catholic, and her friends supported her resolve to live chastely. Katie loved it immediately. "Right now, I could have drinks with any one of five hundred people from school and enjoy myself," she said of her new friends. "They're like-minded, caring, and faithful, which is such a nice difference. They asked me, 'Who wants to go to Mass today?'" Katie said. "This school, with its tight knit community, may not be for everyone, but it was just right for me," she said. Katie graduated and now works as a journalist.

Katie transferred for moral encouragement, but Kevin postponed college altogether for emotional reasons. "I just didn't feel ready for college when it came time to go," Kevin said. "Most kids were excited about getting away and partying and that wasn't appealing to me at all. And I wasn't very responsible about my school work. So if I wasn't going to do the work and wasn't into partying, it was just going to be a waste of money," he explained. His parents and friends frequently offered their "two cents" about the importance of a college degree, Kevin said, but instead, he worked construction and then took a nine-to-five job in residential real estate. For nearly three years, he worked while his friends finished college.

Over time, Kevin began to realize that schooling might improve his business prospects. "I started to think a degree would give me more credibility among certain kinds of real estate clients," he explained. At the same time, a good friend of the family talked "man-to-man" with Kevin about going to school. "The timing was everything. I was ready to listen," Kevin said. Kevin now treats school like his job. "When I don't have classes, I get up and study," he said. "I want to finish quickly, but I'm not going to compromise on my grades," he added. Kevin plans to study year-round while working part-time and should graduate in three years.

Nelly, now a mother and grandmother, jokes that "my son majored in universities and my daughter majored in majors." Years ago, when Nelly's son went far away to college, "I remember how my heart was wrenched," she recalled. Her sorrow didn't last too long because, after the second semester, he transferred to a local university and then to another…Nelly's daughter also took a circuitous route, studying for years accumulating courses without a degree in mind. They both graduated eventually, and Nelly now chuckles about it. "Back then, we didn't think it was very funny, but now I see how the best plans can get waylaid by a fork or two in the road. We all somehow got through," she said.

Not all young adults "get through" nor do some even go to college. They enlist in the military, start a business, go to trade or vocational school, or volunteer, foregoing the traditional four-year college option. Whenever life veers out the confines we imagined, it's easy to forget that Our Father is near, and He loves us and our children more than we do. God expresses His infinite love for us through the actions of His Divine Providence. "Creation has its own goodness and proper perfection, but it did not spring forth complete from the hands of the Creator. The universe was created 'in a state of journeying' (*in statu viae*) toward an ultimate perfection yet to be attained, to which God has destined it. We call 'divine providence' the dispositions by which God guides his creation toward this perfection" (CCC 302).

In His Divine Providence, God assures us of His temporal help and all the grace we need to manage life's twists and turns to reach eternal salvation. What does temporal help from God look like? For women of faith, coincidences are "God-incidences." Perfect timing is "God's timing." An unexpected college acceptance is "miraculous." News of financial aid is a "Godsend." A failure is an opportunity to let God be our strength. When our college-aged young adults stray from the path *we* planned for them, we cling to God's Divine Providence, knowing, as Jesus tells us, that our loving Father is in ultimate control of our lives and can be trusted with everything. "Are not two sparrows sold for a small coin?" Jesus says, "Yet not one of them falls to the ground without your Father's knowledge. Even all the hairs of your head are counted. So do not be afraid; you are worth more than many sparrows" (Matthew 10:29-32). As time passes, we one day, like Nelly, chuckle at these days, relishing the good we now see was God in action.

Our Part

Divine Providence is mysteriously all-encompassing, but it does not liberate us from cooperating with God's movements in our lives. To the contrary, God graciously empowers us to be "coworkers" (1 Corinthians 3:9) through our actions, prayers, and sufferings (CCC 307). We don't always recognize God's invitation to cooperate with Him because faith may require us to jump into a scary void without any immediate assurance of God's presence. We blindly acquiesce, for example, when our child transfers from one college to another unexpectedly. We pray and gently nudge him when he decides to postpone college for what seems like forever. And we suffer through moments, or even years of darkness and confusion, until one day we bow low before the Divine Providence of God, realizing He was there the whole time.

The next time we're tempted to wave a wand to rewrite the future our son or daughter seems to have chosen, let's remember that all genuine power rests in God alone. With prayerful actions, intercession, and the merits of our suffering as parents, we can rely on His Divine Providence to bring us all, as the Catechism says, to our ultimate perfection, straightening every crooked turn we take!

"In all your ways acknowledge him, and he will make straight your paths." (Proverbs 3:6)

PRAYER

Dear Father, Son and Holy Spirit, triune God, Creator, and Deliverer, through your Divine Providence you work all things for good for those who love You (Romans 8:28). I praise You and acknowledge Your sovereignty in my life and over my child _____. I want to o surrender my dreams for _____ to You, Lord, o give over my expectations of _____ to You, Lord, o trust in your governance when chaos erupts in _____ life, o and love _____ unconditionally.

Please help me, Father, to work hard to fulfill Your will in my life and for the sake of _____, believing that by cooperating with Your grace, all will be accomplished for your great glory and the salvation of our souls.

Questions for Reflection:

What short- and long-term goals do I have for my college-aged young adult during this time in his life? Does he corroborate these goals? What concrete things can I do to help him achieve his goals?

God enlivens our weak faith when we exercise it by trusting Him. At times, He strengthens our faith with very tangible answers to prayer. When has God answered my prayer in a surprising way? What characteristics of God are expressed by an answered prayer, and how does that experience invigorate my faith?

Prayer Intentions:

Answered Prayers:

Prayer Practice:

I will watch for little signs of God's Divine Providence in my life this month and offer a little prayer of thanksgiving each time I recognize His action in my day.

Where can I go from your spirit? From your presence, where can I flee? If I ascend to the Heavens, you are here; if I lie down in Sheol, there you are. If I take the wings of dawn and dwell beyond the sea, Even there your hand guides me, your right hand holds me fast. (Psalm 139:7-10)

Lord, how can I love you more today than I did yesterday?

_____

_____

_____

_____

_____

_____

_____

_____

_____

_____

_____

_____

_____

_____

CHAPTER 30:

TRUSTING THROUGH TRAUMA

Teresa was really looking forward to visiting with her son Nate over the Thanksgiving holiday, even if just for a few days. It had been a financial sacrifice to pay for a cross-country flight during the most highly travelled season of the year, but Teresa had listened to her sister who advised long ago to bring the children home during breaks their first couple of years in college. "You need to look at them. You need to see them to really know how they are doing," her sister urged.

Hours before he was expected at home, Nate called with words that gravely concerned his mother. "I don't feel well. I mean, *I really don't feel well.*" Coming from her normally happy, energetic son, this news was particularly unsettling. When Nate arrived, Teresa's instincts told her something was terribly wrong. "His pallor was just gray," she recalled. Nate needed medical attention, and fast. How fortunate Teresa was to have listened to her sister's advice. "God must be at work," she thought.

The next several days were filled with a flurry of examinations by doctors who had no satisfactory answers. As Nate's condition worsened, Teresa realized with a dreaded sense of urgency that she had to relentlessly advocate for Nate to get an answer. Nine doctors later, Nate was admitted to the hospital and blood work was finally done. Nate's hemoglobin was 5. Worst-case-scenario thoughts started to enter Teresa's mind, but confirmation was still needed.

In the hospital elevator that day, Teresa ran into a friend who was visiting another patient. He had just seen a priest friend and summoned him to Nate's room moments before Teresa learned of Nate's diagnosis. His priestly presence was a great consolation to the family as they heard from the doctors that Nate had a very rare form of leukemia. Life was slipping away from him at an alarming rate.

As Teresa recalls, God continued to reveal his tender presence as events rapidly unfolded in the following days. The oncologist who diagnosed Nate was an older, unmarried man who had dedicated his entire life to medicine. Providentially, he had just returned from a medical conference which addressed new treatment for Nate's specific but very rare type of leukemia. A lesser informed oncologist might have subjected Nate to traditional, far harsher chemotherapy. Teresa had wanted a voice in choosing her son's doctor but that decision-making power was placed entirely in God's hands, she realized. Teresa stated with great conviction: "God selected this doctor for Nate."

The oncologist told her chemotherapy would begin that same day. She wanted a second opinion, but it was clear that every second mattered at this point. She was told unhesitatingly, "Your son will be dead in two weeks if we don't begin today." Teresa placed her trust in God.

During the next two weeks of intensive chemotherapy, Nate agonized in horrible pain. At one point, Nate spiked a high fever. His entire body was packed in ice. Life hung in the balance. All the while, Nate's family and friends hounded Heaven.

Back at Nate's Jesuit college, his 80-year-old spiritual director, a three-time cancer survivor himself, offered Masses and prayers. Young men in Nate's fraternity prayed for him. They would later tell him, "I've never been to Mass before" or "I've never really prayed before" but they did for him.

Nate, himself, invoked St. Michael the Archangel in prayer because "this really is a battle," he told Teresa. Priests visited him every day and brought Holy Communion. The Missionaries of Charity came and prayed the Rosary and the Chaplet of Divine Mercy. Teresa offered countless rosaries during the ordeal.

On December 12, the feast of Our Lady of Guadalupe, Teresa proclaimed, "Nate started to live again." His fever broke and he emerged victorious from the first and most important battle against cancer. To begin his long recovery on the Blessed Mother's feast day meant the world to Teresa—her prayers had been heard by Mother Mary.

Nate's chemotherapy spanned the next nine months. Teresa recounted that Nate had seven bone marrow biopsies, which involved piercing his back with long needles. The first was full of abnormal platelets. The next six were clean. "The treatment worked beautifully," she reported.

Although Nate's schooling was interrupted by chemotherapy, God's Providence continued to work little miracles on his behalf. With support from the priests back at college, Nate gained entrance to a local Jesuit university until his treatment ended and he was cleared to return. Nate could not rejoin his fraternity brothers because of his compromised immune system so another praying college mom found him convenient off-campus housing. God's love and care for Nate revealed itself in those whose prayers and sacrifices had sustained him in his time of great trial.

One day during Nate's treatment phase, a friend of Teresa's, a mother of ten with a disabled child, saw Teresa and told her, "You're going to thank God for this." She went on, "This will bring your family closer. Your family will learn to love more." At the time, Teresa did not receive these words well. Her heart still ached as she saw her son endure tremendous suffering. Yet, today Teresa can see that Nate's leukemia *did* draw the family together and drove people who otherwise had never even prayed before to their knees. Although she wouldn't have wished illness on her son or anyone, she saw no shortage of miracles surrounding Nate's battle with cancer. Teresa and her entire family witnessed how one soul's suffering can bring so many together in communion with one another and with God.

Nate has been fully cured for three years now. He still possesses a happy heart, but it's now anchored in a much more profound faith. He has such empathy and love for anyone who has suffered with this illness that he has been asked to talk to people in similar situations. Teresa, too, has felt accompanied by the Lord, his Mother, and all the saints, as well as by so many in the community. "We were truly carried through it all," she said.

Even non-believers have been touched by the seemingly miraculous circumstances surrounding Nate's cure. The oncologist, a non-Christian, who marveled at Nate's recovery asked Teresa many times, "Who do you know? *Who* do you know?" Teresa shyly looked at him and replied, "Well, *God.*"

Divine Providence—the action of God in our lives— can be hard or even impossible to perceive without faith. Yet, Fr Jean-Pierre de Caussade, author of the spiritual classic, *Abandonment to Divine Providence*, confirms "There is not a moment in which God does not present Himself...All that takes place within us, around us, or through us, contains and conceals His divine action."[132] Throughout Nate's life-threatening illness, Teresa prayed, invited others to pray, and sought to attribute any good she observed to Almighty God. The Lord blessed her superabundantly by deepening her faith, working in Nate's heart, and even reaching out through Nate's suffering to the larger community of believers and non-believers to illuminate their lives with the radiant light of His grace. These days, Teresa can, indeed, thank God with a sincere heart.

132 Jean Pierre De Caussade and J. Ramière, Abandonment to Divine Providence (London, England: Catholic Way Publishing, 2013) pp. 26-27.

PRAYER

Lord God Almighty, Your ways are not ours. "As the Heavens are higher than the earth, so are my ways higher than your ways and my thoughts than your thoughts" (Isaiah 55:9). With the eyes of faith, help me to see that You accompany my child _____ and me through hardships of every kind. When I cannot see clearly because of worry or doubt, help me to trust in your Providence anyway. Help me to believe ever more strongly in the power of prayer to change lives for the better and so become a prayer warrior, not a worried prayer.

Questions for Reflection:

There's nothing more difficult than watching a child suffer. Through the eyes of faith, Teresa attributed apparent "coincidences" to Divine Providence. Think of a time when you noticed an inexplicable coincidence in your life; how could that have been God's hand at work? Journal and/or discuss.

Divine Providence is the action of God in our lives as we cooperate with His work.

Read this excerpt from the Catechism below and discuss and/or journal about a time in your life when you saw, perhaps in retrospect, how God had worked things out for the better in your life.

CCC 313 "We know that in everything God works for good for those who love him" (Romans 8:28). The constant witness of the saints confirms this truth:

St. Catherine of Siena said to "those who are scandalized and rebel against what happens to them": "Everything comes from love, all is ordained for the salvation of man, God does nothing without this goal in mind."[133]

St. Thomas More, shortly before his martyrdom, consoled his daughter: "Nothing can come but that that God wills. And I am very sure that whatever that be, however bad it may seem, it shall indeed be the best."[134]

Dame Julian of Norwich: "Here I was taught by the grace of God that I should steadfastly keep me in the faith...and that at the same time I should take my stand on and earnestly believe in what our Lord showed in this time—that 'all manner [of] thing shall be well.'"[135]

133 St. Catherine of Siena, Dialogue On Providence, ch. IV, 138.
134 The Correspondence of Sir Thomas More, ed. Elizabeth F. Rogers (Princeton: Princeton University Press, 1947), letter 206, lines 661-663.
135 Julian of Norwich, The Revelations of Divine Love, tr. James Walshe SJ (London: 1961), ch. 32,99-100.

Prayer Intentions:

Answered Prayers:

Prayer Practice:

I will look more closely this coming week at the circumstances in my life and ask for the grace to see God's presence and action, so as to foster more gratitude in my heart.

We can never achieve anything great except through surrendering ourselves; therefore let us think no more about it. Let us leave the care of our salvation to God. He knows the way…let us be content to love Him unceasingly and walk humbly in the path He has marked out for us…. - Jean-Pierre de Caussade, The Sacrament of the Present Moment

Lord, how can I love you more today than I did yesterday?

_____

_____

_____

_____

_____

_____

_____

_____

_____

_____

_____

_____

CHAPTER 31:

———✦———

A SLOW DRIFT FROM FAITH

Early one morning, delirious with exhaustion from helping my daughter recover from childbirth, I held my newborn grandson in my arms and dreamt. I imagined his first steps, his first grade-school performance, his t-ball and soccer games, and then, suddenly, my thoughts turned south. As he grew older in my imagination, I wondered where my grandson would go to college. I began to recall my own sons' college years and prayed, with a heavy heart, for this little one to keep his faith. That two of my own sons no longer practice their faith is my greatest heartache.

Writing, speaking and blogging puts me in touch with hundreds, if not thousands, of other praying college moms who lament with me, "We tried to teach him the faith…we baptized him…brought him to the sacraments…modeled it at home…then we sent him to college! How can it be that he no longer believes?" We mothers work hard to transmit our faith, doing our best to see that our children receive age-appropriate faith formation, spiritually enriching activities, and a weekly Mass experience. What did we miss? Is it their age? Or the college? Or the culture? Or just a regrettable stage of development? What causes them to lose their faith during college? And, what can we, as praying college moms, do about it?

Peter's Story

Peter went off to his senior retreat a typical high schooler—a rule-following, duty-bound, Sunday Mass goer—and returned *alive in the Spirit*! He was so moved by the weekend, in fact, that he abandoned Catholicism because he says it limits his ability to love God purely. "God is bigger than that," he says, much to his mother's dismay. He's headed to college with a strong belief in "the God according to Peter."

"At least Peter has faith," some parents might say, watching their zombie-eyed kids leave Mass early or skip it altogether to attend swim meets or soccer games. Any faith is better than nothing, right? Not necessarily. "Catholic doctrinal truth and sound spirituality are companions,"[136] says Fr. Donald Haggerty, author and professor of moral theology. "They support and protect each other; they shed luminosity on the importance of the other. But they also starve together when either is neglected, when one does not nourish the other," he says.[137]

In essence, it's impossible to really love someone we don't know. Catholic doctrine reveals who God is. We've never had easier access to Church teachings than we do in our modern era, yet our youth tend to prioritize experiences of God over learning the truth about Him.

---

136 Fr. Donald Haggerty, Contemplative Provocations (San Francisco: Ignatius Press, 2013), 99.
137 Ibid, 99.

To some of our children, the Church is the "great enforcer" of irrelevant rules like the Ten Commandments and Sunday Mass attendance. If these truths don't relate to their immediate experience, they're not germane. Young people think this way because, according to Professor Michael Hout, sociologist at New York University, "Many Millennials have parents who are Baby Boomers, and Boomers expressed to their children that it's important to think for themselves—that they find their own moral compass. Also, they rejected the idea that a good kid is an obedient kid. That's at odds with organizations, like Churches, that have a long tradition of official teaching and obedience. And more than any other group, Millennials have been and are still being formed in this cultural context. As a result, they are more likely to have a 'do-it-yourself' attitude toward religion," he says.[138]

The nebulous "God of Peter" so many young people embrace *feels right*, but what happens when the feelings dissipate, as they always do? How will Peter and the rest worship their god? How will they express their love for god? What delights this god? Has this god conquered death for them? Is he preparing a place for them after their death? Faith does not exist in a vacuum. Eventually, seriously minded spirituality demands a definition rooted in reality.

As Praying College Moms, we know that the Church has a treasure trove of more than two thousand years of documented human experience to confirm what God our Father has revealed to us through Jesus by the power of

---

138 Michael Houk, "Why Millennials are less religious than older Americans," interviewed by David Masci, Pew Research Center, January 8, 2016.

the Holy Spirit. "I am the way, the truth and the life," said Jesus to his disciple Thomas and to each of us (John 14:6). The total body of Divine Revelation is so compelling, in fact, that martyrs still die every day for these truths.[139]

Nevertheless, faith is a gift from God, not from us to our children. "Before this faith can be exercised, man must have the grace of God to move and assist him; he must have the interior help of the Holy Spirit, who moves the heart and converts it to God, who opens the eyes of the mind and 'makes it easy for all to accept and believe the truth'" (CCC 153).

We can educate our children, model the faith, and pray for them, but we can't give faith to them. And we can't control whether they've had faith and lost it.

Carrie, a college freshman home for her first summer, says she has recently begun searching outside Catholicism for truth about God. Carrie was raised as a Catholic but now feels she is being more authentic to herself by searching for something else. "I feel bad knowing my mom is praying for me about things that are important to her but are not that important to me. She tries in nice ways to talk to me about my faith, but we're just not on the same page," she says.

The worst thing we, as mothers, can do in cases like Carrie's is panic and try to "encourage" them. Our sincere efforts to encourage faith in our children can sometimes be misinterpreted so that we push them away instead of drawing them closer to Christ. Katie, a recent graduate,

---

139 At least 7,100 martyrs died in 2015, triple the number from 2013. Kevin Jones, "The number of Christian martyrs has tripled in two years," Catholic News Agency, Washington, DC, January 15, 2016.

says, "My boyfriend's family is still very focused on raising him to be really Catholic. They seem to think the world is a bad place. They say things like, 'We prayed for you, and obviously *this* is God's plan for you.' He feels they're out of touch and don't understand him at all. They're old-school, and that makes for a lot of drama."

There may be many reasons for what I call my children's "slow drift" away from faith during the college years, but let's take a look at one of the more identifiable causes—the old-fashioned, traditional notion of sin. In a word, the Church teaches that sin can erode faith until there's none left. It's a sad truth that merits closer reflection.

A Three Letter Word - SIN

Sin is an unpopular topic in our day. Some people don't believe in sin and others believe but don't want to know anything about it. "See no evil, hear no evil, speak no evil," seems to be our modern maxim. St. Paul apparently had the same trouble with the Galatians. So that it was perfectly clear to them, he enumerated some serious sins in his letter, Galatians 5:19-21. "Now the works of the flesh are plain," he said. "Fornication, impurity, licentiousness, idolatry, sorcery, enmity, strife, jealousy, anger, selfishness, dissension, factions, envy, drunkenness, carousing, and the like." If St. Paul were writing today from a college campus, he might add hooking up, internet pornography, and abortion. St. Paul goes on to admonish the Corinthians [and us] in his letter, "I warn you, as I did before, that those who live like this will not inherit the kingdom of God." Sounds permanent, doesn't it?

How many of our sons and daughters drink too much at school or succumb to sexual sin in varying degrees? The college environment is fraught with this behavior. One mother reported of her son's college football tailgate, "We went to the pre-party ready to grill our steaks and there were no grills anywhere. There wasn't even any food. The kids were drinking like crazy with no end in sight. It was like a big mosh pit."

According to a national survey, 58 percent of full-time college students reported drinking on campus,[140] so let's consider how the sin of drunkenness, which is related to gluttony, might contribute to the "slow drift." A college student might imbibe because he likes the taste of beer, enjoys the feeling of being tipsy, or because everyone else is drinking. At some point, however, he makes a decision to have one too many, effectively choosing his own pleasure over what God says is good for him. The result? Hopefully it's only a wicked hangover. The physical components of a hangover might include a headache, stomach upset, and lethargy. Emotionally he might feel slightly depressed or regretful. We're familiar with this much. Spiritually, however, drinking too much adversely affects the life of grace in his soul. His resolve to "sin no more" weakens. His spiritual discernment dims. His conscience has gradually taken on a vague queasiness and loses its ability to guide him trustworthily. Additionally, guilt from this sin can

---

140 "SAMHSA - Substance Abuse and Mental Health Services Administration," Veterans and Military Families | SAMHSA - Substance Abuse and Mental Health Services Administration, May 04, 2018, accessed May 24, 2018, https://www.samhsa.gov/data/sites/default/files/NS-DUH-DetTabs-2015/NSDUH-DetTabs-2015/NSDUH-DetTabs-2015.htm#tab6-84b.

make him restless and sorrowful. He might end up sick, tired, depressed, guilty and sad. By drinking too much, he has done a disservice to himself and has offended God who loves him beyond measure.

If our actions are gravely wrong [the list Paul sent to the Galatians, for example] and we knowingly and willfully do it anyway, God regretfully departs, only to stand at a respectful distance and unceasingly invite us back home. Our Catechism teaches that sin cuts us off from God 1) if it is of a serious nature 2) we know its gravely wrong, and 3) do it "with deliberate consent" CCC 1857.

God will not leave us alone unless we force him away. What do our college-aged young adults think of sin? Has the topic arisen? If they fall, do they avail themselves of sanctifying grace of Confession? Do you?

Surprisingly, college-aged young adults engaged in serious sin may not identify with a feeling of remorse. Their spiritually deprived state will not likely manifest itself as it would if they were physically starving or psychologically suicidal. Instead, the spiritual appetites of souls in serious sin are deadened and we long for we know not what. As our conscience becomes murky, we cease to care, or simply deny that sin is real. We become forgetful of God. Unrepentant, the Church teaches that we will be barred from eternal life. "For the wages of sin is death..." (Romans 6:23).

There's a second consequence to our sin as well. "No man is an island," the saying goes. Flu outbreaks send the general population scurrying for vaccines, nervously watching the news, fearing shortages. Imagine, for a moment, how sick we'd be if one man's sin produced flu-like contagion among us all. Yet, spiritually speaking, that's what happens. Every sin affects the whole community, even the most private of sins. We live in solidarity with all men and women. We are, in actuality, one body in Christ, so that every sin of man harms our unity and has the potential to lead others into sin.

Is It Really All So Serious?

Scripture tells us that the just man falls seven times a day (Proverbs 24:16). Truly, everyone sins. But just because we're weak, we are not excused from trying to do the right thing. It simply means, like St. Paul, we know it's hard to do the good we want to do, (Romans 7:15). We must work to form a strong will and avail ourselves of God's grace through the sacraments to strengthen ourselves to battle against temptation. By waging war against personal sin, we are, in effect, showing God that we love him. Conversely, allowing ourselves to be slowly carried away by repetitive sin, such as binging drinking every weekend on campus, separates us from God. Yes, that's very serious! The consequences can be eternal.

Does the Devil Make Us Do It?

Adam and Eve weren't alone in paradise. They were tempted by a serpent—the devil. That evil incarnate still lives today, tempting us as he did Adam and Eve. The manifestations of evil are often easier to identify than their source. Consider, for example, the alarming rise of internet pornography or the prevalence of violent video gaming. We parents rile against these influences but can't quite put our finger on the cause. We feel powerless to stop it. The devil encourages this train of thought. He prefers, actually, that we doubt his existence. Once in a while, however, we're suddenly and shockingly reminded. *The Exorcist,* a famous movie made in 1973, depicts the devil in all of his fascinating and horrific evil. It was one of the most profitable horror movies of all time and attracted worldwide attention, perhaps because the story was… true.

Dramatic demonic possessions are thankfully rare, and, as Christians, we need not concern ourselves too much with the devil's more colorful shenanigans. There are, however, some basic things we should know so as to arm ourselves and help our children fight against him. Let's start with what Jesus has to teach us through His example in Scripture.

As we discussed in Chapter 7, following His baptism in the Jordan River, Jesus was led by the Spirit into the desert where he prayed and fasted for 40 days.[141] In this weakened physical condition Jesus encountered the devil. Three times the devil tempted Jesus and all three times Jesus resisted, modeling how we can do the same.

Satan is an opportunist! Jesus was hungry from fasting when the devil taunted, "If you are the Son of God, command that these stones become bread." Satan knows our vulnerabilities and will exploit them if we let him. (Think of the freshman girl who drinks at a party to impress her new boyfriend.) Jesus rebuked Satan, quoting Scripture (Deuteronomy 8:3), "Man does not live on bread alone but on every word that proceeds from the mouth of God." Jesus is reminding each of us how important it is to

---

141 The story is found in Matthew Chapter 4.

know the Scriptures so that we can pray with them in the face of temptation. Scripture has power against evil!

Satan cleverly rallied to tempt Jesus a second time by drawing on Psalm 91:11. "If you are the Son of God, throw yourself down," he said, "for it is written, 'He will command his angels concerning you' and 'on their hands they will bear you up lest you strike your foot against a stone.'" Jesus answered him, "Again it is written, 'You shall not put the Lord, your God, to the test.'" Jesus reminds Satan (and us) that He is God and that He asks us to trust Him, not test Him.

For his third temptation (the devil can also be very persistent), he promised Jesus all of the kingdoms of the world if only Jesus would worship him. Again, quoting Scripture, Jesus answered, "Get away, Satan! It is written: 'The Lord, your God, shall you worship and him alone shall you serve.'" If Satan is pestering us or our family, a simple command in the name of Jesus, "Get away, Satan!" will send him packing.

If the devil is a clever, persistent opportunist, perhaps he is, indeed, too much for our weak natures. How can we expect ourselves and our children to resist this evil?

Jesus is stronger than the devil and all of us receive sufficient grace to ward off evil attacks. Jesus promises as much through is word.

- At the name of Jesus every knee must bend, those who are in Heaven and on earth and under the earth. (Philippians 2:10)
- St. Paul declares, "I can do all things through Christ who strengthens me." (Philippians 4:13)

- Put on the armor of God so that you may be able to stand firm against the tactics of the devil. (Ephesians 6:10)
- God resists the proud but gives grace to the humble. So, submit yourselves to God. Resist the devil, and he will flee from you. (James 4:6-7)

Sin's Remedy

Sin and its consequences likely contribute to the "slow drift" of our children who fall away from the faith in college. As a praying college mom, I am full of hope they will return to the Church one day. For every sin— public, private, communal, serious or not—God's grace is our remedy. "Grace is so excellent, so beautiful…it makes us resemble God."[142] God's grace acts as a coat of armor shielding us from blows as we engage in a battle for our family's sanctity.

While we wait for God to draw our children back to the faith in answer to our prayers, we can't let the heartbreak manifest itself as fear, negativity, or controlling behavior. "Don't be a sourpuss," Pope Francis warns.[143] "Live Christian joy," he says. "Joy is a gift from God. It fills us from within. It is like an anointing of the Spirit. And this joy is the certainty that Jesus is with us and with the Father," says the pope. If we can live with supernatural joy, peace floods into our hearts, and suddenly we find ourselves more cheerful, attentive, interested, and

---

142 Luis M. Martínez, The Sanctifier (Boston, MA: Pauline Books & Media, 2004), p. 209.
143 Homily, May 11, 2013, Rome, Italy.

merciful—attributes that may one day attract our children back to the faith!

In the meantime, wisdom assures us that, if Peter, Carrie, Katie and her boyfriend, and so many others, look for Christ, they'll find Him. We surrender, fearless and confident, knowing that we fight these battles most effectively on our knees.

PRAYER

Dear Lord, I ask you fervently to watch over my child _____ and protect him from all danger, and the near occasion of sin while he studies, works and socializes in college. I implore You to guard my child with the words your priests say at every Mass:

Deliver us, Lord, we pray, from every evil, graciously grant peace in our days, that, by the help of your mercy, _____ may be always free from sin and safe from all distress, as we (all) await the blessed hope and the coming of our Savior, Jesus Christ.

Rekindle his heart to understand how much You love us, so that he chooses virtue over vice, self-giving over selfishness, and obedience over disobedience.

Questions for Reflection:

Pope Pius XII said, "The sin of the century is a loss of the sense of sin" (Â cf. Discorsi e Radiomessaggi, VIII, 1946). What evidence is there in our culture and on college campuses of the "loss of the sense of sin?" How does this reflection make me feel? Talk to Jesus in your journal and/or discuss with the group.

How often do I go to the Sacrament of Reconciliation? If I don't go often, why not?

- *After confession a crown is given to penitents.* - St. John Chrysostom
- *Confession is an act of honesty and courage—an act of entrusting ourselves, beyond sin, to the mercy of a loving and forgiving God.* - Blessed John Paul II, September 14, 1987 Homily

Do I pray for the supernatural gift of Joy? What moments of "pure joy" can I recall from my past? From yesterday? From this morning?

Prayer Intentions:

Answered Prayers:

Prayer Practice:

Recognizing sin and its consequences, I will go to the sacrament of Reconciliation and prayerfully look for an opportune time to share with my child my experience of forgiveness and fortification against further sin that we receive at Reconciliation.

So for one who knows the right thing to do and does not do it, it is a sin. (James 4:17)

Lord, how can I love you more today than I did yesterday?

_____

_____

_____

_____

_____

_____

_____

_____

_____

_____

_____

_____

_____

_____

_____

CHAPTER 32:

MOM-TO-MOM ADVICE

"You're a saint," we commonly remark to the stranger who lifts a heavy bag into the overhead bin on a plane, or the store clerk who finds just the right size on the sale rack. Yet, that casual turn of phrase has more gravitas than we may realize. We are, in fact, surrounded by saints... in-the-making. Looking for the wisest, holiest, most reliable advice for raising children who want to live their Catholic faith brought me into touch with many saints-in-the making: mothers of college-aged young adults with dynamic, active, faithful lives, marked by a naturalness and authenticity with which they live out their personal relationship with Jesus Christ. In a beautiful spirit of humility and magnanimity, they offer some advice for helping young adults live their Catholic faith. I hope, as we wind up this time together, that you find inspiration from the women who share below their varied perspectives, their words of wisdom, and, perhaps most importantly, their humble unassuming approach to raising faith-filled children.[144] Read, however, with the following caveat:

---

144 As with all of the women who shared their stories with me for this book series, these too were interviewed under the condition of anonymity. Rather

Parents feed, clothe, shelter, kiss and hug, instruct, guide, advise, educate, financially support, and so on...but "success" is the Lord's.

Getting to Mass

- *When we do the college tour, I make a point of finding the Catholic student center. I walk them there so they won't have to find out where it is on their own. I introduce myself to the person in charge. Then I take my child to the chapel. I tell him or her, "This is where you come for some quiet. No one will ever bother you in here."*

- *My daughter called freshman year to say she was having trouble making good friends. I encouraged her to go to Mass, even daily Mass, because she would be very likely to find nice people there! I don't know if she actually went to daily Mass but she did go on Sundays and she met some good friends before the year was over.*

- *I always found the Church to be one of the few places on campus where I could find some quiet time. I can't say I prayed very well there but I used to stop in often and just sit in a pew. When my kids call from college saying they're overwhelmed, sometimes I suggest that they go sit in the chapel and I tell them about my experience.*

- *Once in a while, I pull the "Mom Card." This past Christmas season was the first time everyone was home for months. That first night, I texted them all and said, "Please, please let's all go to 9 a.m. Mass together tomorrow morning. That means my car will be leaving*

---

than create names for each, I have left them unattributed.

at 8:45 a.m. You don't have to go. I am just inviting you." Even though it was a Tuesday daily Mass, they all got out of bed and hopped into the car. Afterwards, we went to Dunkin Donuts and they joked, saying that, if they'd known they'd get doughnuts, they'd go to Mass every day.

- *We have always gone to Mass as a family, so when the kids come back from school, it's natural that they come with us on Sunday to Mass.*

- *I always make it a point to be familiar with the Mass times on campus, so I can offer it up to my children in the form of a conversation...always a soft sell and just enough to give direction.*

- *After Confirmation in high school, it became increasingly difficult to get my daughter to go to Church. My husband and I had divorced. He had never been much of a Church goer and unfortunately she was following in his footsteps. "Why do I have to go? I pray in my own way. I'm still a good person." The litany of reasons were endless. It was exhausting—explaining, cajoling, threatening, dragging, begging her to come with me. Sometimes it worked, mostly it didn't. I blamed myself on so many levels and this was absolutely not the way my family was when I was growing up. Fast forward to college and not much has changed. She has never once gone to Mass in college. It doesn't help that she's in a huge secular university in a big city. I tried linking her with the Neumann Society, suggesting she bring up going to Mass at certain holidays as a way to find out what roommates/ classmates might be interested. She actually went so far as to find a Church, ask a friend...but didn't end up attending. Now on her internship in a major city, alone, afraid, she actually found her way to a major cathedral...Small steps...I know she prays. I know she thinks about it. I know she believes. It's going to be on her own schedule and when the call from God hits her on the head. I'm sure of it. So I pray that she accepts prayer as part of her life. She's stubborn. So was I. She's searching. I still am. My daughter, myself. He is with us. I believe...He's with her...she just doesn't know it yet.*

Going to Confession
- *We go to Sunday Mass where they offer Confession before Mass. When my kids are home from school, they almost always take advantage of the availability of Confession right before Mass starts.*
- *I don't have that conversation with my college kids about when they last went to Confession, but when we are together before Mass and I see a priest in the Confessional, I point it out and they usually get in line.*
- *When I know that Confessions are being offered and they're home, I sometimes text them, more as an informational thing, but they go.*
- *Our family has a habit of attending a parish-wide reconciliation service on the Sundays before Christmas and Easter. Soft music is played, there is a short service where the Act of Contrition is said as a group, and then the priests are introduced. It's the least "in your face" way to go to confession I've ever seen!*

Keeping the Faith Through Service

- *My husband took our sons on a mission trip to El Salvador and it was a life-changing experience for all of them. They came back right before Christmas saying, "We are so blessed. We live such a luxurious lifestyle. These people have nothing." The group had brought soccer equipment to hand out, but they also said the rosary, prayed and sang with the families there. My husband had never experienced that they could share their faith with others as well as have the fun that comes with soccer.*

- *I asked my daughter to consider teaching religious education at the parish she attended at college, knowing that service would keep her looking outward. She decided, instead, to babysit for the morning Masses, making $15 an hour. Then she went to Mass in the evening. I liked that her "job" kept her at Church.*

- *After going to Ash Wednesday service, my daughter, with her Catholic friends, took bags of clothes they collected from their closets and distributed them to the homeless downtown.*

- *My daughter got involved in a program at college that does community service. It wasn't particularly spiritual, but I believe that the experiences she had in the inner city helped her to appreciate her faith and her many blessings.*

Spiritual Accompaniment

- *All the while my kids were growing up my husband and I went monthly to spiritual direction as part of our regular routine. When my daughter was in high school, she had spiritual direction as part of a retreat and she sometimes got extended guidance during Confession at her high school. When she went to college, she sought out a lay consecrated woman who lived nearby and came to campus once a month to see her. I don't know what they talked about but I'm convinced that's what helped her keep her faith through college.*

- *When anything big happened at college, the kids would call and ask for our prayers. "Pray for my test, please," or "Pray for this big presentation." They always knew we would. And my husband and I tell them often that we pray for them every day.*

- *I tell them I am praying for them, especially when they are experiencing difficulties or having exams. They laugh that "prayer" is Mom's answer to everything. I just raise my eyebrows, smile and shrug. I tell them to just keep seeking the Truth.*

All in the Family

- *I make a point to appreciate when we're all together— so much so that the kids tease me about it. But I think it's important to relish and call attention to those times, which become rarer and rarer as they're growing into adulthood, that we can be together and enjoy each other's company.*

- *We are a big family, and there are lots of weddings and funerals. Every time we go to a funeral we are all in the same car, so I start the Divine Mercy Chaplet... and they all pray it with me. On the way to a wedding we pray for the bride and groom and for their future. I*

> *try to pray like that out loud just in certain moments so that they learn how to pray, and can roll up their sleeves and make good use of their faith.*

- *My older daughter asked me why I suggest we give up something every Lent as a family. "Isn't it supposed to be about loving more, not being told what to do?" one asked. I reminded her that we are a family. We eat together, do fun things together, pray together, and sometimes we sacrifice together. We are asking God to bless us as a family, and so we make a "family sacrifice." She wasn't convinced but she acquiesced. I hope she is learning something about the importance of unity in the family.*

- *I have to remind myself that they are good, loving kids, who seem to have absorbed and practice many of the basic tenets of faith that we tried to instill in them, and that God is in charge of this. And my husband reminds me that they have to make their faith their own—by this age they should be questioning and coming to an understanding of what they believe. Instead of stressing about my children's faith, which I cannot force upon them, I have found that perhaps I need to do a little soul searching myself and work on developing my faith...and become more dependent on [God.]*

As Praying College Moms know, the most important parenting tool God gives us is our capacity to pray. When we pray, we avail ourselves of the gifts of the Holy Spirit: wisdom, understanding, counsel, fortitude, knowledge, piety, and fear of the Lord (wonder). There are no better parenting skills!

Remembering that we are beloved daughters of Our Heavenly Father, we intercede for our children with childlike trust and confidence, accomplishing the ultimate good for our children. When we wait for prayers to be answered, we can draw consolation from our friend, Saint Tèresé of Lisieux, who captures the earnest desire of a mother for the salvation of her children in these words she wrote about the souls for whom she prays:

> O Jesus, it is not even necessary to say: "When drawing me, draw the souls whom I love!" …All the souls whom [the soul] loves follow in her train; this is done without constraint, without effort. It is a natural consequence of her attraction for You.

> Just as a torrent, throwing itself with impetuosity into the ocean drags after it everything it encounters in its passage, in the same way, O Jesus, the soul who plunges into the shoreless ocean of your love draws with her all the treasures she possesses…I have no other treasures than the souls it has pleased You to unite to mine."[145]

It is my personal prayer that the irresistible truth of our spiritual daughterhood motivates you to pray continually and to ever-deepen your personal relationship with God, for your personal benefit, for the sake of your college-aged young adults, and for all of us who are raised up by the prayers of other saints-in-the making!

God's fatherhood in regard to us is the deepest reality there is, the richest and most inexpressible, an inconceivable abyss of life and mercy. There is no greater

---

145 John Clarke, OCD, Story of a Soul: The Autobiography of Tèresè of Lisieux, 3rd ed. (Washington, DC: ICS Publications, 1996), 254.

source of happiness than being a son or daughter, living in the moment of this fatherhood, receiving oneself and receiving everything from God's goodness and generosity; confidently expecting everything, at every moment of our lives from God's gift."[146]

---

146 Fr. Jacque Philippe, *Thirsting for Prayer* (New Rochelle, NY: Scepter Publishers, 2014), 25.

PRAYER

Dearest Father in Heaven,

You delight in me, as a mother delights in the first smiles of her infant child. Praise Your Eternal Parenthood, Heavenly Father.

You nourish me with the Eucharist, as a mother tenderly feeds her infant. Praise Your eternal provision, Heavenly Father.

You graciously heal my woundedness through the Sacrament of Reconciliation, as a mother kisses wet cheeks and dries the tears of her toddler. Praise Your eternal benevolence, Heavenly Father.

When I'm fearful and anxious, You offer me "peace that surpasses all understanding" (Philippians 4:7), a peace much more transcendent than an earthly mother can give to her child. I praise You Father, giver of every good gift.

With awe and reverence, I praise you for Your Holy Spirit, and for the gift of your Son, Jesus Christ, my savior and redeemer, and His Mother Mary who has become my mother. We are family, Heavenly Father.

Father, I thank You for the gift of my children and I ask You most solemnly for the grace to be the best possible parent in imitation of You. Knowing that "without You I can do nothing" (John 15:4), I entrust my children to Your care, confident that You will guide us all to fulfill Your will on our earthly journey, and reunite us one day with You in Heaven.

Questions for Reflection:

Knowing that prayer is a powerful aid to my children, how am I doing with my commitment to pray regularly? Am I still riddled with anxiety? Unsure of what to pray for? Highly distracted? Doubting that prayer makes a difference and, therefore, praying infrequently or not at all? Discuss or journal about how embracing the truth about our spiritual daughterhood can combat these and other obstacles to prayer.

Prayer Intentions:

Answered Prayers:

Prayer Practice:

I will prayerfully evaluate my spiritual progress this past year, thanking God for all the good, and resolving, with God's grace, to improve in one area of weakness as discerned in prayer.

They shall not appear before the Lord empty-handed, but each with his own gift, in proportion to the blessing which the Lord, your God, has given to you. (Deuteronomy 16:16-17)

Lord, how can I love you more today than I did yesterday?

_____

_____

_____

_____

_____

_____

_____

_____

_____

_____

_____

_____

_____

_____

CHAPTER 33:

LIFE AFTER COLLEGE?
NOT WITHOUT OUR MOTHER!

I often wondered what would become of my children after they graduated from college. It had been fun watching them enjoy their studies, travel a little, and make life-long friendships during their college years. I was sure our oldest would become a judge one day (it's a family joke) and, ironically, he's headed in that direction, having graduated from law school and clerked for two seasons in the Washington DC courts. My daughter, a social work major, always wanted to "help" others. She now works as a college advisor for boys in a Catholic high school and when she's not counseling them, she's counseling me. (She's good at it.) Our son who excelled at languages now lives and works in France. And our youngest pursued engineering, married, and works in a lighting lab on the West Coast. None of them are currently rich, famous, nor otherwise noteworthy, except in their own right as children of God…but their mother is exceedingly remarkable!

Mary, the mother of God, has no rival.

Balkis, a monarch of unsurpassed wealth, showered King Solomon with treasures, so overwhelmed was she by his wisdom. Yet, a more prosperous queen reigns over our lives. Marie Curie won the Nobel Prize for her work in chemistry and physics, discovered two new elements and conducted groundbreaking work in radioactivity that aids in the treatment of cancer. If you can imagine, a more accomplished woman loves us like a mother. Amelia Earhart flew faster and farther than anyone of her era. Even so, we have a mother even more single-minded and mission-oriented. Anne Frank, a Jewish teen, wrote of her victimization by the Nazis with innocence, naiveté, and child-like simplicity. Another Jewish teen, embodying the perfection of childlike innocence and purity, by a single word of affirmation, enabled Christ, on our behalf, to conquer every kind of evil for all time.

Mary is God's most perfect creature. She speaks more eloquently of God's goodness than the Grand Tetons with their snowcapped majesty or the Bee hummingbird, a two-inch marvel, the world's smallest bird. She is at once awe-inspiring and completely accessible. She is our mother.

A most accomplished queen and mother, Mary is intent on mothering us here and now. Her missionary heart, so pure and gentle, beats for each one of us and each of our precious children, as well. Let's take a closer look at some of her defining attributes.

Mary Our Queen

Scripture and tradition tell us that Mary was born to Anne and Joachim, an ordinary couple from an unremarkable town called Nazareth. This Queen of Heaven lived her young life clad not in jeweled robes but in peasant clothes. She grew up not in a palace with attending servants, but in a modest home where she did the chores. Yet, Mary's treasures surpass all the riches we can imagine, as revealed by the Angel Gabriel when he greeted her, "Hail Mary, full of grace."

Destined one day to carry the Son of God in her womb, Mary was conceived without original sin—a gift granted to no other mortal.[147] The Church teaches that she acquired this spiritual disposition in anticipation of her son's passion and resurrection. Her soul was created and remained throughout her life immaculate and virginal...altogether empty of even the subtlest forms of vanity, selfishness or pride. God filled Mary's soul with every known spiritual good, and others, no doubt, beyond our wildest imaginings. To this day, her soul is a veritable treasure-trove of grace. "God the Father made an assemblage of all the waters and he named it the sea. He made an assemblage of all his graces and called it Mary."[148]

Never in her Earthly life did Mary enjoy the trappings of material wealth or royalty, yet her queenly authority extends to every corner of the world, even beyond Christianity into other faiths, like Islam, where the Mother of God is revered. St. Louis de Montfort, well-known for one of the most eloquent and thorough treatises on the Blessed Virgin, noted that Mary the Queen is protectress of kingdoms, providences, dioceses and cities. Altars to Mary grace every Catholic Church. Confraternities, congregations and religious orders are founded under her name. And prayerful people everywhere ask her

---

147 Ineffabilis Deus, 8 December, 1854. Pope Pius IX, CCC 491.
148 St. Antoninus, Summa Theologica Moralis IV, Tit. 15, cap. 4, no.5, as cited in True Devotion to Mary, p.14.

intercession daily through the "Hail Mary." [149] She is truly the Queen of countries, queen of the Church and queen of our hearts.

Queen though Mary is, with motherly tenderness she teaches us how to share in her most precious spiritual treasures. "Say the rosary," she implores us.[150] By recitation of the Joyful, Sorrowful, Glorious or Luminous mysteries of the rosary, we contemplate Christ's life and Mary leads us affectionately to her son. The rhythmic repetition of "Hail Mary's," "Our Father's," and "Glory be's" promotes a meditative stillness in us as we ponder each mystery. The rosary is a powerful antidote to the hectic pace of life and an excellent "training in holiness." [151]

Church tradition holds that St. Dominic, who founded the Dominicans, first promulgated the rosary in its current form. Mary appeared to him in the 13th century in a vision after St. Dominic pleaded for her intercession fighting heresies. The devotion has been endorsed by dozens of popes and, most recently, Pope John Paul II declared it to be his favorite prayer. "It's a marvelous prayer. Marvelous in its simplicity and depth," he says.[152] The Rosary, the Pope says, is clearly Marian in character, but centers on Christ and the gospel message. By saying the rosary, we sit "*at the school of Mary*…contemplate the face of Christ and experience the depths of his love. Through the Rosary the

---

149 True Devotion to Mary, no. 9. P. 6.

150 See Appendix 6 for an explanation of how to say the rosary.

151 Apostolic Letter, ROSARIUM VIRGINIS MARIAE, no. 1, Oct. 16, 2002

152 Ibid,

faithful receive abundant grace, as though from the very hands of the Mother of the Redeemer."[153]

Mary, our Queen, connects with us through her rosary, promising spiritual wealth to those who say it reverently. Throughout the ages, innumerable miracles have been attributed to our Queen's power through the rosary. In 1571, for example, Christians triumphed over the Ottoman empire in the pivotal Battle of Lepanto, prompting Pope Pius V to establish an annual feast commemorating the victory. The win was attributed to Our Lady's intercession, obtained by the recitation of the rosary in all of Europe for the success of the mission.

Praying College Moms in Northern Virginia say the rosary monthly for more than 500 college-aged young adults by name. "When we come together like this," says PCM founder Laurel Howanitz, "we really bond together and feel the power of the Blessed Mother interceding for our children. Praying the rosary for our kids is an essential part of our mission."

Mary, Most Accomplished

Scriptures record no miracles worked by Mary. She rose to no political heights, obtained no advanced degrees, had no career, nor achieved social standing. Her titles while on earth were rather unspectacular: "Nazarene," "carpenter's wife," "rabbi's mother." With the passage of time, however, the list of titles praising Mary has grown in proportion to our understanding of her unparalleled sanctity. Modern Catholics regularly recite Marian litanies, honoring her with hundreds of poetic phrases…queen of angels, mirror

---

153 Ibid, no. 1

of justice, gate of Heaven, star of David, to name a few. What did she *do* to merit these accolades?

Mary's greatest accomplishment was her ability to love God with an incomparable depth and perfection. She surrendered to God's will every time He asked. Hers was an intimate relationship with the Holy Trinity. Truly, Mary was given extraordinary graces from the moment of her conception with which to love the Lord. We could assume that these gifts made loving God much easier. Yet, Mary's life experiences were intensely human and, by scriptural accounts, full of uncertainty, trials, and tribulations. But for Joseph's intervention, Mary, unwed and pregnant, would have been stoned to death. Days before she delivered, Mary rode a mule on a long grueling trip to Bethlehem. The family fled to Egypt because Herod was trying to kill her infant son. She lost the child Jesus in the temple for three days. According to Tradition, Joseph passed away, leaving Mary a young widow. For three long years, Mary watched from a distance as her son ministered to a largely ungrateful people. There was, of course, the scourging, crucifixion and death of Jesus she witnessed and mystically shared. (Who can look upon Michelangelo's Pieta and not be moved by the mother's grief?) Finally, Jesus ascended into Heaven, leaving Mary behind to mother all peoples and shepherd the new Church. Throughout her life, Mary felt pain and grief in proportion to her heart's capacity to love. She chose to love in every difficult circumstance, and her docility, her courage, her perseverance—all of these virtues and many more—originated in her unfathomable love for God, the depth of which is her greatest accomplishment.

As we strive to imitate Mary's courage when life seems overwhelming, she stands ready to shower us with graces from her Son. Our supremely maternal, accomplished Heavenly mother Mary has been most recently made herself known as "Mary Undoer of Knots," —a favorite Marian title of Pope Francis'.[154] The devotion dates back to 1700 and was inspired by a Baroque painting that portrays Our Mother Mary untying a long white rope with the help of several adorable cherubs.[155]

We need Mary, Undoer of Knots, more than ever as our children leave college and progress through their 20's, making decisions about who to marry, where to live, or what career to pursue. Their choices will likely define them for the rest of their lives. How blessed we are to have a mother like Mary to watch over their every move!

Cora sought Mary's intercession through the "Mary, Undoer of Knots" novena when her daughter, Gina, landed an enviable, paid internship in a large metropolitan area many miles from home. The initial excitement of the internship news faded fast once Cora learned there were free co-ed housing arrangements provided by the company. As a practicing Catholic, Gina could not accept the co-ed arrangement. Determined not to miss this once-in-a-lifetime opportunity, she used all human means possible for several weeks to find affordable alternative

154 "The Pope's Personal Devotion to Mary, Untier of Knots," CatholicHerald.co.uk, September 24, 2015, , accessed June 09, 2018, http://www.catholicherald.co.uk/commentandblogs/2015/09/24/the-popes-personal-devotion-to-mary-untier-of-knots/
155 The painting is entitled Wallfahrtsbild, by Johann Georg Melchior Schmidtner (1625-1707) and displayed in the St. Peter am Perlach in Augsburg, Bavaria.

housing while joining her mother in praying the "Undoer of Knots" novena.

"This housing crisis was a huge knot for Gina, but if anyone could undo it, I knew Mary could," Cora said. About a week after the novena ended, Gina received an unexpected grant. Although deadlines had passed already, Gina so impressed the grantor with her stirring objections that he decided to fund her housing. Gina's internship far surpassed her expectations and the Blessed Mother continues to answer Cora's prayers for Gina's success and safety so far from home in a big city.

Mary's Missionary Heart

Mary's motherly love for each of us extends to the whole world, as evidenced by the frequency with which she visits her children in their home towns, back yards, farm lands and Churches. Marian apparitions, carefully recorded by the faithful and authenticated by the Church, reveal to us a woman whose mission it is to reassure, warn, prophesy, and mother, so as to bring everyone closer to her Son. She has appeared to children, teens, men, women, clergy and consecrated in every country on the globe, with increasing frequency during the last century. She unfailingly urges repentance and prayer (often recitation of the rosary) and her messages sometimes carry warnings about war, the retribution of God the Father, and/or the coming of Christ's kingdom.

In her earliest documented appearance, Mary visited a 51-year-old peasant, Juan Diego, in 1531, dressed in an Indian garb, which indicated by its design that she was pregnant with the baby Jesus. As a result of the apparition,

10 million Indians converted to Catholicism in Mexico. Mary left her image in the tilma of Juan Diego which is still on public display in Guadalupe, Mexico.

At Lourdes in France in 1858, Our Lady revealed herself as the "Immaculate Conception" to a young farm girl, Bernadette Soubirous. She asked the young visionary to scratch in the mud and from that shallow hole sprung water that flows with healing qualities. Millions of pilgrims visit Lourdes, France, annually seeking cures by submersion into those waters. Countless miracles have since been recorded.

In her most well-known apparition, Our Lady of the Rosary visited nine-year-old Lucia dos Santos and her cousins Francisco and Jacinta Marto, ages 8 and 6 on May 13, 1917 for six consecutive months in Fatima, Portugal. The children received three secrets, the first of which was a frightening vision of Hell. Jacinta, the youngest, had been so moved by the reality of Hell that, as a child of 9, she offered all of the sufferings on her deathbed because, as Pope John Paul II said at her beatification, "no mortification or penance seemed too great to save sinners."[156] In the second secret, the Blessed Mother asked that Russia be consecrated to her Immaculate Heart, and warned that World War I would end but another war would begin [WWII] following a strange light in the sky. She also asked for devotions on five consecutive First Saturdays. The very controversial third secret was released by the Vatican more than 80 years after the visionaries received it and predicted the assassination attempt on the life of Pope John Paul II,

---

156 Homily of His Holiness Pope John Paul Ii, May 13, 2000, Beatification of Francisco and Jacinta Marto Sheperds of Fatima

which happened on May 13, 1981, the 64th anniversary of the first apparition at Fatima. The Holy Father credited his survival to the Blessed Mother's protection.

More recent visitations by Our Lady have been reported in Akita, Japan, in 1984; Chontaleu, Nicaragua, in 1987; Kibeho, Rwanda, in 1988; and Betania, Venezuela. In each case, the Bishops of those jurisdictions took time to study, interview, document, and pray before recommending them to the faithful. Once discerned by the Church, we Catholics may draw from these "private revelations" anything we find helpful for our spiritual progress.

When she visits, Our Lady, missionary and mother, always urges her children to bring our desires and concerns to her Immaculate Heart. Of her repeated admonitions to do penance and reparation, Pope John Paul II says she "seems to read the signs of the times—the signs of our time—with special insight…The insistent invitation of Mary Most Holy to penance is nothing but the manifestation of her maternal concern for the fate of the human family, in need of conversion and forgiveness."[157]

Today is the feast of the Immaculate Heart of Mary and I draw comfort from the knowledge that my mother's heart beats for my children more perfectly and purely than mine can. When I find my heart divided—wanting for my children what I think is best without proper acknowledgment that they're all grown up now—I turn to my Mother, contemplate her undivided heart so ready and willing to sacrifice for love, and ask for the ability to parent with more grace. It is a prayer I believe she loves to answer.

---

157 Pope John Paul II, Message for the 1997 World Day of the Sick, N. 1, Insegnamenti, vol XIX/2, 1996, p. 561

Mary Most Pure

We tend to think of purity as a modifier for vanilla extract, spring water or olive oil. Much more profoundly, purity is a quality of soul which implies the heart is clear of all selfish imperfection and ingratitude, the mind is guileless, and the mouth speaks only goodness and truth, reflecting its habit of thinking the very best of others. Looking into the eyes of such a soul, one may penetrate, almost infinitely, and find refreshment.

The Church lavishes the Blessed Virgin Mary with titles that reflect our understanding of her perfect purity: Mother Immaculate, Undefiled, Inviolate, Most Chaste. So pure is her soul! She is capable only of love for us. Her purity, however, is not meant to intimidate. Rather, when we, poor and imperfect as we are, take our concerns and worries to Mother Mary, we can be confident, because of her pure love, that she receives us with open arms and a heart full of motherly care. We will never perceive criticism, impatience, distractedness...those dispositions are not within her.

The Blessed Mother would have us imitate her purity so as to more worthily welcome Christ into our hearts and lives. She will even become our protectoress, if we ask. Michelle, mother of six-year-old Joe, called on Mary Most Pure in this capacity one warm spring day. "Joe and I walked to McDonalds and sat by the window, across the room from six boys who were probably students at the nearby college," Michelle explains. "The amount of loud profanity coming from their mouths was unbelievable... every word in the book," she said. When Joe went to the bathroom, Michelle mustered up her courage and asked the boys to tone it down. "Of course, they didn't," she says. "Joe returned—the slowest eater in the world, by the way—all I wanted to do was leave," she says. Instead of nagging Joe to hurry up, Michelle began to pray Hail Marys under her breath. "After Hail Mary number 3 or 4, every single one of them put on their headphones and quieted down. Joe and I enjoyed the rest of our lunch in peace."

Purity in sexual terms implies virginity. The Church teaches that the 14-year-old Mother of God conceived and gave birth to Jesus without losing her virginity and remained virginal throughout her life. [158] We affirm this belief ourselves when we say "born of the Virgin Mary" as part of the Creed at Mass every Sunday. "Virginity is not merely a characteristic of her personality, or a description of her biological state," says Scott Hahn. "Virginity is so much a part of her that it has become like a name." Historic references in literature or song to "the Virgin" refer only to Mary, he says.[159] Only Mary can claim perpetual virginity *and* motherhood as personal qualities. How unique and total is her purity!

Some of the gospels and epistles mention that Jesus had brothers and sisters.[160] "This is virtually a non-issue for anyone who has a glancing familiarity with Hebrew customs," says Hahn. The Hebrew word for "brother" was interchangeable with the word for "cousin," he explains. The term "firstborn" found in Matthew's gospel, says

---

158 CCC 495-511
159 Scott Hahn, Hail, Holy Queen: The Mother of God in the Word of God (**Seoul: St** Pauls, 2004), p.103.
160 Some examples are Matt. 12: 46, Luke 2:7 Mark 3:31-35; 6::3; 1 Cor 9:5; Gal 1:19

Hahn, was a legalism implying that the child opened the womb whether or not others were born later.[161] Our Church has the final word: "Jesus is Mary's only son, but her spiritual motherhood extends to all men he came to save."

Mary, Jesus' mother and our mother, is at once a Queen and a Missionary. Her accomplishments are incomparable and her purity unmatched. Mary possesses through her Son all the graces we could want. And her heart beats with perfect maternal love for each one of us. She aches, as we can see by her tear-stained face at Lourdes and Fatima, to bring us closer to Jesus. Will we be like rebellious children who ignore the pleas of their mother, or will we respond to the love Mary shows us, allowing her to lead us and our children to Jesus, to present us to Him as we peek from under the protection of her mantle? There is no safer way to approach the throne of God on behalf of our children than in the care of His mother...our Mother...Mary.

---

161 Ibid, p.104

PRAYER

Dear Lord, in imitation of every pope and so many great saints, it is my honor and privilege to end these weeks of prayer and reflection by honoring Mary, Your mother and mine. Thank you for the great gift of Mary's motherhood. Her genuine concern and affection for me and my family is my life's singular blessing.

Blessed Mother, please continue to intercede for my children as they grow through college to the adult years beyond. Help me to parent these young adults you have entrusted to my care as I strive to draw closer to the Trinity: your Father, your Spouse and your Son.

Questions for Reflection:

What aspects of Mary do I find most edifying? Her humility? Maternal love? Her purity? What about Mary do I find mysterious, inaccessible? Journal and/or discuss.

Prayer Intentions:

Answered Prayers:

Prayer Practice:

It takes less than 5 minutes to say a decade of the rosary and there are 20 themes from which to choose. The next time I find myself driving to the grocery store, sitting on the metro, behind a long red light, making copies at the office, raking leaves or folding laundry, I will say a decade of the rosary and reflect on Mary's love for me and my children.

We never give more honor to Jesus than when we honor his Mother, and we honor her simply and solely to honor Him all the more perfectly. We go to her only as a way leading to the goal we seek—Jesus, her Son. - Saint Louis Marie de Montfort

Lord, how can I love you more today than I did yesterday?

_____

_____

_____

_____

_____

_____

_____

_____

_____

_____

_____

_____

_____

_____

_____

APPENDIX 1:

ABOUT PRAYING COLLEGE MOMS

Praying College Moms was founded on the belief that mothers have a unique opportunity to lift our children to the Lord in prayer and entrust them to His care. Our network of praying moms is founded on the following six pillars of our faith:

- We follow the example of the Holy Mother to pray for our child(ren).
- We trust God to have a bigger, better plan for our children than any of us might envision for them.
- We believe in the power of prayer to change the lives of our students as they are away from our care.
- We cede control of our children's lives to the Father and enter into intercessory prayer on their behalf.
- We pledge support, mentorship, guidance and prayer to our fellow mothers of college-aged children and those transitioning from having a high school senior to a college freshman.
- We bless our children with regular care packages with a Catholic twist to bolster their emotional and spiritual health.

Who we are:

As a new small-faith community group, Praying College Moms offers a place for moms to share what they are praying for—and how—and offers support and advice as needed. Every college-age student's experience takes them to new levels of questions and maturity. Sometimes college-age students don't want help navigating these challenges, but moms know their kids still need the basics: love and understanding! Talking through one student's darkness and another student's light, our group's focus is on hope, optimism, and care. These moms feast on prayer and fast from worry—and help each other along the way!

Laurel Howanitz, the mother of four children, founded the original group at Saint Mark's in Fall 2012. "I began this group to help moms with college age kids forge a camaraderie with other college moms through Christian fellowship. We used to live in Knoxville, Tennessee, and our parish there had a similar group that really helped me a lot when my older children went off to college."

Praying College Moms groups typically meet once a month for approximately one and a half hours. The group facilitator makes introductions and opens the meeting with prayer. She may solicit prayer intentions from the group. After the opening prayer, the leader initiates a discussion based on the theme suggested by a chapter of the book. She may read the "Questions for Reflection" and/or highlight some lines from the chapter she feels are thought provoking. To close the meeting, the leader prays aloud or invites another team member to do so.

Periodically, the group meets to prepare care packages, say the rosary, or provide some service for the parish, all at the discretion of the group members. PCM groups may go on hiatus during the summer months. Once a month allows for busy moms to fit it in their schedule without being overwhelmed. The chemistry and easy flow of our groups make it so easy to share problems, ideas and joys! It is a great sounding board.

The care packages are a way for parents and families to engage in supporting their college children around the country. Many parents don't think to make care packages, and our care package program makes it easy to send your child a token of your love on a regular basis. The groups gather an enjoyable and fun variety of items for the boxes, and the positive student feedback confirms that our children love receiving their goodies.

The shared experiences of mothers going through the empty-nest college years instills trust in group members. If a situation arises with our college age child, we trust that we can confidentially share our concerns in our group and receive helpful input and insights from other mothers. Some come to gain support as they guide their kids on their journey of discovery and maturation, from a spiritual foundation. We also recognize the power of a group praying together with one voice as a vital force in our lives. This power helps us cede control and trust that all is in God's hands.

We believe this prayer helps the students see God's role in planning and directing their lives more to God as they leave the nest. Our fervent hope is that our students will learn to recognize that any peace and joy they experience is from God. It is also an indication that they are making the "right" choices in their curriculum choices, career planning, relationships, and general good health and well-being. In a time when their rational mind still isn't fully formed, they need to learn to trust in God *and* seek the advice of professionals to make their decisions. We all know the result when they learn only from their peers!

The moms pray hard for all college-age young adults. Most pray daily for all the college age students in their parish, that they may hear and recognize God at work in their lives, keep their moral integrity, achieve their academic goals, experience intellectual growth and academic success, make good interpersonal choices, maintain good health and sleeping routines, and daily inspire and help those in need around them.

APPENDIX 2:

HOW TO USE THIS BOOK IN PCM SMALL GROUPS

...*And So We Pray* was written to help individuals or women meeting in small groups to draw peace and consolation from God as children go off to college.

PCM small groups support each other in prayer and friendship, meeting during the school year to explore themes from one chapter each month.

The first chapters lay the groundwork for the rest of the book, emphasizing the importance of a filial relationship with God and constancy in prayer. Small-Group leaders may want to spend more time with this material, referring to it repeatedly, to reinforce the importance of fidelity to prayer and love of God the Father·

The Praying College Moms community is a welcoming, Christian environment where every member of a small group can share with confidence their innermost concerns, assured of confidentiality and compassion on the part of the other members. Through mutual support, prayer, and friendship, the group is meant to be a pillar of strength and an indispensable resource for women at this stage in life.

A Sample Meeting (approximately seventy-five to ninety minutes)

- Opening prayer and welcome—fifteen minutes
- Chapter review—PCMs review one chapter during each monthly meeting. Share thoughts or comments from the chapter, addressing any questions that arise—thirty minutes
- Discussion of questions—Read aloud the Questions for Reflection and discuss—fifteen minutes
- Review the Prayer Practice—Is this doable during the next month? Why or why not? —five minutes
- Closing prayers sharing intentions—ten minutes

Other optional elements:

- Care Package planning and/or assembly (see the website for details)
- Extended prayer/monthly rosary

For more information, go to www.prayingcollege moms.org. Individuals are also very welcome to contact the author through that website or www.andsowepray. com to share their own stories with the author.

APPENDIX 3:

HISTORICAL AUTHENTICITY OF SCRIPTURE[162]

Author	Date Written	Earliest Copy	Approximate Time Span between original & copy	Number of Copies	Accuracy of Copies
Lucretius	died 55 or 53 B.C.		1100 yrs	2	----
Pliny	A.D. 61-113	A.D. 850	750 yrs	7	----
Plato	427-347 B.C.	A.D. 900	1200 yrs	7	----
Demosthenes	4th Cent. B.C.	A.D. 1100	800 yrs	8	----
Herodotus	480-425 B.C.	A.D. 900	1300 yrs	8	----
Suetonius	A.D. 75-160	A.D. 950	800 yrs	8	----
Thucydides	460-400 B.C.	A.D. 900	1300 yrs	8	----
Euripides	480-406 B.C.	A.D. 1100	1300 yrs	9	----
Aristophanes	450-385 B.C.	A.D. 900	1200	10	----
Caesar	100-44 B.C.	A.D. 900	1000	10	----
Livy	59 BC-AD 17	----	???	20	----

162 "Christian Apologetics & Research Ministry," CARM.org, March 16, 2018, accessed July 06, 2018, https://carm.org/manuscript-evidence.

Author	Date Written	Earliest Copy	Approximate Time Span between original & copy	Number of Copies	Accuracy of Copies
Tacitus	circa A.D. 100	A.D. 1100	1000 yrs	20	----
Aristotle	384-322 B.C.	A.D. 1100	1400	49	----
Sophocles	496-406 B.C.	A.D. 1000	1400 yrs	193	----
Homer (Iliad)	900 B.C.	400 B.C.	500 yrs	643	95%
New Testament	1st Cent. A.D. (A.D. 50-100)	2nd Cent. A.D. (c. A.D. 130 f.)	less than 100 years	5600	99.5%

APPENDIX 4:

TEN WEEKS TO FINDING JOY

Week 1] I will humble myself—Joy is a gift and can't be manufactured. It is a fruit of the Holy Spirit (CCC 1832). I open my heart to acknowledge my weaknesses and neediness and ask You, Lord, for the gift of Joy.

Week 2] I make a covenant with You, Lord. I commit wholeheartedly to living more joyfully by growing in knowledge and love of you by being faithful to ten to fifteen minutes of morning prayer, even on weekends and during vacations.

Week 3] I will stop complaining…out loud. It's impossible to change a habit of negative thought overnight but I will begin by catching the ones that escape through my lips. I will listen to myself and resolve to silence criticism, pessimistic comments, or little or big complaints. Instead, I will exchange those thoughts for "praise You, Lord, in all circumstances." It may not feel natural at first, but that's OK. With Your grace, I will succeed in changing my negative thought patterns.

Week 4] I will find more time for silence by turning off the radio in the car…taking the dog for a walk alone… deleting social media apps. I will use these newfound moments to seek Your presence and appreciate my surroundings.

Week 5] I will be fully present to the other. I will give eye contact, affirmation and full attention to the person in front of me at each moment of my day. I will not look to see who else is around, anticipate my next comment, or wish their presence away.

Week 6] I will do one thing at a time. When I'm driving, I'll ignore the cellphone. When I'm eating, I won't read the paper. I will focus on the task at hand, do my best work, and finish it before I move on to the next thing.

Week 7] I will cultivate an attitude of gratitude. Not everyone is born an optimist, but everyone has the capacity to change thought patterns, so I will fill my mind with gratitude for the people in my life, with appreciation for my creature comforts, with love of nature. I will celebrate the blessings in life! I will savor the glass of wine, steep in the bubble bath, rejoice with others in their accomplishments, and relish my own. I will live the virtue of Eutrapelia—a playfulness that refreshes the soul…I thank You, God, for these things. I will write them down in a gratitude journal.

Week 8] I will examine my friendships. Am I a good friend? Loyal, cheerful, steadfast? I resolve to improve wherever necessary. Do I have good friends? "Whoever walks with the wise becomes wise, but the companion of fools suffers harm" (Proverbs 13:20). I will pray, asking You for good friends and to be a better friend.

Week 9] I will observe and reflect. With more silence in my life and a regular habit of prayer, I am starting to recognize patterns in my behavior. I will appreciate my

God-given talents. This is not a lack of humility: I'm practicing humility by recognizing in truth who I am before You, Lord. I will take my weaknesses and faults to You in the Sacrament of Reconciliation to be healed and strengthened.

Week 10] I will look for opportunities to share my joy with others, especially those less fortunate. Present me, Lord, with the "poor" You wish for me to serve...the poor in temporal gifts and those poor in spirit.

APPENDIX 5:

———— ⌒ ————

WHAT IS MORTAL SIN?

Excerpts from the Catechism of the Catholic Church

1855 *Mortal sin* destroys charity in the heart of man by a grave violation of God's law; it turns man away from God, who is his ultimate end and his beatitude, by preferring an inferior good to him.

Venial sin allows charity to subsist, even though it offends and wounds it.

1856 Mortal sin, by attacking the vital principle within us—that is, charity—necessitates a new initiative of God's mercy and a conversion of heart which is normally accomplished within the setting of the sacrament of reconciliation:

When the will sets itself upon something that is of its nature incompatible with the charity that orients man toward his ultimate end, then the sin is mortal by its very object...whether it contradicts the love of God, such as blasphemy or perjury, or the love of neighbor, such as homicide or adultery...But when the sinner's will is set upon something that of its nature involves a disorder, but is not opposed to the love of God and neighbor, such as thoughtless chatter or immoderate laughter and the like, such sins are venial.[130]

1857 For a *sin* to be *mortal*, three conditions must together be met: "Mortal sin is sin whose object is grave matter and which is also committed with full knowledge and deliberate consent."[131]

[138] *Grave matter* is specified by the Ten Commandments, corresponding to the answer of Jesus to the rich young man: "Do not kill, Do not commit adultery, Do not steal, Do not bear false witness, Do not defraud, Honor your father and your mother."[132] The gravity of sins is more or less great: murder is graver than theft. One must also take into account who is wronged: violence against parents is in itself graver than violence against a stranger.

1859 Mortal sin requires *full knowledge* and *complete consent*. It presupposes knowledge of the sinful character of the act, of its opposition to God's law. It also implies a consent sufficiently deliberate to be a personal choice. Feigned ignorance and hardness of heart[133] do not diminish, but rather increase, the voluntary character of a sin.

1860 *Unintentional ignorance* can diminish or even remove the imputability of a grave offense. But no one is deemed to be ignorant of the principles of the moral law, which are written in the conscience of every man. The promptings of feelings and passions can also diminish the voluntary and free character of the offense, as can external pressures or pathological disorders. Sin committed through malice, by deliberate choice of evil, is the gravest.

1861 Mortal sin is a radical possibility of human freedom, as is love itself. It results in the loss of charity and the privation of sanctifying grace, that is, of the state of grace. If it is not redeemed by repentance and God's forgiveness, it causes exclusion from Christ's kingdom and the eternal death of hell, for our freedom has the power to make choices forever, with no turning back. However, although we can judge that an act is in itself a grave offense, we must entrust judgment of persons to the justice and mercy of God.

APPENDIX 6:

HOW TO SAY THE ROSARY

End with
Glory Be
Hail Holy Queen

First Mystery
Our Father

Glory Be

10 Hail Marys
(A Decade)

Three Hail
Marys

Fifth Mystery &
Our Father
Glory Be

Glory Be
Second Mystery
& Our Father

Our Father

10 Hail Marys
(A Decade)

10 Hail Marys
(A Decade)

Begin by making the Sign of
the Cross and Apostle's Creed

Glory Be
Third Mystery &
Our Father

Fourth Mystery
& Our Father
Glory Be

10 Hail Marys
(A Decade)

USING THE ROSARY BEADS
TO PRAY THE ROSARY

1. At the Crucifix make the Sign of the Cross, then recite the Apostle's Creed.
2. Say one Our Father on the first large bead.
3. One Hail Mary on each of the three small beads.
4. On the next large bead say One Glory Be, Announce the first Mystery then say one Our Father.
5. Move around the right side of the rosary. On each of the ten small beads recite one Hail Mary while contemplating on the Mystery.
6. At the end of the last decade, on the medal or large bead, recite the Glory Be, followed by "Hail Holy Queen." It is then customary to kiss the crucifix followed by the Sign of the Cross.[163]

Praying College Moms groups say aloud the names of the students for whom they pray after each mystery of the rosary (approximately 100 names per decade).

The Mysteries of the Rosary:

Joyful Mysteries of the Rosary
Prayed on Monday and Saturday
1. The Annunciation of the Lord to Mary
2. The Visitation of Mary to Elizabeth
3. The Nativity of our Lord Jesus Christ
4. The Presentation of our Lord
5. Finding Jesus in the Temple at age 12

---

163 Courtesy of St. Elizabeth Catholic University Parish, Lubbock, Texas. http://stelizabethlubbock.com/index.php/prayer/the-holy-rosary/how-to-pray-the-rosary.

Sorrowful Mystery of the Rosary
Prayed on Tuesday and Friday
1. The Agony of Jesus in the Garden
2. The Scourging at the Pillar
3. Jesus is Crowned with Thorns
4. Jesus Carried the Cross
5. The Crucifixion of our Lord

Glorious Mystery of the Rosary
Prayed on Wednesday and Sunday
1. The Resurrection of Jesus Christ
2. The Ascension of Jesus to Heaven
3. The Descent of the Holy Ghost
4. The Assumption of Mary into Heaven
5. Mary is Crowned as Queen of Heaven and Earth

Luminous Mystery of the Rosary
Prayed on Thursday
1. The Baptism of Jesus in the Jordan
2. The Wedding at Cana
3. The Proclamation of the Kingdom
4. The Transfiguration
5. The Institution of the Eucharist

ABOUT THE AUTHOR

Maribeth Harper began as a professional writer 35 years ago, working in Washington DC for a national telecommunication publishing house. More recently, she has co-chaired the Something Greater Ministry, (somethinggreater.net) for which she edits and writes; edited for a national women's Bible study program, Walking with Purpose (walkingwithpurpose.com); and provided website development and consulting for a variety of mission-based clients. She spent six years working with adolescent girls in Catholic faith formation programs and eight years as the co-chair and business manager of the largest fashion show on the East coast—Pure Fashion, which promotes modesty among high school girls. She speaks to women at retreats and Bible studies on topics of prayer and family life. She has four grown children, five grandchildren, and lives in Maryland with her husband of many years, Denis.

It is Maribeth's ardent wish that the stories shared by women of faith in this book will help all women with college-aged young adults—individuals and Praying College Moms—to grow in their relationship with God through prayer, and thereby provide the most effective and fruitful help to their children and their families.

www.andsowepray.com

Made in the USA
Columbia, SC
14 November 2018